T0346739

TALISMANIC
MAGIC
FOR
WITCHES

About the Author

Frater Barrabbas Tiresius is a practicing ritual magician who has studied magic and the occult for more than forty years. He believes that ritual magic is a discipline whose mystery is unlocked by continual practice and by occult experiences and revelations. Frater Barrabbas believes that traditional approaches should be balanced with creativity and experimentation, and that no occult or magical tradition is exempt from changes and revisions.

Over the years, he found that his practical magical discipline was the real source for all of his creative efforts. That creative process helped him build and craft a unique and different kind of magical system, one quite unlike any other yet based on common Wiccan practices. So, despite its uniqueness, this magical system is capable of being easily adapted and used by others.

Frater Barrabbas is also the founder of a magical order called the Order of the Gnostic Star, and he is an elder and lineage holder in the Alexandrian tradition of Witchcraft. Visit his blog at fraterbarrabbas.blogspot.com.

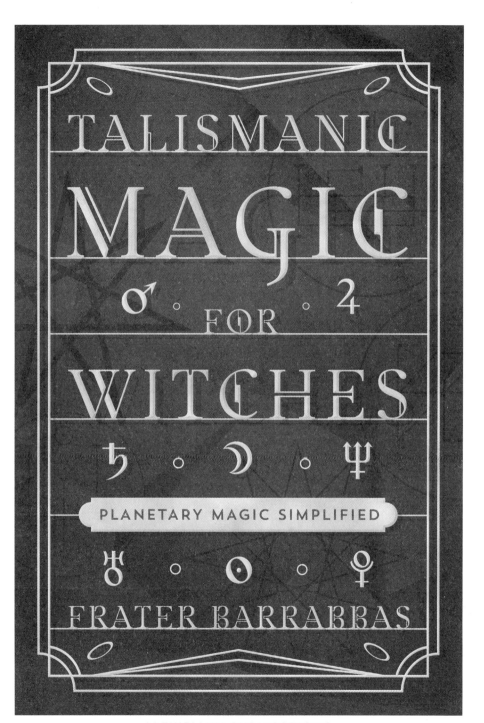

TALISMANIC MAGIC

for

WITCHES

PLANETARY MAGIC SIMPLIFIED

FRATER BARRABBAS

LLEWELLYN PUBLICATIONS
WOODBURY, MINNESOTA

FIRST EDITION
First Printing, 2023

Book layout by Mandie Brasington
Cover design by Kevin R. Brown
Editing by Laura Kurtz

Llewellyn Publications is a registered trademark of Llewellyn Worldwide Ltd.

Library of Congress Cataloging-in-Publication Data (Pending)
ISBN: 978-0-7387-7416-9

Llewellyn Publications
A Division of Llewellyn Worldwide Ltd.
2143 Wooddale Drive
Woodbury, MN 55125-2989
www.llewellyn.com

Printed in the United States of America

Other Books by Frater Barrabbas

Elemental Powers for Witches (Llewellyn, 2021)

Spirit Conjuring for Witches (Llewellyn, 2017)

Magical Qabalah for Beginners (Llewellyn, 2013)

DEDICATION

This book is dedicated to Erich and Alana Brown, to my wife, Joni, who taught me how to write books, and Lynxa, my feline muse. Also, to Max, our amazing tuxedo cat, whose sudden passing was most tragic and forlorn.

ACKNOWLEDGMENTS

Many thanks to Keith Ward for his artistic assistance, Jake Stratton Kent for his hints about the temporal model of magic and its myths, and Christopher Warnock for his peerless classes on traditional astrology and magic. Also, many thanks to Lon Milo Duquette who inspired me to write this book and for his excellent quote about the psychology model of magic.

AUTHOR NOTE

Talismanic Magic for Witches is the third book in this series. While I may have written the other two books, *Spirit Conjuring* (Llewellyn, 2017) and *Elemental Powers* (Llewellyn, 2022), as standalone works that have certain points in common and can be approached separately and distinctly, the case is not the same with this, the third book. *Talismanic Magic* incorporates many elements of the other two books and cannot stand alone. This work must therefore be based on the foundation of the other two, since it will use both evocation and energy magic in combination.

Talismanic magic is the combination of evocation techniques, energy workings, and the introduction of planetary and zodiacal archetypes fused into a single, powerful magical discipline. Anyone who would seek to master celestial magic, the magic of the planets and the zodiac, must first master the arts of evocation, invocation, and energy workings. There just simply isn't any shortcut. The only exception to this rule would be for someone who was gifted in the art and practice of astrology, since that discipline alone might prepare one to master celestial magic.

I would recommend purchasing and studying the other two books in this series before attempting to master this work. Celestial magic is definitely not for beginners. It is the final jewel in the diadem of a longstanding and productive practice of Witchcraft magic. Since this work is built upon the shoulders of the other two, I won't delve into basic ideas and structures covered in those books. I will assume that you will know what I am discussing, since the material was covered in depth in those works. I have taken this approach because there is so much material on celestial magic alone that must be covered that the book would become too large and redundant if everything you would need to know in order to master this work was also included.

Throughout this book you will find footnotes that will help you locate relevant passages in the other two works to help you get the necessary background needed to keep up with the material that will be covered. It will help you either to learn the background in greater detail or just refresh what you already have learned for the topics of magical evocation and magical energy workings. Still, to make the best use of this book, I believe that you should also learn and practice evocation and energy work before advancing to celestial magic.

FRATER BARRABBAS

CONTENTS

INTRODUCTION TO PLANETARY AND ZODIACAL MAGIC   1

CHAPTER ONE: APPROACHING THE PRACTICE
OF CELESTIAL MAGIC   15

Celestial Magic and the Psychological Model of Magic ... 16

Astrology Is the Key to Celestial Magic ... 18

Celestial Magic and the Magical Model of Time ... 20

Planetary and Astrological Deities ... 22

Active and Passive Forms of Planetary Magic ... 25

Talismanic Magic: Combining Planet and Element ... 26

Celestial Magic Topics ... 28

CHAPTER TWO: HISTORICAL OVERVIEW OF
CELESTIAL MAGIC   31

Astrology and Magic Parting Ways ... 33

Astrology and Magic—A Troubling Affair ... 35

CHAPTER THREE: MODELS OF MAGIC: PSYCHOLOGY
AND TIME   39

Psychological Model—Gaming Reality ... 41

Temporal Model of Magic—Fixing the Moment of Magic ... 44

Mythic Elements about Time—Greek and Persian ... 47

CONTENTS

CHAPTER FOUR: PLANETARY CORRESPONDENCES: QUALITIES, DEITIES, AND SPIRITS 51

Archetypal Qualities of the Planets ... 53

Practical Planetary Correspondences ... 58

Table: Table of Basic Planetary Correspondences ... 60

Table: Table of Gods and Goddesses from Various Pantheons ... 61

Table: Table of Archangels, Angels, and Olympians ... 62

Table: Table of Libations and Offerings ... 62

Lintel or Threshold God of Time ... 63

Building a Planetary Magical Domain ... 64

Olympian Spirits or Governors ... 67

Planetary Movements and Locating Them
Using an Astrological Calendar ... 71

CHAPTER FIVE: ZODIACAL CORRESPONDENCES: QUALITIES, DEITIES, AND SPIRITS 75

Archetypal Qualities of the Twelve Signs of the Zodiac ... 76

Practical Zodiacal Correspondences ... 83

Table: Basic Zodiacal Qualities ... 85

Table: Magical Zodiacal Qualities—Gemstones, Archangelic
and Angelic Spirits ... 86

Table: Zodiacal Deities—Roman, Greek, Egyptian,
and Babylonian Names ... 87

Sectional Divisions of the Twelve Signs of the Zodiac ... 88

CHAPTER SIX: LUNAR MANSIONS: TALISMANIC ELEMENTALS 91

Talismanic Elementals ... 93

Lunar Mansions and Talismanic Elementals ... 96

Fire (Mansions of Aries, Leo, and Sagittarius) ... 98

Water (Mansions of Cancer, Scorpio, and Pisces)... 100

Air (Mansions of Libra, Aquarius, and Gemini)... 102

Earth (Mansions of Capricorn, Taurus, and Virgo)... 104

CHAPTER SEVEN: ASTROLOGICAL DECANS: TALISMANIC DOMAINS 109

Tarot Cards, Decan Domains, and Hierarchy of Spirits... 113

Table: Table of the Angelic Hierarchy of the
Zodiacal Signs and Decans... 116

Table: Table of the Planetary Rulers for the Decans... 117

Table: Table of the Egyptian Ptolemaic Decan
Demigon Names... 118

Table: Table of Archangels, Angels, and Olympians... 119

Table: Table of Lesser Arcana Pip Cards and
Decans—Thoth Tarot... 120

Decan Components for Summoning the Decan Domain... 121

Thirty-Six Decan Domains and Attributes... 121

CHAPTER EIGHT: ASTROLOGICAL SEPTANS: TALISMANIC SUB-ELEMENTALS 131

Table: Structure for Zodiacal Septan Divisions... 132

Forty-Eight Dukes and the Talismanic Sub-Elementals... 133

Fire Segments: Southern Quadrant–Activity, Energy,
Ambition—Element Emperor: Caspiel... 134

Air Segments: Eastern Quadrant—Knowledge, Decision,
Analysis—Element Emperor: Carnesiel... 135

Water Segments: Western Quadrant—Feelings, Emotions,
Clarity—Element Emperor: Amenadiel... 136

Earth Segments: Northern Quadrant—Material, Practicality,
Fortune—Element Emperor: Demoriel... 137

CHAPTER NINE: TALISMANIC TOOLS AND RITUAL ARTIFICES 139

Star Polygon Icons ... 140

Other Ritual Devices and Structures ... 145

Celestial Magic Tools and Paraphernalia ... 154

CHAPTER TEN: ASTROLOGICAL AUSPICES 159

Selecting Talismanic Spirits and Workings ... 161

Lunation Cycle ... 165

Table: Eight Phases of the Lunation Cycle ... 167

CHAPTER ELEVEN: DETERMINING DATES, TIMES, AND PREPARATIONS 171

Planetary Hours Tables ... 174

Table: Planetary Hours of the 12-Hour Day ... 176

Table: Planetary Hours of the 12-Hour Night ... 177

Preparing for Celestial Magical Workings ... 178

CHAPTER TWELVE: PLANETARY AND ZODIACAL RITUAL WORKINGS 181

Ritual Patterns for Planetary and Zodiacal Invocations ... 183

Planetary Intelligence Invocation Rite ... 183

Zodiacal Intelligence Invocation Rite ... 187

Zodiacal Intelligence Invocation Rite 2 ... 191

Example: Invocation of the Planetary Intelligence of Jupiter ... 196

Table: Planetary Hours by Day for December 9, 2021—Proportionate Hour Calculation ... 199

Table: Table of Planetary Hours by Night for December 9, 2021—Proportionate Hour Calculation ... 200

CHAPTER THIRTEEN: TALISMANIC MAGIC USING THE LUNAR MANSIONS 205

Invocation of the Talismanic Elemental Ritual ... 206

Stellar Vortex for Talismanic Charging Ritual ... 213

Example: Talismanic Elemental Venus of Water ... 215

CHAPTER FOURTEEN: TALISMANIC MAGIC USING THE DECANS 225

Invocation of the Talismanic Decan Ritual ... 228

Example: Decan Invocation Rite for Mashephar / Semtet 20°–30° of Virgo—10 of Pentacles ... 234

CHAPTER FIFTEEN: TALISMANIC MAGIC USING THE SEPTANS 243

Invocation of the Talismanic Septan Ritual ... 246

Example: Septan Invocation Rite for Duke Ornich of Taurus of the Quadrant Segment of Air ... 252

CHAPTER SIXTEEN: APPLYING TALISMANS IN EVERYDAY MAGIC 263

CHAPTER SEVENTEEN: INVOKING SATURN: RITUAL WORKING FOR JUSTICE 271

Invocation of the Planetary Intelligence of Saturn in Scorpio for Justice Ritual ... 275

CONCLUSION: THREE WORLDS OF WITCHCRAFT MASTERY 281

APPENDIX 1: ALPHABET WHEELS FOR HEBREW AND ENGLISH 289

APPENDIX 2: ELEMENTAL QUALITIES 291

BIBLIOGRAPHY 295

INDEX 299

INTRODUCTION TO PLANETARY AND ZODIACAL MAGIC

"He lost himself in the words and images conjured
in his mind and for a while forgot … He found himself flying among stars and planets …"

CARLOS RUIZ ZAFÓN, *THE PRINCE OF MIST*

Planetary and zodiacal magic fall under the category of celestial magic because they work with the planets and the zodiacal constellations. The purpose of celestial magic is to wield the spirits of the archetypal celestial deities and to produce magical artifacts called talismans. This is an old magical methodology consisting of talismanic magic and celestial deity petitions referred to collectively as Scholastic Image Magic (SIM) that had precedence during the European Renaissance.[1] Prominence has risen once again in the last several decades through the reunion of the disciplines of magic and astrology. These two methodologies have long been separated; changes in attitudes within the astrological community toward magic, as well as in the various magical groups and organizations who have rigorously adopted astrology once again have brought a kind of rebirth to both disciplines.

---

1 Clifford Hartleigh Low, "On Scholastic Image Magic," Sorcerer's Domain (blog), accessed January 2, 2022, *https://sorcerer.blog/2016/12/03/on-scholastic-image-magic/*.

So, what exactly are planetary and zodiacal magic, and how do they relate to talismanic magic? Until the twentieth century, it was popularly believed that the planets and zodiacal constellations had a powerful influence on all living things and that these energies left a deep impression in the mind of individuals at birth and continued to influence them throughout their lives. It was thought that the configuration of the planets and the zodiac could completely determine a person's fate and even predict their death.

Although modern astronomy has, for the most part, repudiated the belief in cosmic forces that affect human nature, many people still actively and successfully employ an astrology practice and its magical capabilities are still very effective and in use today. There is something operating within astrology and celestial magic, but it is likely not an actual cosmic force so much as it is a collection of psychological forces similarly to the function of magical energy, the occurrence of the realm of spirits and the effectiveness of systems of divination.

Celestial magic was used to harness these celestial portends for both good and bad outcomes and to manipulate the apparent underlying cosmic forces so as to render them subject to the will of magicians. There were also spirits associated with these cosmic forces, and some believed that such spirits were the intelligences and powers behind the potency of celestial magic. A thorough mastery of astrology and astrological magic was required for someone to even begin to plumb the depths of this kind of magic, in addition to a kind of knowledge of invocation. Talismanic magic was a discipline within which these cosmic forces and intelligences were summoned and projected into a metallic piece of jewelry that held the charm in place through the virtues of its metallurgy and the symbolic signatures inscribed upon it.

It would therefore seem that celestial magic and astrology represent a level of knowledge and capability that would be daunting to some and particularly exclusive to others. While ceremonial magicians have been tinkering with celestial magic long before the nineteenth century, it was the Golden Dawn that brought it into greater practical use with the introduction of the ritual workings employing the lesser and greater hexagram. The hexagram was an important device used for actively generating planetary energies so that they could be used in magical workings, producing an active planetary signature or quality based on the drawn hexagram angle. Prior forms of this kind of magic, those established in antiquity, used passive mechanisms for capturing the powers of the stars, briefly exposing consecrated gemstones or jewelry at a strategic time and place. In some cases, the final work of inscribing the talisman also occurred under the auspices of the elected time. Practitioners were required to cast and delineate an *electional* chart to determine the most auspicious timing for such a magical operation.

The Golden Dawn's use of an active methodology for performing planetary magic was a powerful innovation, and it deserves to be considered one the of great breakthroughs in celestial magical workings. While some find the Golden Dawn system quite adequate for working celestial magic, others have developed alternative methodologies that are just as capable and appropriate. Some have gone back to the methods derived in late antiquity with a modern perspective. Most of them, however, use the active or a combination of methods instead of the passive method alone, as we shall see.

To generate an active planetary energy signature using a star polygon, as this device is called, first denote each of the seven positions in the hexagram with one of the seven planets. The focus is on the point associated with the planet that one seeks to invoke. Next, deliberately draw a line using a finger or tool from the opposite point to that point and follow the lines as they pass through all of the rest of the points and back to the opposite point. A final thrust to the point of the target planet produces the final planetary energy signature.[2] This method follows the same basic pattern that is used to generate an element energy using the invoking pentagram. Here is an example of the greater hexagram used to invoke the planet Jupiter:

---

2 This drawing method is used only for the unicursal hexagram. The hexagram that consists of two triangles is drawn in two parts: the operator draws one triangle and then superimposes the second over the first.

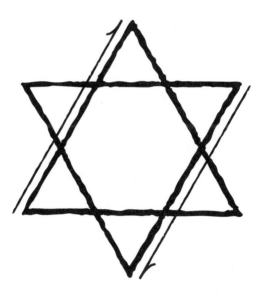

Figure 1: The Greater Invoking Hexagram of Jupiter

For myself, I approached the problem of working celestial magic years ago pretending that I had a completely clean slate. I was knowledgeable about the Golden Dawn rituals that used the hexagram, but I found them cumbersome and not very appealing. The one problem I had with the Golden Dawn technique is that I didn't like using the hexagram device to determine and project the planetary angles that are a necessary part of actively generating a planetary energy signature. Even the unicursal hexagram seemed contrived to me, and I had found a much better device in the septagram.

My system of magic uses a septagram (a seven-sided star) to invoke a planetary intelligence. I like the septagram because there is a separate and distinct node or point for each planet. However, the septagram is much more difficult to draw in the air as a device, so I have adopted the use of a consecrated icon of a septagram, where the device is painted on a special wooden plank and placed in the center of the temple on a central altar. I then trace the angular lines to invoke a specific planet only once on the icon instead of having to do it four times at each cardinal direction, as it is done in the Golden Dawn ritual of the Superior Hexagram. I have used this technique for decades and find it quite efficacious. While I might not use the device of the superior hexagram, I have found uses for the lesser hexagram of the elements in my magical workings.

I will admit that I was besotted with the septagram—it was so unusual looking and somewhat obscure, and I found a way to use it in planetary magic that was concise and effective. My premise was that the septagram had seven points, one for each of the seven archetypal planets of traditional planetary magic. One had to draw all six of the double triangles of the hexagram to invoke the Sun with the traditional Golden Dawn hexagram device. The unicursal hexagram was slightly better, since the center point in the hexagram became the node associated with the Sun. And yet, I still felt it was contrived. Why not use a device that had seven points for the seven planets? It seemed so obvious to me! Perhaps the Sun as the center of the classic Golden Dawn hexagram was due to a heliocentric instead of geocentric perspective.

My use of the septagram is not exclusive; Denning and Phillips also employed this device in their 1989 book *Planetary Magick*. Unfortunately, that book came out years after I had already built a magical system from my Witchcraft magical foundation to perform celestial magic. Since I had chosen the septagram to use as my planetary magical device, I ended up not using much of the GD tradition for this kind of magic. That was the beginning point where my path diverged from the ceremonial magical tradition regarding planetary magic, and it only accelerated from there as time went on.

In my previous books on evocation and energy magic, I had shown a remarkable pattern of diverging from established magical traditions. I think that this was because I felt so connected to the Witchcraft way of looking at and doing magic. I never really considered the modern tradition of ceremonial magic as something foreign to my magical workings on the one hand, nor was it a required discipline to be adhered to without any significant change on the other.

I think that Gardner had already plotted that divergent course decades ago when he established the Witchcraft praxis for his tradition. By now, that course had been well established. We Witches were already deep in unmapped territory; moving forward in this manner seemed both logical and prudent. I thus assembled a system of magic that Witches and Pagans could use to work celestial magic many years ago. I felt that it was a very important step and, as a system of magic, was completely missing in either the Gardnerian Book of Shadows or in any of the inter-coven magical traditions.

Witches I knew in the 1970s and 1980s tended to pick up the Golden Dawn tradition of planetary magic and use it for working that kind of magic. Anyone who found that system to be either unpalatable or too complex and contrived had few options: invent their own methodology, seek out older grimoire traditions and attempt to make them work, or opt out of this kind of magic altogether. Of these basic choices available to Witches in those days, I decided to fashion my own system. What I learned and discovered by traveling that route was a system of magic with many more possibilities and potentials than the one the GD had incorporated. It is the very same system described in this book.

However, I am getting a bit ahead of myself. What we really need to discuss in this introduction is explain why anyone would want to adopt the rather involved and complex system of magic that is planetary and zodiacal magic. What is the most compelling reason to engage in this kind of magical work, particularly when there are so many other kinds of magic available to the competent practitioner? The question is important, and it is one that needs answering to justify taking on this kind of work.

Why Should Witches Master Celestial Magic?

Of all of the forms of magic available to a Witch that are either underrepresented in the Gardnerian Book of Shadows or are completely absent is celestial magic. Some would think that celestial magic is the highest of the highbrow forms of magic, making it the exclusive property and proclivity of the ceremonial magician. Is it another one of those off-limit subjects that Witches should justifiably shrug off and ignore? Anyone could have said the same thing about evocation and advanced energy magic, yet I have shown through my published works using the artifice of Witchcraft magic alone that even these methodologies are readily accessible. I have the same opinion regarding celestial magic. However, adopting celestial magic will necessitate the addition of tools and techniques that pushes the methodologies of Witchcraft magic into an area of ritual magic proper.

Some might say that there is no difference between ceremonial magic and ritual magic. I would disagree—ceremonial magic assumes that the magician must abrogate the authority of God to command and master the spiritual domain through the artifice of magic. The ritual magician, who has a completely Pagan spiritual approach actually assumes the godhead of their deity and performs these operations through that guise. Witchcraft and polytheistic Paganism allow for this approach to magic, but magicians operating under monotheistic creeds cannot assume the godhead without the dispensation of the holy orders of priesthood (if such orders exist in their creed), restricting them to a regimen of begging their deity for such power and authority as their inherent piety and purity will allow. I therefore make a distinction between ceremonial magic and ritual magic; according to my definition, they operate under completely different spiritual perspectives.

Adding celestial magic to the repertoire of Witchcraft would not be as easy and simple as adding evocation or advanced energy magic. So the question stands: why would a Witch want to engage in the effort to adopt this method of magic to their regimen? What benefit does celestial magic have that cannot be found in other methodologies of magic? These are important questions that need to be answered before committing to the additional work required for performing celestial magic.

The core product of celestial magic is the creation of a talisman. We are thus considering talismanic magic as the basic purpose for performing most celestial magical operations. Yet it is the production of this magical artifact that will inform anyone's decision whether or not to master celestial magic. This is because talismanic magic is the art of making for yourself and others a charmed life, a life in which reality seems to consistently bend to the will of the talisman's owner at all times and places, lessening the possibility of misfortune and empowering great good fortune. A talisman is nothing more than encapsulating a wish or desire and continually setting the powers of the elements, celestial spirits, and archetypes of the gods upon it.

In other words, a talisman is a materialized spell that is continually and perpetually operating for the benefit of its owner. That owner can be the practitioner or their family, friends, or clients. A talisman makes a charmed life possible, and building up a battery of them to act on several fronts simultaneously for the benefit of the owner is the final magical mechanism that makes this kind of overall effect possible. The magic of talismans is thus considerably more potent, consistent, and autonomous once charged and activated. Other than talismans, I am not aware of any other magical artifact with these qualities. Learning to produce a talisman would therefore be the best of all possible magical practices a Witch could master.

Advanced energy magic has its uses; usually it is deployed to make a very specific and strategic event materialize in the practitioner's life. Evocation can conjure a spirit to do the same in a more nuanced, deep, and intelligent manner. Yet it is talismanic magic that offers the ability to work on a given objective perpetually. Evocation and energy, as forms of magic, are performed for each and every objective, whereas a talisman can be produced to cover a given area of one's life and allowed to work all the time, day in and day out. Because a talismanic artifact is generated for broad purposes such as wealth creation or career success, it will continue to work on that objective indefinitely, as long as the owner takes special and conscious consideration of it and acknowledges its existence, purpose, and the auspices under which it was created.

Because talismans can only be terminated through complete physical destruction of the artifact itself, they can be passed on to a family member, friend, or client and will continue to work their magic long after the creator is gone from this world. A talisman can become inactive through long-term neglect, but even one that is inactive due to inattention can still carry the potency it had in a latent and quiescent manner, only needing to be reawakened to become potently actualized once again.

A talisman is a magical treasure, and a good practitioner of celestial magic will create a series of them to act on every aspect of their life, tapping each one for a specific purpose when the need arises. This capability alone represents the quantitative wealth or richness of talismanic magic. Who would pass up a chance to acquire this wealth to make a charmed life for themselves? This is also why I refer to talismanic magic, and to celestial magic as its organizing principal, as the veritable *crown jewel* of Witchcraft magic.

I am sure that the attraction of talismanic magic, as I have defined it here, will doubtlessly intrigue and motivate you to engage in it. I may have appealed to your desire to better yourself at all levels by describing the wonderful qualities of the charged talisman and what it can do for you. I should state that there is a cost for learning how to work this magic in terms of time and materials. It is not a simple process, and it has more stipulations than simpler forms of magic. I would compare celestial magic and the production of talismans to any other laborious process, such as complex herbal magic; the making of magical medicines, potions, ointments or elixirs; or the crafting of magical tools. It is a skill that has to be practiced and developed over time. It also requires some additional tools and a knowledge of the celestial sciences; in particular astrology and also astronomy.

What is required to work celestial magic is a practical regimen of work, both from a liturgical and a magical perspective. These, of course, are above and beyond the basic practices of integral Witchcraft liturgy and magic. Where the advanced practices of energy work and evocation still fit in the basic practices of Witchcraft, practicing celestial magic requires a more dedicated approach. If you are going to work celestial magic, you will have to dedicate more time and resources to making it happen. Here are five of the more practical requirements needed for working celestial magic:

Characterizing planetary archetypes as personal deities: Probably one of the most important steps that a Witch will take when starting a magical discipline of working celestial magic is to embody the seven planetary archetypes as living and breathing deities within their practice of Witchcraft liturgy. What this means is that the person will select deities in their own ethnic tradition (or one of their choosing) and bring these into their personal pantheon. The person will give offerings to these deities during full moon esbats and celebrate them at the eight sabbats. They will enshrine these deities in some form within a special altar, using consecrated objects, emblem tools, or even some kind of statues to represent them.

Ultimately, the Witch may even invest these objects with a talismanic charge and activation to make them into living icons that house the deities. Knowing celestial magic will also allow them to charge and activate other statuses and icons, so that their shrine of deities is empowered, alive, and fully conscious of the Witch's life and objectives at all times. Possessing such an empowered shrine will require a regimen of periodic and continuous offerings to each of these icons.

A deeper liturgical investment: A Witch practicing celestial magic will need to pay more attention to the cycles of the moon, the seasons of the sun, and any highly auspicious astrological event. Celebrations of the esbats and sabbats will become more engaged with the natural occurrence of astronomical and astrological events, since these will be seen as spiritually significant. Times for performing regular religious observations are also necessary, based on the chosen discipline. A Witch working celestial magic is one who is more religiously engaged than one just following the typical praxis.

Becoming a competent astrologer and astronomer: Because celestial magic relies heavily on the actual occurrence of celestial events and determining their significance as well as when such magic should be performed, it is critical to have good, strong knowledge of astrology and astronomy. The reason is that celestial magic has the determinants of constant change, event-based auspices, and knowledge of one's celestial life potential that is derived from them. Working celestial magic requires a working knowledge of natal astrology and astrological transits because these are affected and activated at the moment that celestial magic is performed. You don't have to be an expert, but you do need to be competent and knowledgeable to make the most out of celestial magic.

Guiding and restricting the magical schedule to temporal factors: Celestial magic is determined by the auspices of the moment, and that means this kind of magic has to have a rigorous schedule that uses planetary hours, planetary days, the periods when the lunar mansions or the astrological decans are active, and when certain auspicious transits occur. This is the kind of magic that can only be worked at certain times of the day or night, and the Witch who seeks to work celestial magic must comply with that kind of restriction in order to get the best results.

Building and using additional tools, furniture, and stocking supplies: Practicing celestial magic requires the use of a new magical tool and a secondary piece of furniture. The magical tool is what I call a septagram icon, and the secondary piece of furniture is a small portable central altar. The septagram icon is a wood plank that has a septagram (or some other star polygon) painted on it. As an icon, it is consecrated and charged after being built so that it becomes a specialized magical tool. I call it a magical icon because it is a focus for magical workings; in the case of the septagram icon, it is used to draw and invoke the planetary angles of the septagram. There are other kinds of magical icons that have many uses, but this is the only one required for celestial magic. The septagram icon is placed on the central altar and used as the principal focus for celestial magic.

The rest of the tools and supplies I typically use for celestial magic are optional aesthetic additions to this kind of magic. You can choose to use any or all of these in your magical workings, or you can stick to just the essential elements and keep your celestial magic as basic and simple as possible. It is up to you to manage the level of sophistication in enhancing and embellishing this kind of magic. This book focuses on both the required elements and suggested enhancements so you can decide how to build up your own method for celestial magic.

I use different kinds of metal stock to make talismanic disks and metal etching equipment. Finding metal stock is not very easy, but many stores that specifically cater to jewelry making can provide plates of metal for working on.[3] You will need a good pair of tin snips or heavy-duty craft scissors to cut the plate stock into disks.

Other items would include seven colored scarves, stoles, or scapulars; planetary incenses; planetary music or specific tones; and specific planetary offerings such as colored devotional candles, liquors/spirit libations, flowers, oils/perfumes, herbs/drugs, and food. All of these items should fit into a set of celestial correspondences that you would use to tailor the magic to a specific planet or zodiacal sign.

I will, of course, cover all of these elements in greater detail later, but as you can see, celestial magic can become quite elaborate and involved, depending on your tastes and sense of magical aesthetics. What it all represents together is quite an investment of time, materials, discipline, practice, and training in the elements of astronomy and astrology. And like any investment, it will be well worth it if you are able to master this method and build for yourself, family, or clients a charmed life. I believe that the compensation will be considerable when compared to the overall work required.

If you have added both evocation and advanced energy magical workings to your Witchcraft magic regimen, adding celestial magic won't be so challenging. The rituals and the disciplined practice for celestial magic are above and slightly beyond what you have already mastered with the other two forms

---

3 I recommend Rio Grande jewelry supply online store for metal stock, wires, chains and tools: *https://www.riogrande.com/category/metals*. For etching, the UTool engraver or a Dremel as found on Amazon or in any other hobby store should suffice.

of magic; it is likely much more involved for a Witch who has not attempted to master either magical technique.

Therefore, my principal reading audience for this book on the topics of celestial magic and talismanic magic would be those who have already added the disciplines of evocation and advanced energy workings to their regimen of magical skills. Whether or not they have purchased and studied my two books on these subjects is immaterial, but having this skill set would be important. A Witch who has a competent knowledge of astrology and skill in performing advanced Witchcraft workings should be able to derive their own practice of celestial magic by studying the contents of this book. This kind of magic will not be beyond their abilities.

However, a beginning magical practitioner who doesn't have much knowledge of astrology would find the instructions and contents of this book to be prohibitively difficult, particularly determining the timing of a working. I would recommend that a beginner learn to master the basics first and then take on evocation and advanced energy workings before attempting to engage with the material presented here. Celestial magic is complex and requires a greater level of discipline and tool usage in order for one to become competent and capable of regularly using it.

While this book is devoted to celestial magic, the student will want to study astrology in order to get a deeper understanding of that sacred science. There are many books on this topic; a list appears at the end of this introduction for your purchase and study. I won't get into deep discussion about basic astrological topics in this book (e.g., natal chart interpretation), but I would expect that the student will want, at the very least, to have a working knowledge of natal astrology and be able to perform a delineation of their own natal chart.

Additionally, I would recommend knowing how to use an astrological calendar to determine the relevant transit aspects, their meaning, and how they would affect one's natal chart. It bears repeating: one doesn't need to master astrology to get the best results out of celestial magic. And it is *also* true that the more one understands about astrology and astronomy, the greater the clarity when planning a working.

I would recommend the following books to anyone who wants to study astrology and get to know it better in preparation for working planetary and zodiacal magic. If you collect and read these books and also purchase the Daily

Planetary Guide for the current year, you will have more than enough information to plan a celestial working. In planetary and zodiacal magic, knowledge is power!

Practical Astrology for Witches and Pagans by Ivo Dominguez Jr. (Red Wheel/ Weiser, 2016)

The Only Way to Learn Astrology, Volume 1—Second Edition: Basic Principles by Marion D. March and Joan McEvers (ACS Publications, 2008)

The Only Way to Learn Astrology, Volume 2—Third Edition: Math and Interpretation Techniques by Marion D. March and Joan McEvers (Starcrafts Publishing, 2009)

The Only Way to Learn About Tomorrow, Second Edition: Progressions, Directions, Solar and Lunar Returns, Transits by Marion D. March and Joan McEvers (ACS Publications, 2010)

Llewellyn's Complete Book of Astrology: The Easy Way to Learn Astrology by Kris Brandt Riske (Llewellyn Worldwide, 2007)

Llewellyn's Daily Planetary Guide (for the current year)—this is more useful to me than lugging around an ephemeris and having to calculate the planetary positions to my local time.

Additionally, the online classes taught by Christopher Warnock are also highly recommended, since he is both an astrologer and a magical practitioner. He has also written several books that are still in print.

https://www.renaissanceastrology.com/astrologyandmagiccourses.html

Chapter One
APPROACHING THE PRACTICE OF CELESTIAL MAGIC

"Though my soul may set in darkness,
it will rise in perfect light;
I have loved the stars too fondly to be
fearful of the night."

—SARAH WILLIAMS, *TWILIGHT HOURS:*
A LEGACY OF VERSE

Because celestial magic is such a complex topic, it must be broken down into smaller topical areas to really give a complete perspective on the depth and breadth of this magical discipline. The full spectrum of this topic covers many areas: the psychological model of magic, the importance of astrology and its role in celestial magic, and the time or temporal model of magic, a model that has been only rarely covered in any work.

Also included is an examination of the two types of celestial magic, the passive and the active methods, and how the best approach is to use a combination of both. We will look at the nature of planetary and zodiacal spirit intelligences and how they are one of the important keys used in celestial magic, thereby incorporating the spirit model of magic. We will examine the nature of talismans, the importance of the lunar mansions and astrological decans in this work, as well as other techniques and mechanisms, such as the astrological septans. We will, of course, discuss the ritual structures used to create a talisman, and explain the astrological underpinnings and how they are integrated into this kind of magic.

So, let's briefly look at each of these topics with the implicit understanding that they will be covered in far greater detail in subsequent chapters. My purpose is to help you to understand the components that must be included in a complete study on celestial and talismanic magic.

Celestial Magic and the Psychological Model of Magic

Many of the oldest books about magic and the most famous grimoires of all time feature some form of planetary or zodiacal magic, known as celestial magic within their pages. Such grimoires were famously known as the *Picatrix* and the classical *Key of Solomon* variations. The beautiful and mysterious planetary talismans in the *Key of Solomon* are a good example of this kind of magic, but variations on planetary and zodiacal magic are ubiquitous. We can find planetary magic as one of the pinnacles of ceremonial magic in the Golden Dawn tradition, and it is a staple of the Enochian magic of John Dee and the Hermetic magical writings of Ficino.

It is quite apparent that planetary and zodiacal magic has its roots in antiquity, and even before that when it was a way to communicate with the gods. The origins of this magic can be traced to Assyria and Babylon, where it was part of the religious practices of those times and places. Therefore, the magic of the planets and the constellations has an obvious ancient provenance. There should be no surprise, then, that astrology and planetary magic are still relevant, popular, and part of the worldwide cultures of the modern world despite the powerful cultural contradictions imposed and promoted by modern astronomy and physics.

If I were to list the three most important techniques of magic, I would include celestial magic along with elemental magic and magical evocation. A competent ritual magician would be able to use all three techniques of magic either separately or in combination to fulfill whatever they required regarding the unquenchable desire to know all things and to master the material world. Since I have written books that have delivered to the modern Witch the methodologies of elemental and evocative magic, I felt it would be important to also produce a book on planetary and talismanic magic.

While elemental magic covers the energy and information models of magic and magical evocation covers the spirit model of magic, the techniques of planetary magic cover the psychological model of magic. It also employs the spirit and energy models, but it is the psychological model that has precedence. This is because planetary magic is based on the planetary archetypes, which are considered the constituents and the building blocks of conscious being. They are the stuff of the mind itself and what colors the characteristics of the human personality.

Planetary spirits are called intelligences because they represent the very components of the mind of the individual and the culture of the collective consciousness. These spirits are associated with and embody psychological archetypes or meta-symbols that interreact in a dynamic and implicit part in the personality and characteristics of a sentient human being. A personality is therefore defined as the dynamic interplay of psychological archetypes acting within the inner sphere of the mind and reflecting and refracting the external material world. However, a personality can also exist without a physical body, since that would explain such phenomena as complex spirits, thoughtforms, cultural motifs and tropes, egregores, and the paradoxical phenomenon of deities, demigods, angels, demons, and the ghosts of our ancestors.

The psychological model of magic stipulates that magic is a phenomenon of the mind but that its domain extends beyond the mental sphere of the individual into the collective conscious mind and beyond. Psychological magic uses the "as if" paradigm and the powers of the imagination to make what was merely psychic fully realized and actual. By extending the mental sphere, the psychology model of magic would therefore include all forms of celestial magic, talismanic magic, as well as the inner domains of the psyche called the inner planes. It would include forms of magic that produce illusions, visual and mental paradoxes, as well as triggering forms of psychic transformation and transcendentalism.

Psychological magic is the provenance of the stage magician, the magical actor who engages in spectacular and mysterious theatric presentations. Magicians with this knowledge and ability are those who wield and engage with the powerful psychic transformational processes or ordeals for the benefit of themselves and all of humanity. This kind of magic establishes a powerful link between the inner mind, the collective mind (culture), the universal mind (god-consciousness), and the material world. It binds the microcosm to the macrocosm such that it becomes a singular instrument in the hands of the ritual magician. The essential paradigm of this kind of magic is found within the point in consciousness where *thought becomes form,* and conversely, *form becomes thought.* It is the bridge between the mind and the material world. Psychological magic is therefore a linguistic phenomenon and also a social phenomenon, meaning it also covers the informational model of magic.

Because it is an integral part of psychological magic, the use of celestial magic cannot only change the material world, it can also affect the psyche of individuals, collective groups, and populations. It is a source of self-knowledge and an instrument of teaching, self-transformation, and realization. The world we live in has both internal and external cultural symbols, archetypes, and tropes that the knowledgeable magician can employ to manipulate the psychic reality of consciousness itself.

Even today in our modern world, our culture is saturated with planetary and zodiacal references, from the days of the week to the months, seasons, and events that occur in the world from age to age, those mythic cycles of the greater human personality. There is a reason for the continued prevalence of what are obviously antiquated beliefs and traditions. Yet it has more to do with the psychic profile of the human personality and the cultural collective than it does the astronomical phenomena it seeks to corroborate with regarding the fate of individuals and nations.

Astrology Is the Key to Celestial Magic

The foundation of planetary and zodiacal magic is, of course, astrology itself. When used to divine events and the reasons for personal and collective choices, astrology is used in a passive or divinatory manner. Here, the powers of the symbolic constructs of zodiacal house, sign, planet, and aspect are used to inspire and delineate a kind of powerful and psychic purview of possibilities and, on occasion, actual prophecies. However, there also exists an active or magical way of making things happen, and it is here the same powerful symbols and archetypes are used to energize and force a potential outcome into becoming a materialized realization. Conversely, this kind of magic can easily and readily operate on the mind of the individual as well as the cultural collective.

It is my belief that the divinatory and magical techniques have always been used in astrology but these two disciplines were separated somewhere in time. This division split astrology and planetary magic into two distinct disciplines when they should in fact be one and the same. We should examine the history of astrology to see where the split occurred, and through that knowledge, propose uniting the divinatory and magical parts of astrology once again. We will do this so that astrology will be a powerful divination tool *and* a method of practical magic.

In antiquity, the astrologer who prophesized events through mundane astrology was also the wizard who produced talismans to draw, filter, or repel astrological and planetary influences. However, in today's modern world, astrologers assume that their methods are rational and scientific such that any dabbling in magic would probably scandalize the astrological community or the public at large. Of course, this separation of magic from astrology has its basis in the conceit of modern astrology as a philosophical and scientific discipline, even though the scientific community has thoroughly rejected astrology as a science. This has left planetary magic in the hands of ritual magicians, where it would be more ideally utilized by astrologers who have mastered the symbols and constructs used in astrology. Luckily, in today's world many magicians are also studying and mastering astrology.

The emphasis of astrology on being a rational and philosophical (scientific) discipline is based on the iconic astrological work of Ptolemy, as found in the *Four Books*, or *Tetrabiblos*. We will briefly examine the history and foundation of astrology to discover where this philosophical root has its origin so that we might rectify it and bring astrology into a more modern (and paradoxically) ancient perspective. This rectification is already occurring in astrological circles, yet it is important to restore astrology to a system of divination as it originally was so that it can be united with the occult practices of planetary and zodiacal magic.

What this means is that if a Witch performing ritual magic seeks to master planetary and zodiacal magic, then they should also seek to master astrology. These two separate practices are truly one complete system of divination and magic. You cannot approach planetary magic without a rudimentary knowledge

☉

of astrology, and if you are a competent astrologer, you cannot really change much in the world without also using planetary and zodiacal magic. They are integral to each other—to be an effective practitioner of one does indeed entail the use of the other. I will get more into the details of why this is such an important perspective a bit later on and will also show how some of the techniques of astrology are quite magical, regardless of whether some professional astrologers accept this as true.

Celestial Magic and the Magical Model of Time

Astrology teaches us that just like the material world it emulates, the world of archetypes is subject to constant change. While there are changes stochastically occurring in the sky, such as comets, supernovae, or unexpected meteorite showers, most occurrences are predictable, e.g., eclipses, apparent retrograde planetary movements, lunar phases, and the shifting of the seasonal ecliptic.

The movement of the planets across the sky and the constellations that mark the seasons are all predictable, as are the constant movements of houses and angular aspects between them. It is the combination of the planet, sign, house, and aspect that constitutes what I call an archetype in celestial magic, and this construct is undergoing continual cyclic change through time. However, electing a specific time and place for a magical working or casting a horoscope represents a snapshot of this continual movement, since it is this frozen moment used for both divination and magical operations.

The background or foundation for planetary and zodiacal magic is therefore the ever-changing positions and interactions (aspects) of the planets within the field of astrological houses and signs, something I call the eternal dance of the archetypes. Planetary magic is not based on static definitions and attributes—the archetypes are constantly transforming in their interactions, just as the four elements are transforming. Yet that elected moment or snapshot is what gives the most meaning to the configuration of astrological elements.

If the magic to be worked is for a strategic life-changing event, it is important that the magical practitioner finds and uses the most auspicious influences for the event of a specific planetary working. Not only are the current transit aspects that are happening in the sky when the magical event is performed important, the planetary hour and day of the week are also significant.

These correspondences can make a stronger or weaker alignment that will affect the magical working. The practitioner should strive to use the strongest alignment possible to ensure that the magical artifact produced will help result in a successful outcome for important workings. This is unlike any other type of magic, because the practitioner should always be concerned with timing to get the maximum effect out of their magical working, if that working is for a strategic life change. For lesser kinds of workings or magical effects, these considerations are not as important.

What this means is that there is a second magical model involved in planetary and zodiacal magic, and that is the model of cyclic time and the snapshot of the moment. This is an obscure model since it is possible to work planetary magic without any concern for the auspiciousness of the time or place. Similarly, it is important to perform mundane actions to help a magical process successfully complete and that these actions increase the odds for the outcome to be as the operator desires it to be. However, a powerful astrological alignment captured in a celestial magical working will require far fewer accompanying mundane actions to help complete a magical objective simply because it is done at the right time. The timing is the single most important reason for performing an astrological analysis and checking the celestial auspices for a working.

If a practitioner wants to maximize the possibilities for a fruitful outcome with a magical working, paying attention to the astrological details is critically important. Incorporating the planetary day, planetary hour, and the various transits associated with the astrological event when planning a working will ensure a much higher probability of success when it is done. This approach uses both the active and the passive methods simultaneously in the practice of celestial magic.

All magical practitioners seek to bend the laws of probability to their will to make a change in the material world. Yet there can be no greater enhancement to this simple objective then when planetary magic is performed at the right time and place. For stimulating the material plane or even the conscious predilection of the mind itself, planetary magic is a superior system of magic if the regimen of timing is carefully followed. If it is not followed, it will suffer the same limitations as any other technique of magic. I would recommend that all practitioners of planetary magic pay attention to the attributes underlying time, since time is a strategic model in this kind of working.

In the cyclic time model of magic, magic is mediated by auspicious events and the cyclic, predictable interplay of astrological phenomena. At a deeper symbolic level, this model represents the attributes and dynamic interplay of the symbols and archetypes of conscious sentience. The cyclic time model of magic is the opposite of the chaos model, representing a predictable cycle of occurrences that, once triggered, allows for the gateway of conscious realization to open for the practitioner and through them as mediator, cause both psychic and material changes to occur.

This model allows for both a passive and active role for the practitioner and the performance of ritual, since the auspicious moment is profoundly transformative in and of itself. Finding that auspicious moment is the part of this magic concerned with astrological divination. Once it has been determined, performing a magical ritual process becomes the actual trigger for that irresistible magic of the moment.

We could therefore say that time is like a powerful deity; in fact, the Greeks knew this godhead as Chronos. To us, he is the personification of that auspicious moment when magic transforms the universal mind and the material universe. The time model of magic and the philosophic deity Chronos are covered in greater detail in chapter 3.

Planetary and Astrological Deities

The symbols of the planets and the zodiacal signs have within them the original attributes of the deity. These deities have associations with ancient Akkadian and Chaldean deities that were used to characterize ancient astrology when it was purely a form of divination that was used to communicate and discover the will of the gods for a given question or request. While modern astrology has sought to bury these associations, Witches and Pagans would do well to take this relationship into account and accord these deities the respect and veneration that engaging with them would normally require within a liturgical magical context.

It is my opinion that planetary and zodiacal magic also have a liturgical dimension to them, since approaching the planetary and zodiacal deities for magical purposes also entails certain religious obligations. We as Pagans and

Witches should not approach planetary magic as if it was some kind of secular operation. We should also seek to make spiritual and liturgical connections with the planetary and zodiacal deities, since that will empower all of our planetary workings and incorporate an antique oracular attribution of divination into our workings.

What I propose is that we treat the great planetary deities as part of our spiritual family to give them offerings, prayers, and some kind of physical representation in our temple shrine. We would do this as if they were a part of our Pagan or Wiccan liturgy. Making an alignment with these deities will help in establishing alignments with the planetary magic that we seeking to perform. I believe that this aspect of worship will keep the planetary and zodiacal attributes of a magical working from becoming secularized and despiritualized. If, on the other hand, it makes them more real and immanent, that will greatly enhance the working. This would include a special place for the deity Chronos to be unofficially part of one's pantheon.

While everything psychic and material changes within the endless cycles of time, the deity Chronos represents that oneness that fosters the endless change but never changes itself. Chronos is characterized by both infinity/eternity and singularity. It is the ever-unchanging fulcrum of continuous change—the eternal now that is the beginning and end of everything.

The planetary system of antiquity in which astrology was made into a rational philosophy consisted of five known planets: Mercury, Venus, Mars, Jupiter, and Saturn, including the Sun and Moon. There were thus seven planetary archetypes attributed to the Roman gods. In its ancient formulation, astrology used these seven planets to qualify and characterize the twelve signs of the zodiac. These have been given the names of mythic beings or animals: Aries (Ram), Taurus (Bull), Leo (Lion), Scorpio (Scorpion), Capricorn (Goat), and Pisces (two fish joined together). These mythic images disguise the underlying character of actual deities, and we will examine these attributes in more detail in chapter 5.

However, since that time we have discovered and added three new planets and included them with the original seven. We have also added a few asteroids as well. Modern astrology uses these new planets and planetoids in its delineations and has produced a kind of hybrid between the traditional astrology of Ptolemy and modern astronomy. Yet planetary magic is still focused on using the same seven-planet system based on older astrology. It works quite well as it is, but there might be more possibilities if the additional planets were incorporated.

Celestial magic includes archetypal deities and spirits associated with the planets. When examining the spirit intelligences and entities associated with the planets, there are basically two approaches: use of the traditional planetary angel pairs or the seven Olympian governors. Typically, an operator would use one set or the other, since they represent two different traditional approaches.

The first method proposes a pair of spirits consisting of the angelic spirit intelligence and the energy spirit associated with a Hebrew-based Qabalistic correspondence. They are typically used together for talismanic workings. These pair of angelic spirits have been used for centuries for higher (intelligence) and practical (energy) forms of planetary magic and are featured in Agrippa's *Occult Philosophy* volumes. In addition to those pairs of angels is a list of archangels that could be used alongside the pair or as a replacement.

The second method is to use another set of spirits referred to as the seven Olympian governors or spirits, introduced in the grimoire called the *Arbatel*, possibly written by Paracelsus or one of his students. I have found that the Olympian spirits are much more to my magical tastes, aesthetically closer to my form of Witchcraft magic. Of course, the Olympian spirits are just the spiritual intermediaries (daimons) for the Olympian gods (in the guise of their Greek or Roman equivalents); one could work with the daimons and also give worship to the deities behind them, which is the approach I use and is present in this book.

Whatever approach the operator uses, they are considered the agents of the energies and intelligence of the planets. They personify the planetary qualities (from an astrological perspective) and can be invoked and approached as any spirit can. Not only do they represent the qualities of the planet, they can also communicate their knowledge and instruct the magician about their utility. They are the active and activating psychic forces for the planet they embody. Invoking one of these spirits places that magical operation firmly in the category of being active rather than passive; like drawing hexagrams or septagrams, it is an active approach to attracting the planetary intelligence and energy in order to energize a working instead of passively using the available astrological aspects.

The operator should approach these spirits with the same reverence they would a minor deity. In addition, I believe that establishing a liturgical relationship with the Deities associated with these planetary intelligences can also empower the working, probably in a manner far greater than if they are omitted.

Active and Passive Forms of Planetary Magic

As was said previously, there are two basic formulations for working planetary magic: actively invoking the planetary intelligence and energies, and waiting for an auspicious time when that planetary attribute is naturally triggered by an astrological event. The first method is called the active technique and the second is referred to as the passive technique.

Most forms of ancient planetary magic used the passive technique to imbue a talisman or some kind of tool with the planetary qualities that occurred at a specific moment in time. Some aspects only last a few minutes, but most last for the duration of a planetary hour. The planned planetary event could occur at any time during the day or night, and the magician would have to plan accordingly. The active technique was likely a recent invention, although Renaissance magicians such as Ficino seemed to use an active method of summoning a planet using colored cloth, incense, and specialized lighting to push the process from passive to more active.

Using the passive method requires focusing the planetary intelligence and energy to bless, consecrate, and imbue a tool with its energies. This tool would be a talisman, a magical instrument typically made of a semiprecious metal and engraved with sigils, seals, or signs to identify the magical qualities it now possesses after the working. The tool could also be a consecrated elixir or an ointment or balm. The tool is uncovered on the altar, exposed to the planetary influence, and then covered up after the influence has passed. The tool must then undergo a period of isolated incubation until the planetary influence is fixed within it, typically three to seven days.

The active method can be used in many different ways, whether to imprint and exteriorize the planetary intelligence and energy with a sigil, to internalize it also using a sigil, or to apply it to an object such as a talisman, elixir, balm or an ointment. The magician can use a sigil to direct the planetary influence because it is contained in the magic circle and, like an energy structure, can be imprinted with a sigil containing a magical link. This cannot be done using the passive approach because there is no way to contain and compress the planetary influence—it is only passively activated at the auspicious moment and absorbed by the artifact. As you can see, the active method is much more efficient. It can be directed and is not bound by an astrological moment, but it is also less effective than if it was performed during a planned event that maximized the planetary and astrological influences.

Using the active method alone does not require the use of planetary days, hours, or any astrological auspices. The passive method is heavily invested in the auspices of the moment of charging and thus requires a greater depth of analysis and even the casting of an elective chart. A hybrid system would use both methods but would be less dependent on the auspices of the moment than the passive technique. This gradation between active with no auspices and passive with extensive auspices is where I propose to work my celestial system of magic.

Talismanic Magic: Combining Planet and Element

A talisman is a specific kind of artifact produced in planetary magic. It is produced through a combination of planet, zodiacal sign, and element. It is generated during an auspicious time associated with a lunar mansion or an astrological decan as well as a planetary hour and planetary day. While a talisman can be generated through a planet or a zodiacal sign alone, the resultant artifact is not as powerful or as sustaining as one that includes an element energy.

This is because the planetary or zodiacal intelligence that is used to charge and imbue its qualities upon a magical artifact has a greater force and longevity when an element charge is used in combination with it. The element charge not only sustains the planetary or zodiacal intelligence imbuing an artifact but also amplifies the talisman's overall power.

Typically, I invoke a planetary or zodiacal intelligence by itself for two functional purposes: when seeking advice, prophecy, or direction; or when I want to affect my mind or alter my psychological profile in a positive and empowering manner. These kinds of workings are direct, immediate, and powerful but only last for a short time. The effects are only long lasting because I am the direct recipient of this kind of magic and the workings have a powerful overall impact on my mind.

These kinds of workings are internalized, not for creating direct effects on the external material world. They can impart a great deal of self-knowledge and cause insights and realizations, but they don't have the capability of generating a talismanic field. Invoking a planet or zodiacal sign can be very beneficial, and it is a powerful kind of working available to the Witch who has mastered celestial magic. It also employs exclusively the psychological model of magic.

To create a talisman, one can either employ one of the twenty-eight lunar mansions or one of the thirty-six astrological decans. Still, perhaps the simplest and most rudimentary talisman can be forged with a combination of a planet and a zodiacal sign. This is because the zodiacal sign has an implicit element as its basic formulation.

I have also created a new structure qualifying the twelve signs of the zodiac with the four elements, thereby breaking the signs up into four equal segments of around 7.5 degrees for each. I call these zodiacal element segments septans because they are around 7 degrees duration. Dividing the twelve signs into four septans per sign produces a total of forty-eight different qualifications, similar to the thirty-six qualifications of the decans. I have developed a system of talismanic magic to use these septans and have included it in this work.

Therefore, a talisman is a magical artifact that is imbued or charged by the spiritual intelligence of a planet or a zodiacal sign (or a combination of both) and empowered by an element. It is generated at a very specific time, using planetary hours, days, and astrological auspices, such as planetary transits. It also incorporates the time factor of either the lunar mansion, astrological decan, or astrological septan, since these occur only at very specific intervals and have a finite duration. Talismanic magic strategically incorporates both the psychological and the time models of magic, but also include the energy, spirit, and information models.

While it is possible that a talisman can be made of any substance as long as it can endure the wear and tear of time and use, the best substance for creating a talisman is a metallic, stone, crystal, or semi-precious gemstone artifact. These substances have the property of enduring the effects of time and therefore will keep the integrity of a talismanic charge at its maximum strength. They can and often are etched with sigils, seals, or characters that denote the nature of their effect and the target of their energy field.

Celestial Magic Topics

We have briefly covered the full spectrum of what will be in this book's contents. It is my hope that this work will instruct and guide you to be able to work planetary and zodiacal magic, to project, absorb, and charge talismans so that the powers and intelligences of these celestial deities and their mediators will be competently wielded by your hand.

As you can see by this second chapter, I will be presenting planetary magic in a manner atypical to the material that you would find in other books and articles. That is because I am proposing both a magical and a liturgical practice so that the astrological attributes come alive and once again live in our conscious minds as the deities that they originally were. I believe that for Witches and Pagans this is the optimal path for working this kind of magic.

These are the subjects that I am seeking to develop in the following chapters of this book. I believe that we should study and discuss these topics in greater detail, from the basic suppositions to the actual rituals and techniques used to perform this magic.

Included will be lists of spirits and the qualities and characteristics of the planets and the signs of the zodiac. We will focus on the three stages of planetary magic, consisting of a simple planetary invocation, engaging the mansions of the moon and the talismanic elementals, and enlarging upon that with the inclusion of the magic of the decans and septans. We will examine all the elements and components not only for working planetary magic but also knowing how to determine the most auspicious time for such a working to make it almost irresistibly effective and successful.

The chapters cover the following topics in detail:

- The relevant models of magic: the psychological model and the temporal model. We will also explore how the spirit, energy, and information models work within this type of magic.

- Planetary and zodiacal magic are based on the cyclic and periodic changes associated with activating aspects of astrology. We will also examine astrology regarding magical auspices, covering the components of timing how they work with celestial magic. We will also briefly discuss the foundation of astrology regarding its history and show that it is to be seen as a system of divination and not so much as a rational science.

- Astrology consists of the interpretation of the symbols of sign, house, planetary, and angular aspects. All these symbols represent the archetypes that make up the personality of the individual and the psychic domain of the collective consciousness. Knowing the symbols of astrology and their application will give the magical practitioner the ability to determine the most auspicious time for performing a given planetary or zodiacal working. Additionally, being able to interpret one's natal chart as well as examining the associated astrological transits of an elected time for a ritual performance will reveal a treasure house of not only self-knowledge but knowledge of the potentials for performing magic at any given time and place.

- We will fully discuss the seven planetary archetypes and their definitions and the twelve astrological signs. We will also go over the septagram in detail and discuss how it is to be used in a planetary working. Finally, we will examine the spiritual entities associated with the planets and zodiacal signs, their character, use in magic, and the deities that underly them. Included will be a discussion of the liturgical practices that I am promoting for Witches and Pagans who seek to include these deities in their pantheon.

- While we have already discussed the methodology of a passive and active mechanism for working talismanic magic, we will focus on the active mechanism used within the determined optimal auspices. The hybrid approach to this work is likely the best practice for getting a successful outcome. As for the passive only mechanism, I will leave the reader to consider the writings of other practitioners who seek a more traditional approach.

- Three forms of talismanic ritual workings will be discussed in detail, and these are the invocation of a talismanic elemental using the lunar mansions, the invocation of a decan using the astrological decans, and the invocation of a septan using the astrological septans. We will go over how to build ritual structures to perform these three kinds of working, including giving examples and discussing how to project into the world, absorb into the psyche, or charge a talisman. We will get into the details about talismanic magic, how to develop your own personalized designs for a talismanic artifact. We will also discuss the practical application and use for a charged and activated talisman, since generating them is only part of the process of making use of them.

- Finally, we will examine the philosophy of Pherecydes and how it works within the definitions and devices of celestial magic. It is the basis for the temporal magical model and teaches us how to conceptualize this kind of magic and how to incorporate a specialized liturgical practice to engage and honor the god of time, Chronos. I will use this philosophy to define and reveal this mysterious and peculiar deity and its impact on all modern earth-based religious practices. Because they exist outside of the cycles of change, they are seen as a lintel deity, as Chronos, Herne, Eris, also Saturnus, Laverna and Janus, who are the Lord and Lady of Misrule and the Preserver of Celestial Order.

These topics will help you master the third and final magical system of celestial and talismanic magic, bringing them into your repertoire of Witchcraft practices. As I have covered the techniques and methods of spirit conjuring and energy work in my previous two books, in this one together we will complete the training of a Pagan Magus.

Once you have developed all of the rituals covered in these three books and have practiced them, you will be able to master every challenge and opportunity that life could possibly present to you. This is especially true if you learn to actively work planetary and zodiacal magic while simultaneously determining the most auspicious time and place for that work to be done.

What I present here are the techniques and systems that I myself have developed and used for decades. While I have not been deemed any kind of a miracle worker, I have discovered how to live a life that is guided by a magically empowered life process that is compassionate to my needs and helpful to my life-long search for wisdom and ultimate personal fulfillment. I hope that you will join me in examining all the rich details for working celestial magic.

Chapter Two

HISTORICAL OVERVIEW
OF CELESTIAL MAGIC

"Mortal as I am, I know that I am born for a day,
but when I follow the serried multitude of the stars
in their circular course, my feet no longer touch
the earth; I ascend to Zeus himself to feast me on
ambrosia, the food of the gods."

—CLAUDIUS PTOLEMY, ASTRONOMER

The origins of astronomy, astrology, and celestial magic in human endeavors are lost in the mists of time. We can only conjecture based on archaeology and the newly devised field of archeoastronomy as to when and how human beings began to develop a sophisticated knowledge of astronomical phenomena and how they affected their lives. The most important fact is that astrology was not the invention or possession of one people. It evolved over time and passed through many cultures from the Middle East, to Greece and India, the Islamic world, Europe, and the rest of the world. Every culture has some form of astrology to offer its people or has revitalized an existing antique practice.

As we would understand it, astrology was first developed by the Babylonians and the Assyrians in Mesopotamia. While I could write a number of books about the historical origins of astrology, for the purpose of learning to practice celestial magic, here's an outline of some basic events in history that had a great impact on how astrology and celestial magic are viewed today.

Babylonian astrology was a fully developed system of divination, its aim being to determine the will of the gods by way of the apparent motions of planets and constellations, not to mention the phenomena of eclipses, comets, meteor showers, and even weather patterns. It was a sacred science practiced by a literate and priestly caste and was limited to determining the fate of kings and nations, a practice that today is called mundane astrology. It also included various forms of priestly magic to enhance the good influences and inhibit the bad as determined by astrological auspices. The Babylonians also operated through a calendar that was full of auspicious and inauspicious days that highly regulated the life of the king and his court. Their system of religious astronomy was based on the understanding that the macrocosm, as defined by the heavens, determined what would happen in the microcosm, or the material world.

The Babylonian empire quietly fell to the Persian empire and was quickly absorbed, to include the sacred study and practice of astrology now divorced from the Babylonian court and Babylonian theology. From here it was developed to serve multiple interests, from kings and princes, to wealthy merchants. It is likely that natal astrology had its beginning at this time, along with electional and horary astrology. Itinerant astrological mages wandered through the towns and cities of the Persian empire and migrated to Anatolia and Syria, and eventually to Greece.[4]

When Alexander conquered the Persian empire, it kicked off a process for the mingling of ideas both east and west, especially the knowledge of astrology. It therefore found its way to Greece, where it became a newly acquired topic that Greek scholars could examine, thereby ultimately spreading its influence far and wide throughout the Hellenistic world. Astrology had evolved somewhat, becoming disassociated with Babylonian religious practices, but it retained the divinatory and magical practices as established by the Babylonian priesthood.

Scholars in the Hellenistic and later Greco-Roman worlds had mixed opinions about astrology. While some decried its divinatory and magical elements and the

---

4 Nicholas Campion, *A History of Western Astrology: Volume 1—The Ancient World* (London: Bloomsbury Academic Press, 2012), 83–84.

cosmic determinism that it implied, others were drawn to it and further developed it into a rational discipline. Cicero excoriated astrology and condemned it as a superstitious absurdity, and others harshly criticized it as a corrupt foreign import and a dubious collection of eastern omens and superstitions.[5]

What astrology needed was to be reformed and made into a rational science. Aristotle had laid the cosmology groundwork for considering astrology as a form of philosophy, so it was up to someone to pull the philosophic elements together to produce a philosophical based discipline of astrology, which happened starting in the early second century CE, unsurprisingly in Alexandria, where scholars who were already very sympathetic to astrology resided.

Astrology and Magic Parting Ways

The first scholar and author who sought to reform astrology and bring it into the study of proper philosophy was Claudius Ptolemy, who was born in Alexandria at around 70 CE. His two books, the *Almagest* (astronomical mathematics) and the *Tetrabiblos* (astrological interpretation), fully established astrology as a rational and natural philosophical science. He was no doubt influenced by the negative opinions about astrology that were all the rage in the community of writers and scholars when he started his project of reforming astrology. Based on his writings and defense of astrology, it is likely that the writings of Cicero were very much on Ptolemy's mind when he wrote the Tetrabiblos.

Ptolemy removed the divination and magic of the quasi-religious system of astrology that had come from the Persians and Babylonians, instead building a philosophic framework for it so that it might thereafter be considered a respectable discipline.[6] While there were several other individuals involved in this work, Ptolemy's *Tetrabiblos* became the ultimate source of astrological interpretation. His books forever changed the study and practice of astrology. What he put into the mainstream of belief and practice managed to survive through the centuries until today. Other scholars and practitioners would later add and expand the lore of astrology, but its basic premise remained unchanged throughout all that time.

---

5 Campion, *History of Western Astrology*, 209.

6 Geoffrey Cornelius, *The Moment of Astrology: Origins in Divination* (New York: Penguin, 1994), 84.

Ptolemy's pulling together the writings of Plato and Aristotle brought astrology into a scientific context with a material-based determination of causality. Without magic, religion, or mysteries, the celestial spheres shaped and influenced the fate of all living things, humanity in particular. Astrology was the key to understanding and perhaps mitigating to a limited extent the impact of that fate.

From here, the disciplines of astrology and celestial magic proceeded on two separate tracks. While there were some astrologers who crossed over between astrology and magic, over time and likely due to the later influences of Christianity and Islam, the boundary between astrology and magic became ever wider and more distinct. Astrologers sought to appear respectable and rational to the public that they served, and it would seem that trafficking with celestial magic was something of a forbidden taboo, not to mention that it became a practice that would invite authorities to prosecute and punish the perpetrators.

Throughout the Middle Ages, the study and practice of astrology became an important part of the knowledge and training of the educated person. The western church relaxed its condemnation of astrology until even church prelates studied and practiced astrology. It had finally become mainstream, and there even seemed to be a way to merge the teachings of the Christian church and the will of God as the final arbiter of destiny and that the stars captured what God had willed as found within the natal chart.

When astronomy changed from a geocentric system with concentric celestial spheres circling around it to one that was decidedly heliocentric, astrology was able to adopt and adapt to this change. It didn't change the method for calculating a chart and its interpretation. Astrology was based on the apparent motion of the sky as observed by people watching from the ground, a fact that didn't seem to deter scholars from accepting astrology as a natural science. However, it is around this time that the practice of philosophical astrology was abandoned for the practices of natal, elective, and horary astrology. Mental conditioning, objectivity, and discipline were replaced with a kind of dogmatic conviction and a need for material employment.

Beginning the sixteenth century, certain scholars began to write and complain about the abject determinism and absolute certainty that practicing astrologers were peddling to a gullible public. Ficino and Pico Mirandola both

wrote harsh criticisms about astrology and astrologers.[7] This criticism continued and increased in volume until the seventeenth and eighteenth centuries
when members of the then-early scientific community began to focus exclusively on astronomy and thereby reject the notion that astrology was even a
science. This breakdown and its resultant fallout continued unabated until the
nineteenth century, when the study of astrology had become the predilection
of the occultist, eccentric, the charlatan or the madman. Of course, such a system of powerful symbolism could not be completely discarded or forgotten,
since so much of our culture today has underpinnings and influences that orig-
inate with astrology. It had to return to a kind of prominence, and it did as an
occult science.

Modern astrology was formed by the Theosophical Society, which seemed
to bring a lot of different and diverse studies and systems from the past to the
present in both eastern and western worlds. Alan Leo, a Theosophist, was one of
the major proponents for a modern astrology, and many others soon followed.
Jung brought astrology into a modern psychological interpretation, for better or
worse, and Dane Rudhyar started a movement for a humanistic astrology.

However, due to the efforts of scientists and cultural rationalists, astrology
was shown to lack much credibility, so it became more of an occult science
than a philosophy or a physical science. If astrology has returned back to its
occult roots, then perhaps it is time for a reunion between astrology and celestial magic.

Astrology and Magic—A Troubling Affair

The practice of celestial magic has always been a part of astrology from its very
beginning. The Babylonians believed that astrological omens could be shaped
and mitigated by the intervention of their gods, so there was always a religious
and magical component to astrology. Without magic, astrology became too
deterministic and not particularly useful. If you could predict an event, then
why not also have a way to enhance the possibility of a desirable outcome or
avert a negative one. When astrology made the transition from a courtly religious and magical practice to one that was performed outside of that context,
the practice of celestial magic followed the practice of astrology.

---

7 Cornelius, *The Moment of Astrology*, 2–3.

However, when Ptolemy made astrology into a philosophical science, he removed from it the religious magic, the qualities of divination and the elements of the psychic and the irrational. Astrology became a secular science that was wholly rational, deductive, and consisting of an accepted physical causality. Those who practiced astrology in this guise no longer adhered to any of the magic and mystery that had made it an important system as practiced in the East. A secular astrology did not threaten the religious tenants of the time and even later, when Christianity and Islam dominated the Western and Middle Eastern worlds.

There were prohibitions against the practice of magic in antiquity (although often ignored), but these prohibitions were more threatening in the Christian and Islamic worlds. Celestial magic therefore became something of an underground practice that surfaced from time to time in various books and manuscripts. It was likely practiced by astrologers or those with a knowledge of astrology, but it was a secret discipline because secular and religious laws forbade it.

An observation of the various books and manuscripts that became available certainly shows that celestial magic was used in the Byzantine empire and that practical knowledge passed on to Arabic astrologer magicians, and then later to Europeans. The earliest representations we have of celestial magic in antiquity are found in the *Greek Magical Papyri* (second century CE), which presents numerous forms of talismanic magic under the auspices of a planetary godhead, a metallic or ceramic artifact, and specific words of power[8].

The Testament of Solomon (third century CE) contained Jewish celestial magical operations and demonology, likely taken from earlier Pagan Greek sources. The earliest versions of the *Key of Solomon* (Hygromantea) were produced in Constantinople in the fourth century CE, written in Greek, and continued to be developed into the fifteenth century. The *Picatrix* (Gayat al Hakim), an Arabic manuscript from the tenth century CE, was translated into Latin in 1256 CE. It was considered the master work of celestial magic. All of the written lore we have today represents only a fraction of what was actually available in the various public and private collections back in those times.

The Renaissance probably produced more magical writings than any previous period, and much of it was published. Ficino introduced a kind of benign

---

8 Hans Dieter Betz, editor, *The Greek Magical Papyri in Translation* Volume 1–Texts (Chicago: University of Chicago Press, 1992), 112–148.

natural planetary magic as part of his celestial-based philosophy in the late fifteenth century. Agrippa published his *Three Books of Occult Philosophy* in the 1530s, one of which was devoted to celestial magic. The occult system of John Dee (late sixteenth century) was based on elemental and celestial magic, and many of Paracelsus's writings concerned themselves with medical astrology and a form of celestial healing magic that accompanied it. One of his students published a book called the *Arbatel* that consisted of a unique system of planetary magic in 1575.

The seventeenth century saw the publication and dissemination of many books on magic, including hardcore grimoires that contained forms of planetary and talismanic magic. That century was something of a watershed for books on magic, because the interest in magic in the eighteenth century—particularly celestial magic—began to devolve and become the published almanacs and remedy books for the gullible public. Collectors and occult connoisseurs continued to copy and sell manuscript versions of the old grimoires into the nineteenth century, but it would seem that the practice of celestial magic was starting to die out.

The late nineteenth century saw the revitalization of the occult through the Theosophical Society and the rebirth of the practice of celestial magic. While two Frenchmen, Éliphas Lévi and Papus, had started to promote Western occultism and magic in the middle to late nineteenth century, it was the British esoteric Order of the Golden Dawn that brought celestial magic into the twentieth century and thus completely revitalized it. While it was not the intent for the members of that organization to make their magical lore public, the fact that it was published started a magical movement that continues today.

Celestial magic and astrology were always two sides of the same coin, each to be used to make the other relevant. However, as in any troubled relationship, they have been separated, reunited, and separated again. As one became quasi respectable and even considered mainstream, the other was forced to wander alone, only finding refuge in dark alleys and the underworld, where they could rub elbows with the most brilliant and also disreputable characters. Now, both are mutually in disrepute, although one much more than the other. Can they reunite in an equitable relationship once again? I hope to show that a reconciliation is already happening in our century, as attested in this work and others.

Chapter Three

MODELS OF MAGIC: PSYCHOLOGY AND TIME

"The world as we have created it is a process of our thinking. It cannot be changed without changing our thinking."

—Albert Einstein

The foundation of celestial magic is based on two models: the psychology model and the time or temporal model. The psychology model is important because celestial magic consists of the building blocks of human consciousness—the planetary and zodiacal symbolic character archetypes. These symbolic character archetypes are integrated seamlessly into a fabric that represents the persona and characteristics of each individual human being.

These archetypes are also found beyond individual minds and represent the super symbolic collective that is our culture and heritage. All of these artifacts are connected and interact, both within our minds and outside in our cultural world, residing in a continuum or domain of consciousness itself. Clearly, celestial magic would seem to be wholly described by the psychology model of magic because the inner and outer domains of the mind are preeminent. Yet this is not so because of another model, time.

The temporal model of magic is more subtle and less dramatic than the psychological model. Because of the constant changing nature of celestial phenomena from our vantage point on Earth, there is a distinction between the stream of continual change and a single moment. It is like the distinction between the macrocosm and the microcosm, the greater domain of the cosmos as seen in the night sky and that moment in time when our willpower is unleashed to take a decisive action. The temporal model is therefore focused on the moment that produces a time-slice of the ever changing cosmic dynamic when a magical action is taken.

The time chosen for any chart, be it natal, progressed, horary, or elective, is actually a random event determined by the astrologer. This is why natal charts based on the wrong birth time (e.g., Princess Diana, who had two birth times and no clear accurate one), horary charts, or elective charts can all present interpretations that are revealing and on target. Thus, destiny is not preordained as much as it is created and ordered by one who knows the secret language of the astrological symbols.[9]

In astrology this would be the moment a horoscope is cast, or with the tarot and any other divination system, the moment when the stones, coins, or dice are tossed or cards laid out. In magic, it is the moment when the magic circle is set for a specific magical operation. That moment has the quality of fate or one's personal destiny attached to it, especially if the magical action is one that is critical or strategic.

We can ignore these crucial moments and consider them as nothing more than a single moment in a continuum of moments, or we can mark that moment and examine it through astrological interpretation. We would want to mark and investigate that moment when considering a strategic celestial magical working, since all such workings formulate a kind of elective horoscope. We choose when to work magic, but we can also make a judicious and fateful choice by choosing the right time and place to do such a working.

To fully comprehend the nature and the power of celestial magic, we should thoroughly examine the psychology and time models of magic.

---

9 Cornelius, *The Moment of Astrology*, 232–249.

Psychological Model—Gaming Reality

The psychology model of magic is where magic is seen as a product of the mind, particularly psychological perceptions. Through this model the experience and practice of magic is defined as the product of psychological, perceptual, or sociological dynamics or processes. The psychology model of magic reduces everything to the sphere of mental processes, where all phenomena, whether spirit, energy, or information is a product of the mind. As Lon Milo DuQuette has said about magick in his books and lectures, "it's all in your head; you just have no idea how big your head is[10]."

This model has two components, one very narrow and the other quite vast. The narrow perspective limits the domain of the mind to the individual, and the larger perspective doesn't impose any limits because the mind is perceived as a shared phenomenon between all sentient beings. I believe that the unlimited domain of the mind is the correct definition, because even in my narrow individual case, the mind seems to have no limitations or boundaries when it comes to my imagination.

If all magical phenomena are reduced to a mental process (at least in the unlimited domain), that narrow definition of magic seems to be hardly restrictive or narrow at all. However, there is a way to accept the reality of magical energy and spirits and to understand that it has a place and a reality within the ocean of shared consciousness.

The basis of the psychological model of magic, then, is vested in the power of metaphors, particularly when a metaphor is exemplified. To simplify this idea, we need only to think of the power of actualized fantasy that children engage in when they play. The ability to pretend something and then perceive it as real is embodied in the euphemistic term "as if," which acts as a label for what is actually occurring.

Through this "as if" mechanism, symbols are given specific meaning, metaphors are empowered so that they become real things, and whole worlds are created through a kind of symbolic play acting. Mythic thinking and even mythic dreaming become ways for people to realize religious and magical phenomena

---

10 Lon Milo Duquette, *Low Magick: It's All In Your Head ... You Just Have No Idea How Big Your Head Is* (Woodbury, MN: Llewellyn Worldwide, 2010), 133.

in a tangible and shared manner. It is a way of gaming reality, so to speak, that allows other possibilities to present themselves.

In his 1997 book, *Symbolic Worlds: Art, Science, Language, Ritual*, author Israel Scheffler defines that process of exemplifying metaphors as "mention-selection," a term in the field of semiotics that describes the act of relating a term not to what it really means (denotation), but to parallel representations that have a specific significance.[11] The basis of this phenomenon is the allowance of an active and creative fantasy that uses symbols, artifacts, actions, and a specific context in which one may enact entire worlds of experience not relative to the empirical and objective world. Active fantasy is an important key to the performance and experience of magic.

If we expand this theory just a bit, we could easily see that all models of magic—including magic and religion themselves—are products of this powerful and meaningful semantic manipulation. The worlds of spirit and deities, magical powers and energies, and the meaning of symbols, sacred or magical artifacts, and ritual enactments are all based on the exemplification of metaphors and the creative wielding of symbols and signs. This theory doesn't negate the emotional and cognitive experiences of religious and magical phenomena, nor does it do away with paranormal perceptions and the power of intuition. States of consciousness and the development of one's mind conducive to this kind of metaphorical exemplification are important parts or the foundation to experiencing religious or magical phenomena.

Meditation techniques are the first order of business for anyone who wishes to plumb the depths of the semantic world view of the spiritual. And in the very deepest states of meditation-based consciousness, all the various disparate and separate elements of the world are perceived as being connected in a union of being-ness, a perception of unity that serves as a basic metaphysical fact for the occurrence of all religious or magical rituals. Yet it is a phenomenon of the mind and consciousness. We cannot fathom this unity in the mundane world and its many distinctions and differences. Therefore, controlling one's mind through meditation and altering one's perceptions of reality to synchronize it with the religious or magical world view are the essential tools for the practice of the psychological model of magic. The fact that the other mod-

---

11 Israel Scheffler, *Symbolic Worlds: Art, Science, Language, Ritual* (Cambridge, UK: Cambridge University Press, 1997), 44–45.

els also rely on these techniques should show how interrelated they are and integral to the practice of ritual or religious magic. However, for the psychological model, altering and mastering the ability to perceive and interact with exemplified metaphors is the sole basis to that model of magic. In this fashion, the magical aphorism, "thought becomes form, and form becomes thought" is fully realized.

If we consider meditation to be the base of the psychological model of magic, what are the tools employed in that system of magic? The answer is simple: anything that alters our perception to coincide with the metaphorical world we are seeking to experience. Such tools are visualization, guided or spontaneous, chanting (these can be meaningful words, such as affirmations, or intonations or sounds), visual fascination, hypnosis, trance, concentration, contemplation, mindfulness, or emptying the mind. Other tools would include the use of hallucinogens, post-orgasmic mind states, music, and choreographed dance. Theater becomes the stage of actualized fantasy, and the stage magician with his illusions and legerdemain is an exemplar of the psychological model of magic. Mystical and magical plays such as the staged initiations of the York or Scottish rites of masonry, or the magic theater of Steppenwolf are all a part of this method.

Returning to our considerations for celestial magic, we see a very rich fabric of symbols and signs, myths, expressions of deity, and archetypes of personality, all operating within the domain of astrology. It would seem that if we add heightened states of consciousness, trance, and visualization to our experience of these metaphors, these symbols, signs, myths, and archetypes would come alive, interact with us, and be subject to magical manipulation, thereby allowing us to change ourselves and the material world around us.

Celestial magic is based on the activation of the symbolism of astrology to affect the mind of the operator, and correspondingly, to affect their domain or world. Taken to a higher level, these signs and symbols can affect the consciousness of the cultural body itself—the place of the collective consciousness. Organizing astrological symbols into tables of correspondences has always been the first step for working celestial magic, since it is the use of similar and associated qualities with the planets and the signs that gives the operator the ability to summon and assume the intelligences and powers of those celestial metaphors.

Planetary and zodiacal correspondences include colors, gemstones, metals, herbs, elixirs, incenses, musical tones, deities, demigods, angels, sigils, signs, seals, and psychological types. Celestial magic includes all the models of magic—spirit, energy, mind, and information—in terms of spirits, forces, mental characteristics, and specific symbolic signs. Throughout the ages, these components have been a part of celestial magic, whether in antiquity, the Renaissance (Ficino's natural magic), or in the occult revival of the Golden Dawn. Each age has emphasized certain attributes and practices over others, but in the present age we can avail ourselves of them all.

Temporal Model of Magic—Fixing the Moment of Magic

We live in a day-to-day world that has, for the most part, suppressed any real significance of any date or time except the day we were born. That date is important because laws govern what we can do depending on our age, as well as our status in our culture and society. The seasons come and go, holidays are celebrated and then pushed into the background of routines that we focus on in the name of gainful employment in pursuit of some manner of a livelihood. Our survival and its needs pushes everything else into the background of our lives while we focus on what is important, such as the support of ourselves and loved ones and acting as responsible citizens. Still, everyone has certain events that occur at some point in their lives that are more important and strategic to their life's story than other events. We keep these memories alive in our mind and they become a part of us, acting as the various elements that characterize us and our lives. They are our life stories that we tell ourselves and others.

These strategic events in our lives usually occurred without any determination of cause, although we often dwell on them to shake out some meaningful cause after they are behind us, whether or not it has any basis in fact. Yet, looking at a specific date when something critical happened in our life and examining it from the perspective of astrology, we will discover that greater celestial dynamics were afoot than we imagined at the time. We were not necessarily fated to have a specific experience, but the potential for that experience or something like it was there, based on our natal chart and the active transits occurring at that time.

Examining our natal horoscope can reveal to us not only our essential characteristics but also our ultimate destiny, or what we might undergo in our lives at specific times and places. Much of the analysis of a natal chart will define who we are personality-wise, including potentials and possibilities for future outcomes. Prognostication often consists of conjecture and hindsight, and when you are my age, it is mostly an illuminating hindsight. Those strategic events did not occur based on long-standing choices in most cases, they were events that happened in the course of our lives, often without apparent warning.

In contrast, celestial magic represents a strategic event chosen at a specific time and place, giving us the ability to coordinate that event with astrological auspices that would make it more meaningful and better able to produce the result we are seeking. The manner in which we control the execution of that magical event represents the particulars for the temporal model of magic.

The first step in engaging in the temporal model is to ask, simply, "what date and time should I do this action?" Of course, that question is really asked to determine the significance of the time and place in which the event of magic is to occur. The moment is elected based on astrological possibilities and is also forced as the magical event is actively performed within a specific planetary hour and planetary day.

Also under consideration are the season of the sun, the lunar cycle, transit aspects occurring during the day of the event, geographic location, and even the weather. An elective horoscope can be cast for the magical event and can be compared to the operator's natal chart. The two together produce a large volume of data to examine and delineate. If the auspices for the magical event are weak or even negative, another date and time can be chosen. Chapter 11 covers how to examine this data and make some simple determinations about the auspiciousness of an event.

The whole basis for working celestial magic is the need for something, and whether that need can be fulfilled is determined by examining one's natal horoscope. In fact, the manner in which one approaches a working can and should be shaped by the operator's natal chart. Greater and detailed knowledge and insights into the natal chart will help the operator choose the right combination of celestial components in the magical working. The maxim "know thyself" is critically important in celestial magic. Let me give you an example.

In my natal chart, I have Venus and Saturn conjunct in the fifth house in the sign of Scorpio. Although they are practically out of the orb of conjunction, the Arabic Part of Fortune is between them, thus strengthening the conjunction.

This conjunction has had a negative effect on my ability to find a mate—I was single for most of my adult life. Saturn had a very cooling effect on the passions of Venus, and in the sign of Scorpio there were additional issues of abuse and self-abuse, bondage, and unrequited love. Such an aspect would also ensure a lack of children, an abnormal family life, and social isolation. I was consistently attracted to women who were not interested in having a relationship with me; often they used and abused me. As a desperate and romantic fool, I took that abuse as a substitute for a real relationship.

Throughout many years I attempted to fix my problem with talismanic workings involving the planet Venus, but those workings failed to produce any results. If I had been wiser and more insightful, I would have understood that invoking Venus wouldn't help me! I would have seen that the key to my problem would be using the powers of Jupiter and the Sun to change my life, thereby counteracting Saturn's influences on my Venus position. Curiously enough, Saturn ultimately ensured that this situation would be mitigated later in life, since Saturn has the qualities of time and old age. I was married later in life (at age 59) when Saturn released its hold on me and became a positive force: my age and maturity. If I would have been more knowledgeable about my natal chart and what it meant to me, perhaps I could have found the right celestial magical solution to my problem earlier.

I have shared this example to demonstrate that successfully working celestial magic requires knowing not only what you want to do but also what components will help you achieve the results you seek. Because of my chart configuration, I was able to work talismanic magic to help myself financially and career-wise, but I couldn't help my love life or my social standing. The technique for analyzing a natal chart to get this kind of information is to ask specific questions and then look to those astrological attributes to determine the answer. You can ask about your financial and career possibilities, love life and social standing, your health, or determine blind spots or areas of weakness or inadequacy. Once you know these things about yourself and your chart, mark the planets, houses, and zodiacal signs that contribute to them. This knowledge will offer you the celestial solution to mitigate and resolve your need.

In addition to the planetary hour and the planetary day, is also a time factor based on the lunar mansions and the zodiacal decans. If you are working celestial magic that uses one of the twenty-eight lunar mansions or one of the thirty-six decans, you will also need to determine the event of the magical working based on when that lunar mansion or zodiacal decan is active. A lunar mansion lasts for approximately a whole day each month, but a decan period only changes every ten days. This is because the Moon appears to move faster through the zodiac than the Sun; the difference is twenty-eight days for the Moon versus 360 days and an intercalated period of five days for the Sun.

Mythic Elements about Time—Greek and Persian

Two cultures produced a kind of mythic theology that centered around a deified aspect of time, which is appropriate for our adoption of the temporal model. The first was fragmentary writings of the Presocratic philosopher Pherecydes, a contemporary of Pythagoras (sixth century CE). The second was the occurrence of a heretical sect of Zoroastrianism called Zurvanism after the god Zurvan, a creator god associated with time and fate (Sassanian Persia, third–seventh centuries CE). Whether Greek or Persian, both derivations were unusual and left little impact on the following ages. Their obscurity is almost similar to the obscurity of the temporal model of magic, representing a hidden significant perspective in theology and magic that we will briefly examine here.

It is my belief that behind all the models of magic, there is some kind of fabric of myth and theology that stand as a basic foundation underlying them. We saw that most obviously with our study of the four elements, and I believe that the other models would have a corresponding source of myth and theological philosophy underlying them. Perhaps I shall uncover them all in another book one day, but for now let us examine these two unusual perspectives as they relate to the temporal model of magic.

Pherecydes of Syros was born around 580 BCE and passed from the earth in around 520 BCE. He wrote in prose (the first to do so) and taught a mixture of philosophy and theology that later philosophers believed was couched in a symbolic language hiding a mystical and esoteric doctrine. We possess only fragments of his writings from later writers, but we have enough to outline the basis to his writings and teachings. He taught that the human soul was actually immortal and that it engaged in a ceaseless cycle of transmigrations. He believed that this endless cycle of rebirths could be mitigated through special practices and disciplines. What he taught was very similar to Pythagoras's teachings, and some believed that he himself might have been Pythagoras's teacher. Nevertheless, Pherecydes's lost books expressed an early cosmogonic cycle that will be the focus of our brief outline here.[12]

A reconstruction of Pherecydes's work brings to light the main parts of his theological writings.[13,14] The *Pentemychos* (five recesses or pits) postulated that before the birth of the cosmos, there existed three primary and principal godlike beings. These were Zas (Greek for "life," similar to Zeus), Chronos (time—not to be confused with Kronos, the father of Zeus in another myth), and Chthonie (earth). Time is the eternal and everlasting procreative force in the universe; when joined with Life and Earth, they create the cosmos with the earth as its center. From the seed that Chronos cast forth into the void came the elements of fire, air, and water, which deposited in five hollows, and from these were born a new generation of deities. The gods born of fire resided in the two parts of the sky (Ouranos and Aither), and those of air in the winds that blew in Tartaros, those of water resided in the oceans of Chaos, and those of darkness dwelt in night. Thus, the creation of the cosmos was a form of self-creation, which denied the creation of the cosmos from nothing. These were the five hollows or recesses, or domains of the gods.

After this sorting of the new generation of deities, Zas married Chthonie, and on the third day of their wedding fashioned a sumptuous garment for her, which became the earth. The garment was filled with all varieties of life from their union—all things had their places in the world, from the darkness of Tartaros at the root of the cosmos to the heavens of the stars at the summit, with the oceans encircling the earth, and the ever-cycling day and night. The cosmos flourished and life as Zas rejoiced. However, this perfect state didn't last. There emerged from the darkness of night an antagonist named Ophioneus, who gathered his minions in Tartaros to challenge the new order. A great war was fought between the armies of light commanded by Kronos, the newly elected leader of the gods of fire, and the armies of darkness commanded by Ophioneus.[15] Kronos was victorious and later crowned as king of the gods by Zas, and

---

12 Editorial staff, "Pherecydes of Syros" *Britannica* online, accessed Dec 30, 2021, https://www .britannica.com/biography/Pherecydes-of-Syros.

13 Maria Michela Sassi, *The Beginnings of Philosophy in Greece* eBook, 51–53.

14 *Pherecydes of Syros EN Academic*, accessed December 30, 2021, https://en-academic.com/dic .nsf/enwiki/421387.

15 Not to be confused with Chronos, the ultimate father deity.

Ophioneus and his followers were banished to the oceans of Chaos, never to return. The cosmos returned to its prior state, except the war had its echoes in every cyclic return of chaos threatening to overturn the established order.

The most important part of this myth is the characterization of Chronos as the everlasting procreative force in the universe. This idea has precedence with the temporal model of magic, since it is the event of magic that is similar to the event of self-begotten creation that created the cosmos. While we can consider the other models of magic such as spirit and energy, the fate-filled moment or event of magic is overall significant and primary to acts of magic, and most particularly, to celestial magic.

Similar to the Greek theological philosophy of Pherecydes was the later heretical sect of Zoroastrianism known as Zurvanism. I will recount the mythic theology of Zurvanism and we will see that it seems to oddly match up with the teachings with Pherecydes.

Zurvanism appeared sometime during the period of Sassanian Persia, between the third and seventh centuries CE, nearly a millennium after Pherecydes. Zurvanism is based on the obscure Persian deity Zurvan and was a heretical sect opposed to the dualistic theological beliefs found at this time in Zoroastrianism.[16] According to the sect's beliefs, the god Zurvan, representing time and eternity, was the uncreated creator of the universe. Zurvan was believed to influence the fate of all human beings in a limited fashion, and was seen in two forms, limitless time, and time of long duration. Limitless time was the overall lord and master of the universe, and time of long duration was lord and master of earth. Later on, Zurvanism taught that the god Zurvan was the creator and father of both Ormazd and Ahriman, Light and Darkness. The worship of Zurvan was a synthesis of Zoroastrianism proper mixed with astrological beliefs, possibly as influences from Babylonian astrological theology.

If we focus on Zurvan's two natures—limitless time and time of long duration—we find the two aspects operating in astrology. We see the ever-changing unrelenting cycles of the cosmos as seen from earth, and the moments of fate or destiny occurring in the lives of individuals and nations. These two aspects perfectly encapsulate the nature of the temporal model of magic—the endless cycles and the fateful moment or event that occurs within them.

---

16 Campion, *History of Western Astrology*, 80.

While modern physical science has shown that time is relative to space and perhaps even an illusion, as quoted by Einstein himself, the magic and mysteries of time are represented as they appear to us on the surface of the earth.[17] The relativity of time is taken as fact in modern science, but it is a very real and potent phenomenon from the standpoint of individual humans and the world we live in. On the surface of this planet, the symbology of astrology has the power to predict and change the course of individuals and nations, and time itself is like a sole-creator god, infinite and eternal yet also intimately engaged in the workings of destiny for everyone and for all ages.

17 Jamie Trosper, "What Einstein Meant By 'Time is an Illusion'" *Interesting Engineering* website, accessed December 30, 2021, https://interestingengineering.com/what-einstein-meant-by -time-is-an-illusion.

Chapter Four

PLANETARY CORRESPONDENCES: QUALITIES, DEITIES, AND SPIRITS

"Magic exists. Who can doubt it, when there are
rainbows and wildflowers, the music of the wind
and the silence of the stars?"

—NORA ROBERTS

The very heart of celestial magic consists of the archetypal qualities that define them. We have covered a lot of ground to get to this strategic point in our study of planetary and zodiacal magic, and now we can examine all of the qualities that make up this kind of magic.

First, I would like to state what I believe is the basic and essential talismanic equation. Talismans are strongly and most effectively represented with a combination of a planet and zodiacal sign. The reason for this is that the element quality of the zodiacal sign, its triplicity, combines with the planet to produce a dynamic field that is perpetually empowered and radiant. A planet alone is less effective because there is no elemental power to act as its foundational charge. The same is true for a zodiacal sign without a planet—it lacks the psychic dynamic and spiritual intelligence necessary for it to be guided and given a directive or purpose. The talismanic equation is the combination of planet and sign, or planet and element. For this reason, we must study both attributes thoroughly within the context of the natal and the transit or elective astrological charts.

The seven classical planets, the twelve signs of the zodiac, and the fixed stars mysteriously arrayed behind them represent the various components of celestial magic. Each of these qualities also has associated with it various deities, angels, demigods, and a large assortment of material correspondences. If we are going to tap into one of these qualities, we must also concern ourselves with the associated spiritual hierarchy and the artifacts of ritual magic we will use to summon it. There are various components that affect our sight, hearing, smell, taste, and touch, and all of these sensory experiences will be simultaneously activated to help make the elements of celestial magic realized.

Although I have found a wealth of correspondences associated with the planets and the zodiacal constellations, there are far more correspondences than are really worth the time and effort to collect. I believe that you only need several to really express the qualities of one of these attributes fully; the rest don't really add much more than what has already been assembled. For this reason, I will limit the scope of the descriptions and correspondences to only what is needed to perform the rituals to make them manifest as we examine the qualities and correspondences for the planets and the signs of the zodiac in the next chapter. There are hundreds of different categories of correspondences for planets and zodiacal signs, yet only a handful are used in the rituals that appear in chapters 13 through 15. I will leave the rest of these categories for you to seek at your leisure if you decide later that you want more information.

This chapter will focus on just the planets, as they are the heart of the talismanic equation. We will examine first the archetypal qualities for each of these attributes and then go over the various tables of correspondences. All the correspondences will be used in the associated rituals found in later chapters, making them strategically important to the work of celestial magic. I will explain each of the categories of correspondences before displaying the tables in which they are depicted.

Once I have presented all this information, we will end this chapter with some basic information about planetary movements (retrograde and direct), finding planets in natal and transit or elective charts, constellations and fixed stars in the sky at night, and using an ephemeris or an application to locate them if they are within your viewing sphere.

Let us take a trip through the land of celestial archetypes and get some really detailed information about each of these primary attributes. Note that each of these attributes should be seen as living and breathing components that make up our minds and souls, in addition to the stuff of the gods, goddesses, and their various intermediaries. Everything that is conscious and has sentience is populated with these various attributes, though they are often combined, interacting and even conflicting with each other. We will see them as separate and distinct, even though they never really function alone in dynamic living beings.

Archetypal Qualities of the Planets

We begin our tour starting with the planets. While in antiquity astronomers and astrologers only knew about five planets and included them with the Sun and the Moon, they used this system and defined them as the seven planets. The geocentric perspective used by the astrologers at the time, placed these seven heavenly bodies in orbits around the world, since that is how they appeared from the surface of the earth. Later on, when the heliocentric model replaced the geocentric model, astrologers still considered the seven planets in the same manner, except that the five planets and earth orbited the sun and only the moon orbited around the earth. The earth was not really included in their considerations, which is odd because by then it was considered a planet, so this structure remained popular until the twentieth century.

In the last two hundred years, three new planets were discovered and added to the menagerie of astronomical planetary lists. Although astrology incorporated these new planets, celestial magic continued to use the traditional seven. Because all the tables of planetary correspondences rely on those seven traditional planets, the magic presented in this book will also use them.

I could present these additional planets as archetypes and remove the sun because it is really a star, but there are few situations at present where these additional archetypes would be used in forms of planetary magic. Also, there would be variations on exactly how to organize this different planetary structure using just the planets. Would that list include Earth instead of the Sun, something that even astrology has not proposed? While these thoughts are intriguing, I believe that for our purposes here, we should move forward with just the seven archetypal planets; this speculation is better left for future works.

Let us now examine all seven of these planetary archetypes and their associated tables of correspondence. I have consulted four sources and distilled the definitions for the planets employed below.[18]

Sun: *Rules Leo—365-day geocentric period*

The Sun represents the outer personality or persona of an individual being. Think of it as the light that shines from the collective of their personality. The Sun symbolizes leadership and success. It is the essential creative principle in all conscious beings; therefore, it rules health and vitality. It symbolizes persons in authority, personal dignity and self-worth; it is a person's identity—how they see themselves. It is the energy of progress, dynamic beingness and activity, the will to exist, and the will to achieve greatness. The Sun is the great illuminator, so it is the teacher, the arts and sciences of civilization, and the development of wisdom. It is the ego, the appearance of one's identity and individuality, and the core of the true self—the metaphorical heart of a person. It is our social face and our essential self. The magic of the Sun is for healing, empowering the self, attracting groups of people (charisma), giving instruction and insight, and even prophesizing the future. Greek deity: Apollo or Helios.

Moon: *Rules Cancer—28-day orbit*

The Moon represents the inner personality, feelings, and motivations that may not be readily apparent. Where the Sun is light, the Moon is, as its opposite, darkness. The Moon is the closest planet to the earth, and therefore moves rapidly through the signs of the zodiac each month. Due to its proximity and rapid movement, the ancients believed it to be lowest level or sphere of all of the celestial orbits. Where the Sun emits light, the Moon receives it, thereby representing the receptive principle, the shaper and giver of life. The Sun is the

---

18 Skye Alexander, *Planets in Signs*, beginning of each planetary chapter (Atglen, PA: Schiffer Publishing, 1997); Marion March and Joan McEvers, *The Only Way to Learn Astrology, Volume 1: Basic Principles* (Epping, NH: ACS Publications, 1997), 21–28; Robert Hand, *Horoscope Symbols* (Atglen, PA: Schiffer Publishing, 1981), 47–83; Kim Rogers-Gallagher, "Introduction to Astrology–Planets: The First Building Block" in *Llewellyn's Daily Planetary Guide 2022* (Woodbury, MN: Llewellyn Worldwide, 2021), 5–10.

father and the Moon is the mother. It represents instincts instead of knowledge, emotional tones, and deeper moods that motivate and push in seemingly irrational directions. The Moon symbolizes cycles, reflexes, habits, and personal desires and needs. The Moon is magnetic to the Sun's electric qualities, representing growth, fertility, the internal self, and the symbolic container (womb) of all things. It is the source or origin of all beingness, passive yet persistent, reflective, nurturing but also wild, frightening, and fierce. The magic of the Moon is for revealing mysteries, fertility, creativity, self-reflection, protection, and transformation but also for obscuring and making invisible, projecting illusions, delusions, and overall cursing. Greek deity: Artemis or Selene.

Mercury: *Rules Gemini and Virgo—88-day orbit*

Mercury is the closest planet to the Sun, so its movement through the signs appears to be tied to the astrological Sun—in a natal chart, they are never far apart (always within 28 degrees). Mercury has no gender; it assumes whatever gender is required or useful in the moment. It represents communication, reason, intellect, self-awareness, dexterity, thinking, writing, and the dialectical process. Mercury can take either side in an opinion or an argument and has no vested interest in any particular point. It is volatile and changeable, and represents quick and nimble movements between places and intellectual ideas. Mercury symbolizes curiosity, fascination with novelty, theft, burglary, but also laughter and humor, riddles, and pranks. Mercury represents travel, mercantile trade, money, mathematics, electronics, and mediation. It is the power of symbol-making, language, writing, memory, cartography, and divination. Mercury is the archetypal messenger, helping to connect all things together through a matrix of meaning and knowing; it is also the seeker of truth wherever that leads and the guide of both living and the dead. The magic of Mercury is divination in all its forms, to clarify and make sensible all forms of communication between people, to gain insight and understanding, to probe the depths of knowledge, to reveal hidden things, and to locate and reveal buried treasures both of the mind and the earth. Greek deity: Hermes.

Venus: *Rules Taurus and Libra—224-day orbit*

Venus is the second planet from the Sun; like Mercury, it is always close to the Sun in an astrological chart, never straying more than 46 degrees. Venus represents love—that power which draws together beings and inspires them with a sense of passionate union. Venus is considered the lesser beneficent power to Jupiter's greater. Venus also represents friendship and amity between individuals and groups of people. It is symbolized by art, high culture, aesthetics, beauty, but also material possessions and the refined things in life. Venus qualities are charming, good taste, good manners and the harmonious interaction between individuals and groups. Venus is represented by sweets (honey), poetry, art, theater, music, and entertainments. Venus is illicit love affairs, flirtations, romantic stories, as well as happiness in marriage, business, and institutional organizations. Venus is not so much the sexual act and its variations (and perversions) but instead represents the integrity and innocence of emotional bonds, tenderness, and mutual benefit, all with a degree of decorum and even morality. Venus is luxuriousness, pleasure, sensuality, cosmetics, fashion, and costly adornments. Venus represents voluntary mutual agreements, fairness, and equality. The magic of Venus rules all things of the heart, desires, and passions, in addition to friendship, harmonious interactions among groups and institutions, and the acquisition of material wealth and happiness. Greek deity: Aphrodite.

Mars: *Rules Aries—22-month orbit*

The red planet has had a reputation for violence and bloodshed in their various forms in cultures around the world. In astrology, Mars was considered the greater malefic force. Mars represents physical action, the animal nature of human behavior, sexual energies, ambition, motivation, personal power (over others), work, war, competition, bloodshed, and murder. Mars as symbolized by instruments of iron and steel governs surgery and operations, weapons and cutting tools, but also accidents, inflammation, wounds, and burns. Mars is represented by involuntary action, impulsiveness, assertiveness, coercion, destruction, anger, fighting, courage, physical strength, and protection. Mars gives security to individuals and groups, teaches self-defense, and is also expressed as passion, the urges for adventure, boldness, and cruelty. Mars is self-expression and independence, willpower, impatience, self-centeredness, and the will to survive. The magic of Mars can be deployed for bolstering aggressive enterprises, overcoming obstacles, self-empowerment, defeating enemies in war or peace, beginning a new enterprise, and self-protection against the aggressiveness of others. Greek deity: Ares.

Jupiter: *Rules Sagittarius—12-year orbit*

Jupiter is the brightest star in the sky next to Venus (seen only during sunrise and sunset), and was associated with the ruling deity in ancient times. Jupiter is considered the greater beneficent and thus represents all that is powerfully good and positive in human affairs. Jupiter is wealth, success, the higher mind, philosophical reasoning, aspiration, good luck, and goodwill between subjects and governments. Jupiter represents sporting events, hunting and fishing for sport, but also the love of animals as pets. Jupiter symbolizes legal judgments, legislation, charity, help and financial assistance, divine order, health and growth, inheritance, monarchy and nobility, abundance, optimism, encouragement, generosity, expansiveness, and over-indulgence. Jupiter governs the union of individuals to form practical associations (corporations), academies and universities, patronage, religious piety, and civic gatherings for business, religion, and pleasure. The magic of Jupiter governs material wealth, opportunity for expansion, material success, the help of authorities in legal matters, good luck in gambling, learning new subjects, combating sickness, overcoming the evil of others, building one's public reputation, and winning popularity contests or elections.

Saturn: *Rules Capricorn—28-year orbit*

Saturn is the slowest moving of the original seven planets and was considered to be the most distant, representing the highest level of the planetary spheres and the gateway to the sphere of the fixed stars. Saturn represents rules, slow changes, discipline, responsibility, material ambitions, vocation and career, but also limitations, sorrows, procrastination, and delays. Saturn governs limiting structures, scientific laws, old age, depth, patience, time, tradition, conventionality, orthodoxy, order and productivity (work). Saturn is the inflexibility of truth, representing contraction, reduction, but also evolution and wisdom based on past experiences and misfortune. Saturn symbolizes maturity, the slow but inexorable movement of events, resistance to change, conservation, loneliness, hardship, tests, and fate. Saturn is called the lesser malefic in astrology, and is considered to be emotionally cold and indifferent. The magic of Saturn governs justice, balance, equity, long-term endeavors, protection from the malice of others, retribution, and the projection of malefic misfortune to one's enemies. Greek deity: Kronos.

Practical Planetary Correspondences

Planetary correspondences are used to help invoke a planetary intelligence by using recognizable attributes that assist the mind in identifying and associating with the archetypes embedded in our collective consciousness. These correspondences affect the senses of the operator, making the cognitive impression that manifests the qualities of a particular planet, creating correspondences that stimulate the eyes, ears, nose, fingers, and taste buds as well as the imagination.

Let me give an example of this kind of sensory mnemonic process. When I was a child, I would spend a week or two with my maternal grandparents during the summer. My grandfather smoked a specific brand of cherry tobacco that became entangled with my memories of him. Oddly enough, decades later if I happen to smell this tobacco burning no matter where I am, at that moment I am briefly back with my grandparents in their house on some idyllic summer afternoon.

What I am proposing for a planetary magical working is similar to the cherry tobacco mnemonic in my mind concerning my long-departed grandfather. Although certain colors may readily represent certain planets to the imagination, the incense, perfume, metal, gemstone, and other attributes might not immediately recall a planetary quality. What is required is to gather together these various attributes and explore and experience them together associated with the mental image and qualities of the specific planet. You will need to do this at least a few times so that the experience becomes fixed in your head.

The attributes I have chosen to represent the seven corresponding planetary intelligences are mostly readily available for purchase or can be crafted for planetary workings. I chose firstly a color, then a modern incense, with an accompanied metal and gemstone for the talismanic focus. Also and most importantly, there is a specific deity associated with the planetary intelligence, representing the godhead attribute that truly exemplifies that planet's archetypal qualities.

As part of the process of familiarizing yourself with the planetary attributes, it is important to also bring the worship of this godhead into your practical liturgical work. The planetary deity will also require orisons or invocations, votive offerings or incense, prayers and meditations, and libations and food offerings as token of your spiritual alignment. To top off this collection of attributes, you should also acquire some prerecorded music that will definitely help the working's tone and mood. All of these attributes, including and especially the deity, will unite to create a powerful mnemonic that will invoke the planetary intelligence.

Color is primary because it represents the quality of light associated with a planetary intelligence, making the wearing of clothing and use of an altar cloth of that color an important feature of planetary magic. Incense is important because it associates a specific scent to the planetary attribute, and music, which is by itself evocative, gives a powerful background to the magical environment.

The talisman itself can be made of any material but is best when made from a basic metal enhanced with a semiprecious gemstone. A table of metals and gemstones is included as part of the planetary correspondences for this reason. Since a talisman must have some degree of durability, it cannot be made from cloth or parchment. Wood or artist's board is the minimum of acceptable materials; metal in the form of a metallic disc has the best durability. If wood is used, it should be a certain color and stained to bring out that coloration as associated with the planetary color.

Selecting a deity from a specific pantheon has to be more than just a random association. These deities must be part of the operator's personal spiritual and magical pantheon. For this reason, I include a table of deities from the Greek, Roman, Babylonian, and Egyptian pantheons. From that table, you should be able to put together your own based on deities from the culture and pantheon of your choice. I will also help you to put together some liturgical practices that will help to make these deities alive and active in your spiritual life, an important step to mastering celestial magic.

Additionally, there are various spirits who function as powerful intermediaries for the deities and are used to establish a planetary charge onto a talisman. These can be archangels, angelic spirits of the intelligences, and powers of the planetary deity. There are also what are known as Olympian spirits who act as daemons or intermediaries for the deities. I have found the Olympian spirits to be like demigods that can be approached to work planetary magic independently of the planetary deity.

All these correspondences are more than just a list of interrelated items—they represent the very fabric and core of each of the planetary archetypes, so they must be materially realized as tools and magical components an operator uses to invoke them. Presented here is my own list that I have used for many years; it represents what I think is a consistent approach to planetary correspondences.

You can also look over the various tables of correspondences available in Crowley's *777*, Stephen Skinner's *The Complete Magician's Tables*, Bill Whitcomb's *The Magician's Companion*, or the tables listed in Denning and Phillips's *Planetary Magic*. Still, what I have listed below is fully representative of what I have used despite some differences with the various alternative sources named here—importantly, they aren't in full agreement with each other, either.

The following table consists of the basic correspondences related to color, metal (for the talisman construction), gemstone (if used in talismanic jewelry), and the modern and classical incenses. I tend to use just modern incense or premixed incense blends that are supposed to be more representative of the planet than the simple or raw ingredients. I leave the traditional incense list to those who believe that tradition trumps the modern alternatives.

Table of Basic Planetary Correspondences

Planet	Color	Metal	Gemstone	Modern Incense	Classical Incense
Sun	Yellow	Gold/brass	Topaz	Frankincense	Frankincense
Moon	White	Silver	Moonstone	Jasmine	Myrrh
Mercury	Indigo	Cinnabar/ aluminum	Opal/agate	Sandalwood	Cassia
Venus	Green	Copper	Emerald/jade	Rose/lotus	Spikenard
Mars	Red	Iron/steel	Garnet/jasper	Pine/cypress	Costus
Jupiter	Purple	Tin	Amethyst	Cedar	Indian bay leaf
Saturn	Black	Lead/ antimony	Onyx	Myrrh	Storax

The next table contains the basic set of deities from various pantheons that you might find interesting or even useful, depending on how you work with various deities. These are lists I have used in my workings, so they represent selections I have determined based to some extent on traditional and historical sources. The Greek, Roman, and Egyptian deities are likely of greater interest to most than the more obscure Babylonian deities, but I thought it would be useful to place them here. I have done work with the Egyptian deities since they have more aesthetic appeal to me than the others, but over the years I have also found myself drawn to the Roman and Greek deities. Listed are the archetypal deities of the planets; they represent the final power, intelligence, and authority in planetary magic. I therefore, approach them with respect and reverence as I would any other deity. That kind of approach is the way of polytheistic Paganism and Witchcraft.

Table of Gods and Goddesses from Various Pantheons

Planet	Greek Deity	Roman Deity	Babylonian Deity	Egyptian Deity
Sun	Helios, Apollo, Hyperion	Sol Invictus	Shamash	Ra
Moon	Artemis, Selene	Diana	Sin	Khonsu
Mercury	Hermes	Mercury	Nebo/Nabu	Thoth
Venus	Aphrodite	Venus	Ishtar	Hathor
Mars	Ares	Mars	Nergal	Horus/Sekhmet
Jupiter	Zeus	Jupiter Optimus	Marduk	Amun-Ra
Saturn	Kronos	Saturn	Ninurta	Set

The next table lists the planetary intermediaries used to charge and imbue a talisman with a planetary intelligence and energy. In this list are three approaches to determining intermediaries to the seven planets: the archangel, the angelic intelligence or spiritual power pair, and the Olympian spirits. When we perform planetary magic, we will invoke the intermediary spirit through the authority of the archetypal deity. We will discuss the Olympians in greater detail later in this chapter.

Table of Archangels, Angels, and Olympians

Planet	Archangel	Angelic Intelligence	Angelic Spiritual Power	Olympian Spirit
Sun	Raphael	Graphiel	Serath	Och
Moon	Gabriel	Malkah b'Tarshishim	Chasmodai	Phul
Mercury	Michael	Tiriel	Taphthartharath	Ophiel
Venus	Haniel	Hagiel	Kedemel	Hagith
Mars	Kamiel	Nakhiel	Bartzabel	Phalegh
Jupiter	Tzadkiel	Yophiel	Hismael	Bethor
Saturn	Tzaphkiel	Agiel	Zazel	Aratron

The next table are the libations and offerings for the archetypal deities. I have not been able to find these correspondences in any source material; over the years I have determined through my own experiments what would serve as appropriate libations and offerings for the seven archetypal deities. Use these libations and offerings as part of the liturgical operations when contacting and aligning yourself to one of the archetypal deities before the actual planetary working is performed.

Table of Libations and Offerings

Planet	Libation (Drink)	Offering (Food)
Sun	Sweet white wine	Honey cakes/omelet
Moon	Milk/cream	Yogurt/white cheese
Mercury	Orange/lemon juice	Rice and beans/legumes
Venus	Mead/champagne	Sweet fruits and berries
Mars	Brandy	Beef steak (rare)/cooked beets
Jupiter	Red wine	Wheat bread, butter, and preserves
Saturn	Dark rum	Black bread/pudding, sautéed mushrooms

As for planetary music, there is so much to choose from; because it really depends on the tastes of the operator, I will only give suggestions of purely classical music. Of course, there is Gustav Holst's *The Planets*, which would cover Mars, Venus, Mercury, Jupiter, and Saturn. The Sun would be well represented by Beethoven's Piano Concerto no. 5 in E-flat major ("Emperor"), and the Moon by Claude Debussy's "Clair de Lune" (third movement from his *Suite bergamasque* in D-flat major). Of course, if your tastes lean more in the direction of rock music or some other genre (electronic, ambient, and so on), I believe you can reliably pick out music that would represent the archetypal qualities of the planets. It should be noted, however, that the music must aid the magic, not distract from it.

As for planetary correspondences, we have covered the archetypal Deity, the spiritual intermediary, the color, metal, gem stone, incense, libation, offering and music. Those qualities should help you to collect the components that you need to create an effective mental mnemonic to associate the Deity and the Spirit with the archetypal qualities.

Lintel or Threshold God of Time

While the planets are qualified by deities and given offerings, honor, and respect, there is one deity that stands above and beyond them, and that is the mysterious God of the Double Gateway, the Deity of the Lintel, the changeless guardian of the transformative ordeal. We meet this godhead every time that we pass through the magical gateways to perform talismanic magic or undergo a powerful individual transformation. This deity is neither male nor female; it is both and neither. While I have assumed this entity functions as a male, I have sometimes experienced it as female, and at other times both genders. It is the union of all opposites and also the changeless point within the center of everything.

This is not a deity who can be worshiped or honored in any way—appearing instead as a trickster, a dark mirror image or the Sphinx's ultimate riddle. It is the question that has no answer and the answer that has no question. I have given this entity the name of Chronos, but it could easily answer to the Roman Janus, or Herne, the Lord of Misrule in Pagan and Witchcraft traditions. She could also be attributed to Laverna, Roman deity of thieves, cheats, and liars; or the Greek Eris, Lady of Chaos, or Ate, goddess of delusion or blind folly.

I see this deity as a double-faced and double-bodied entity who is actually one single being. It looks to the west and wards the gateway of the underworld or inner world, and it looks to the east and wards the gateway of the dawning sun and the materialization of dreams and visions. This double-faced deity teaches two lessons, of the guardian and the ordeal. As the guardian, we must overcome our own self ignorance and realize who we are, and as the ordeal, we must surrender and be reduced to nothing before we can rebuild and realize our true potential. The guardian gives to us an allotment of time (Chronos) to live (Zas), so we must wisely use that time to fully know ourselves and our destiny.

What has been omitted in this discussion so far is the nature of Cthonie (Earth), the guide who helps us achieve our cycle of light and darkness, life and death. The guide is our mother, our friends and loved ones, and our place in time and space. The guide is, first and foremost, love, particularly the love we hold for ourselves. This is not the love of narcissism, ego inflation, or the blind adherence to our supposed role in the world. It is the love that informs us who we really are (self-knowledge) and that frees us from our own bondage; it is the inherent unselfish love that resides at the core of our being. It is also the nature of the powerful entity known as the archetypal guide, and it is this power that keeps us afloat and moves us forward. It is the love that teaches us that there is no death, only change, and that we can pass through it all as long as we can surrender the perishable outer parts of ourselves.

Therefore, to honor the lintel god Chronos, we must meditate on the nature of the magic we are about to perform and define our western gateway guide, guardian, ordeal, and the changeless deity behind it all. The ultimate purpose to each and every magical working is to learn the lesson about the meaning of our particular work and its overall significance in our life. If we can pay attention to that unique quality within the center of our magic, we will have given full honor and respect to Chronos.

Building a Planetary Magical Domain

Now that we have covered the attributes associated with the seven planetary archetypes, we can examine the steps an operator undertakes to assemble them and invoke a planetary intelligence. In this process, we create a temporary planetary temple or magical domain within our own temple made exclusively for the planetary intelligence to be summoned.

Collecting and assembling specific items and using them in conjunction will help create the required planetary magical domain. The following items are used to help build this domain and make it part of the work of celestial magic. There are five things that are needed:

1. Artifact, token, or statue of planetary deity

2. Colored scarf or stole in a color associated with the planet

3. Invocation, hymn, or prayer to be addressed to the planetary deity

4. Libations, votive offerings, and various liturgical practices

5. Burning of incense or fragrance, music to set the mood, and other sensory clues

What is most important in this work is having some kind of artifact or token representing the planetary deity. It doesn't need to be elaborate; it can be as simple as a colored stone, handmade icon, or a small store-bought representation (statue or artistic representation). Association and use will make an artifact what it represents, but you can bless the representation with consecrated water, incense, or perfume oil, depending on the nature of the artifact. Do this action of blessing the artifact and recognizing its meaning during the associated planetary hour of the day or night to produce the desired results. You should plan on making seven of these artifacts to be used in your celestial magical liturgy. Artifacts should be kept on your shrine altar where other godhead representations used in your religious devotions reside.

Another important tool is the colored stole or scarf worn by the operator to indicate and express the planetary quality. This can also be a simple item—it can be a piece of colored cloth wrapped loosely around the operator's neck and shoulders that hangs down their chest. It doesn't have to be fancy or feature planetary symbols and characters, but adding them will add to the overall aesthetics of the work.

The hymn, orison, or invocation can be taken from a traditional source (such as the Orphic Hymns to the Greek Gods), or you can write one yourself. In fact, I would recommend that the operator collect or write various orisons, prayers, and invocations for all seven planetary deities, keeping in mind the (optional) inclusion of any accompanying prerecorded music with a length that accommodates several repetitions of the prayer. Whatever you use should be short, succinct, and easy to memorize. In the invocation, describe the qualities and virtues of the planetary deity by name. Once established, implore that deity to come to your aid. Note that at this stage, you have prepared yourself and are now giving offerings to the deity in their honor, showing your piety and your allegiance to the godhead. Some of this material can be memorized and some can be spontaneous, but it must be stated in a passionate and heartfelt manner.

Gathering incense or perfumes and constructing the talismanic device (if it will be part of this undertaking) are also part of the preparatory work. Offerings of libations and food can be made in small amounts, representing a token material offering of what is really an offering of love and devotion—the real food and drink of the gods.

Once this collection is complete, perform the following simple liturgical rite for each of the planetary deities. Focus on one planetary deity at a time, and perform this simple rite several times over the course of a few days so that the various components are able to create mnemonic device in your mind.

1. After a period of quiet meditation in the temple space, at the appointed planetary hour, put on the scarf or stole and stand before the shrine. Anoint your forehead with a perfumed oil associated with the planet. Next, start the prerecorded music selection.

2. Place the iconic artifact in a central place on the shrine and bow low before it. Then light a candle near it and ring the altar bell.

3. Place the token offerings before the icon artifact and light the incense, using the incense brazier (or holding the stick of incense) before the icon and offerings. Thoroughly incense the area of the shrine.

4. Now intone the hymn, orison, or invocation seven times (depending on the number of planetary deities in the planetary pantheon). You can use prayer beads to count the number of repetitions, if needed. This step is done standing before the shrine with arms held out in a position of offering and supplication.

5. Finally, sit in meditation silently before the shrine and seek to have a communion with that planetary deity. This simple rite should last the duration of the planetary hour. Once completed, blow out the candle, put out the incense, and ring the altar bell.

Although a simple rite, it is very important to build up an association in your mind for each of the planetary deities in your pantheon. Over time it will suffice to bring forth the planetary deity to aid in the work by simply anointing yourself, putting on the stole or scarf, lighting the incense, and ringing the bell in front of the planetary icon sitting prominently on the shrine while internally reciting the hymn or invocation.

Olympian Spirits or Governors

As a Pagan and a Witch, I have found the Olympian spirits (or governors, as they are called) to be the most useful and utilitarian spirits to contact when performing planetary magic. While the magical tradition as determined by Agrippa in his *Occult Philosophy* made use of the Hebrew planetary angel pairs to contact and project a planetary intelligence and power (a practice adopted by the Golden Dawn), I have found that the Olympian spirits are more amenable to my sense of aesthetics. This is a choice the practitioner can make, but I have found that working with demigods representing Pagan planetary deities is more in the style of Witchcraft magic. For this reason, I decided to adopt them.

If you are not interested in using the Olympian spirits, you can instead use the archangel or the angelic intelligence and angelic power to get the same effect. It is really your decision as to which direction you choose to go, but first let me describe the Olympians, where they come from, and how I use them in planetary workings. You might change your mind and decide to adopt their use instead of the traditional angelic spirits.

The seven Olympian spirits or governors were a later adaptation produced by the magical school of Paracelsus in the early sixteenth century and published in a book called the *Arbatel*. The date of publication was 1575, and according to Joseph Peterson, is very likely accurate.[19] Paracelsus himself died in 1541, stressing the fact that his school of medical astrology and celestial magic survived into the next century. The *Arbatel* was probably published by one of Paracelsus's followers, since the contents of the book appears to conform to the teachings associated with that group. Needless to say, the book is a brilliant work of planetary magic that is written in a concise and easy-to-follow manner without any of the typical baggage that grimoires of the time typically contained.

The names of the seven Olympian spirits have not been traced to any tradition or previously written work, so we must accept them as inventions of the

---

19 Joseph H. Peterson, *Arbatel: Concerning the Magic of the Ancients* (Lake Worth, FL: Ibis Press, 2009), x.

magical school of Paracelsus. However, I have used these names in planetary magic for decades and can attest that they are powerful intermediaries for the archetypal planetary intelligences. I see these spirits as intermediaries to the planetary deities, allowing for the projection of the intelligences and powers of those archetypes into the material world through the artifice of magical rites.

It is my intention to present these seven Olympian spirits as powerful intermediaries in planetary magical workings to be incorporated along with the planetary deities. The operator focuses first on the planetary deity, performs their planetary liturgical rites, and then once completed, summons the Olympian spirit to act on behalf of the planetary deity. It is really that simple to summon and project the qualities of the planetary archetype using the planetary deity and the Olympian spirit.

We should now examine these seven curious demigods, their qualities, their magical images, and most importantly, the specialized characters used as a link to invoke them. These descriptions and images are taken from several sources, from the original *Arbatel* to more recent traditions.[20]

Here are the seven seals that accompany the Olympian spirits and are used to invoke them:

---

20 Peterson, *Arbatel*, 29–39; Denning and Philips, *Planetary Magic*, 15–123. (I have used the physical descriptions of the Olympians from this work.)

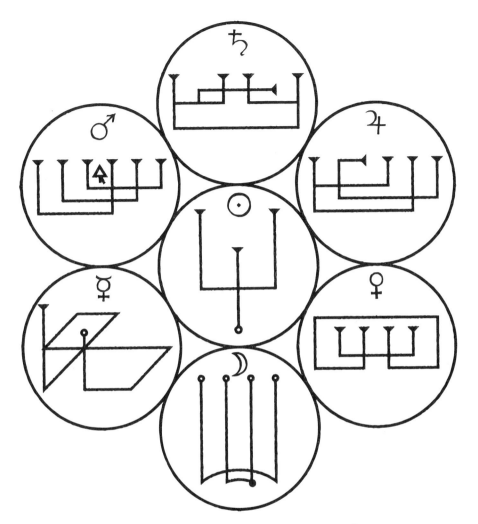

Figure 2: Seven Olympian Spirit Seals in Septagon Configuration

Aratron–Saturn–Image: A tall bearded ancient man with a long gray beard and hair, wearing dark robes made of crystalline metal. Aratron teaches alchemy, magic, and medicine. He can make one invisible and offers familiar spirits to the operator.

Bethor–Jupiter–Image: A robust dark bearded man with large, expressive eyes. He is thoughtful and well mannered. He wears white brocaded robes and a golden turban with a large sapphire and peacock feathers.

Bethor teaches self-exaltation, finds hidden treasures, and gives aerial familiar spirits. He can prolong life to 700 years.

Phaleg–Mars–Image: A muscular man wearing a red tunic and wide leather belt. He is armed with a shield and sword. He has flaming eyes. Phaleg presides over things pertaining to Mars, yet he is the prince of peace. He exalts one to the highest dignitaries in military matters.

Och–Sun–Image: A vigorous youth riding on a red lion wearing a robe of metallic gold. Och presides over Solar things. He gives 600 years of good health, grants wisdom, excellent helper spirits, and transmutes metals into gold as well as plain stones into precious gems. He gives gold and a magic pouch that pours out an endless supply of gold. He causes one to be honored by all the rulers of the world.

Hagith–Venus–Image: A beautiful, graceful woman with long dark hair, wearing a rose circlet and sparkling jewels. She is naked to the waist and wears a saffron colored skirt. Hagith presides over things ascribed to Venus; she gives charms and beautifies one with costly adornments, turns copper into gold and gold into copper. She bestows faithful familiar spirits.

Ophiel–Mercury–Image: A youth wearing a long white robe with a cone-shaped helmet with wings. He holds a silver wand and is standing barefoot on a carpet. Ophiel is the governor of Mercurial things. He teaches the arts and dignifies one's character. He turns mercury into the philosopher's stone.

Phul–Moon–Image: She appears as a warrior maiden, muscular, with a radiant face. She wears a chain mail tunic with trousers of violet. She wears a silver helmet and cape, and carries a bow and quiver of arrows. She is also girded with a crescent sword. She rides a white winged bull. Phul changes all metals to silver, governs lunar things, cures edema, and gives water spirits to serve the operator in physical and visible forms. She extends life 300 years.

Aside from the more archaic uses and capabilities listed above, we can ascribe to these Olympian spirits the full qualities and magical uses associated with the seven planets. The use of familiar spirits is probably a moot point here because the Olympian spirits function as intermediaries and demigods for the planetary deity. In my opinion, familiar spirits are thus redundant in the work of planetary magic.

Planetary Movements and Locating Them Using an Astrological Calendar

To engage with the planetary archetypes, you will use the planetary hours and the planetary day of the week, but most importantly you will need to know the position of the planet in the zodiac. All of these event-driven auspices will qualify the planetary working you are endeavoring to perform. Additionally, if you have an expertise in transit astrology, you will also want to examine if there are any significant aspects occurring during the day of your working for the target planetary archetype.

From the position of the earth, the planetary orbits are not always moving in the same direction. Sometimes some of the planets appear to move both backward and forward, in other words their movement can be direct or retrograde. A planet moving in a direct motion will have the standard quality associated with that planetary archetype, but a planet moving in a retrograde movement will slightly skew the quality that will associated with the planetary archetype. All the planets have positive, neutral, and negative qualities, and what they express in a working is dependent on the purpose the operator has set to them. Yet despite that tight relationship, when a planet is moving in a retrograde direction, it will have some effect on the planetary archetype and thereby effect the working.

While some have made a big deal out of some of these retrograde movements (especially Mercury retrograde, which is supposed to indicate a host of communication and mercantile difficulties), I have found that the influences of such movements are actually slight. First of all, the manner in which a planetary retrograde movement affects an individual depends on their natal chart. If the planet was retrograde at the time of their birth, then it hardly seems to matter when the current movement of the same planet is retrograde. Do two negatives make a positive in this situation?

Since astrological events are so very complex based as they are on transits and natal dispositions, and a planet changing from a direct movement to a retrograde movement occurs with a predictable regularity, it would seem that the changes in quality would be subtle. Mercury goes retrograde three times a year, while Venus may go retrograde once a year. Each of these periods are brief. However, the slower planets, such as Jupiter, Saturn, Uranus, Neptune, and Pluto can remain in a retrograde motion for weeks or even months. Mars sometimes doesn't have a retrograde period during the year because its annual orbit takes slightly less than two years, so it occurs every two years.

Choosing a time to work with a planetary archetype when that planet's motion must only be direct might delay a working for several days or even months for one of the slower planets. Therefore, my advice is to think of retrograde motion as a slight resistance or distortion in the planetary field and to perform the working when it is needed regardless of retrograde motion.

However, there are other considerations when planning a planetary working: the sign that the planet is occupying, the house (if there is an elective chart to consult), and the position in the sky that the planet occupies. Some planets are visible at daybreak and some during the night; knowing where in the sky the planet is positioned during a working is helpful.

All these conditions for a specific planet will have a qualifying impact on the planetary working, yet except for the zodiacal sign, none of these conditions are critical, because the planetary workings promoted in this book are active instead of passive, and the planetary archetype is invoked and set with a combination of planetary deity, Olympian spirit, and the angular vectors used to summon the planet on a septagram. If we were dependent on a passive method, the position of the planet in the sky would be far more important.

All the qualities associated with a planet to be invoked at a certain time can be easily retrieved from an astrological calendar. One of the handiest and the best of these calendars is *Llewellyn's Daily Planetary Guide*. In it, you will find everything you need to know about the planetary events occurring throughout the year and what they mean specifically. There is also an ephemeris for the year showing all of the planetary positions for each day based on Eastern and Pacific US times. You can also examine the astrological events for a specific calendar day and note the phases of the Moon, and the position of the Sun and other planets. If you are going to work celestial magic, having some kind of astrological calendar is very critical.

One thing that you should focus on when examining the astrological calendar is to note the zodiacal sign in which the target planet resides for the time you are planning to do the working. The qualities of a planet will change as it goes through the twelve signs. For instance, performing a generalized love spell based on the planet Venus will be affected whether the planet is in Taurus (sign of its rulership), Pisces (exalted), or Scorpio (detriment). A Venus-Taurus combination has a maternal earthiness to it, whereas a Venus-Pisces will be very spiritual and ethereal; Venus-Scorpio will be quite debauched and excessive. Knowing that this quality will affect the working can help the operator get the right kind of Venus to work for them, depending on what they are attempting to promote. I would advise anyone who wants to practice celestial magic to have a book on their shelf that defines each of the planets as they are qualified by the twelve signs of the zodiac.

We have covered the qualities of the planetary archetypes, the various tables of correspondences, the deities and associated intermediaries, liturgical practices, and determining the location and qualities of the planet at the elected time for the working. However, this is only half of the talismanic equation. In order to complete our analysis for the other half, we will need to examine the twelve zodiacal signs and their associated element qualities.

Chapter Five

ZODIACAL CORRESPONDENCES: QUALITIES, DEITIES, AND SPIRITS

> "Astrology has no more useful function than this,
> to discover the inmost nature of a man and to bring
> it out into his consciousness, that he may fulfil it
> according to the law of light."
>
> —ALEISTER CROWLEY

We have explored the full spectrum of meanings and correspondences, deities and spirits of the planets from both old and new traditions—and they are but the first part of the talismanic equation. The second part is the twelve signs of the zodiac and all of their accumulated correspondences of qualities, deities, and spirits. It is the combination of planet and zodiacal sign that establishes the talismanic equation, so let us examine what we need to know to complete it.

Similar to our analysis of the planets, we begin with examining the archetypal qualities of the twelve signs of the zodiac and then present their various tables of correspondences. Like the planets, there are many layers of deities, spirits, and various qualities that represent the twelve signs of the zodiac.

The twelve signs of the zodiac are qualified by three factors: triplicities, quadruplicities, and polarity. The triplicities are the four elements: fire, air, water, and earth. The quadruplicities are the qualities: cardinal, fixed, and mutable. Polarity is the archetypal gender a sign assumes, referred to here as either the creative (masculine) or receptive (feminine) qualities.

Three quadruplicities represent the energy and the stage of a person's process and perspective regarding their life. Cardinal signs represent the starting or inauguration of a process. Fixed signs represent the inflexible urge to maintain what has been achieved and uphold the status quo. Mutable signs represent a process in its final stages of transition from one state to another. We can examine the qualities of these processes by looking at the three signs that occur in the season of spring.

The beginning of this season is represented by the cardinal sign of Aries, the medial part of this season is represented by the fixed sign of Taurus, and the ending and transitional part of the season where spring becomes summer represented by Gemini. The three processes can be compared to the three phases of the cosmogonic cycle of creation, equilibrium (stasis), and dissolution.

A zodiacal sign is a unique combination of triplicity, quadruplicity, and polarity, thus making each one unique. Additionally, the signs of the zodiac have a ruling planet and characterizations or associations that have been handed down from ancient Babylonia. Therefore, Aries and Taurus, besides being cardinal fire with a creative polarization and fixed earth with a receptive polarization, are also characterized by an association of the ram and bull respectively. Someone born under the sign of Aries would behave in a strong but fleeting and impulsive manner, and someone born under the sign of Taurus would be complacent, plodding, and slow to anger, but terrible when angry. Associations such as these help determine the significance and meaning for each of the twelve signs.

Archetypal Qualities of the Twelve Signs of the Zodiac

Here are the twelve signs of the zodiac and their specific archetypal qualities. As stated previously, "creative" is used in place of the old "masculine," and "receptive" denotes what were denoted "feminine" qualities. In some cases, a sign may have more than one planetary ruler because the Ptolemaic system of seven planets was later enhanced with ten planets. For this reason, I have placed the modern attributions first and the old/classical attributions next to them. In places where they are more apt as rulers of signs, I have also added asteroids. These attributions were taken from Robert Hand's *Astrological Symbols*. Most importantly, I qualify each zodiacal sign with its associated magical abilities and powers. This information will be important to consider when examining the decans and other divisions in the circle of the twelve signs.

Let us now examine the twelve zodiacal sign archetypes and their associated tables of correspondence. I will let you decide which to include in your workings. I have consulted three sources and distilled the definitions employed below.[21]

Aries—Ram: March 21–April 19: Aries is the cardinal fire sign that has a creative polarity. The planetary ruler is Mars. Aries represents the beginning of the Sun's cycle through the year. As the harbinger of spring, Aries is about beginnings and the inspiration and motivation to embark on big projects and engaging tasks. Aries does not lack in ambition nor aspiration but has problems with completing what has been started. Aries is raw power, boundless energy, ego-driven, and expressed as willpower, but it is also impulsive, changeable, and easily distracted. Aries symbolizes the self-made individual but can also show signs of being antisocial and lacking the ability to be a team player. People born under this sign are often leaders, pioneers, and adventurers; they have boundless energy, but they can also be overly assertive, blunt, combative, quick to anger and impatient. They are brave and courageous, highly competitive, but also arrogant, pushy, intolerant, prone to violence, and they have a need to dominate others. The magical uses of Aries are to energize and inspire people, start new enterprises and undertakings, and overcome obstacles and difficulties. Aries magic symbolizes the warrior's power and intelligent cunning.

Taurus—Bull: April 20–May 20: Taurus is the fixed earth sign that has a receptive polarity. The planetary ruler is Venus. Taurus is an earth sign expressed through the planet Venus, making it a sign of fertility, growth, material manifestation, stability, constancy, persistence, focus, steadfastness, earthiness, sensuality, and pleasure seeking. Taurus symbolizes

---

21 March and McEvers, *The Only Way to Learn Astrology*, 12–18; Hand, *Horoscope Symbols*, 211–241; Kim Rogers-Gallagher, "Signs: The Second Building Block" in *Llewellyn's Daily Planetary Guide 2022: Introduction to Astrology* (Woodbury, MN: Llewellyn Worldwide, 2021), 10–14.

wealth and possessions, the ownership of land, farming, and earthly abundance. People born under the sign of Taurus are cautious, methodical, plodding, complacent, and practical. Taurus symbolizes evolution and slow changes, even with a built-in resistance to change. Taurus is patience, solidity, hardworking, conservative, domestic, and responsible, but also stubborn, jealous, self-indulgent, greedy, materialistic, and overly possessive. The magical uses of Taurus are to foster all kinds of creativity, fertility, and material increase. However, this magic takes time to develop and materially manifest, so it is best used for long-term projects, careers, and enterprises. The magic of Taurus is also good for gardening, farming, and animal husbandry.

Gemini—Twins: May 21–June 20: Gemini is the mutable air sign with a creative polarity. The planetary ruler is Mercury. As a mutable sign, Gemini represents transitions, and because it is an air sign, it symbolizes mental changeability. As an exemplar of Mercury, Gemini is quick moving and always changing, logical, rational, and comprehensive in its perception but also shallow and surface-oriented. There is an old saying that the mental scope of a Gemini is a mile wide but less than an inch deep. Gemini has the quality of rapidly changing from topic to topic, but never grasping the root of any of them. Those born under the sign of Gemini are curious about everything, very sociable and casual, but they avoid any commitments or long-term agreements. Gemini people are inconsistent, malleable, humorous, communicative, and literate. They can be a social gadfly or a trickster, whatever path excites them at the moment. They are versatile, dexterous, and quick-witted but can also be two-faced, restless, scheming, and feckless. The magic of Gemini can be tapped to gain ideas, increase mental agility, expand one's literary abilities, or solve a problem with many possible solutions. Gemini magic helps the mind to be open, flexible, loose, and capable of accepting new and novel directions.

Cancer—Crab: June 21–July 22: Cancer is the cardinal water sign that has a receptive polarity. Its planetary ruler is the Moon. Like the Moon and water, Cancer is a sign of the emotions, powerful feelings, and the need to protect oneself from emotional pain. Cancer is emotional depth;

at times it can be inchoate, unformulated, deep, intuitive, and irratio-nal. Those born under the sign of Cancer tend to focus on the past, particularly their childhood, which can cause them to be motivated to seek emotional security. Cancer is the perfect homebody. They like to make a place where they can feel that they truly belong, where they can raise their family and feast with their friends. Cancer represents nurturing, social-cohesion, privacy, and intimacy. Cancers wear their hearts on their sleeves and are vulnerable and easily hurt. They can be needy, dependent, selfish, overly retentive, brooding, paranoid, and manipulative, but they are also very sympathetic, patriotic, and espouse traditional values. The magic of Cancer helps to bring people together, mends family separations, and heals emotional pain. Cancer magic can assist difficult births, protect mothers and children from outside threats, and bring peace to disturbed minds.

Leo—Lion: July 23–August 22: Leo is the fixed fire sign that has a creative polarity. It is ruled by the Sun. Leo is a sign of royalty, pride, and per-sonal charisma. Where Aries starts a project, Leo has the social power and strength to make it realized. Leo symbolizes the ego, one's social iden-tity, and perceived dignity and social worth. Those born under the sign of Leo exude confidence, admiration, and self-fascination, and they are moti-vated to be accepted by nearly everyone. A Leo is more concerned about those who are enemies or indifferent than they are about their friends. They seek personal recognition and the adulation of their friends but comport themselves as if they were actors in a play. Leos are ostentatious, flamboyant, and need the attention of others. They are typically con-trolling to the point of being inauthentic, and they seek to control their loved ones and children to play their part in the act. Leos are generous to a fault, idealistic, ambitious, creative, overly optimistic, and ebullient, but they are also vain, overbearing, boastful, pretentious, and autocratic. The magic of Leo is the magic of charisma, self-confidence, good luck, and success with the opposite sex. Leo magic can be used to create a glamour around oneself to powerfully influence friends and enemies.

Virgo—Virgin Holding a Sheaf: August 23–September 22: Virgo is the mutable earth sign that has a receptive polarity. It is ruled by Mercury or Ceres/Vesta. Virgo represents service to others, efficiency, practical adaptability, realism, orderliness, perfectionism, and conformity. People born under the sign of Virgo are cautious and constrained by self-doubt, even though they seek to change the world by example instead of coercion. They are detail oriented, self-critical, high-minded taskmasters. Virgo symbolizes an aesthetic for organization, perfection, and accuracy; a strong sense of personal humility and reliability makes them the ideal helper and team player. Virgos can be overly serious and humorless; they are also discriminating, analytical, and capable problem-solvers. They are often plagued by feelings of inadequacy and inferiority because they can never meet (let alone exceed) their own expectations. The magic of Virgo is to cause people to think and perceive with perfect clarity whatever problem or issue they might focus upon. Virgo magic reveals the truth despite any complex illusions (even delusions) and cuts through sentiment or fancy to lay bare the facts of a matter.

Libra—Scales: September 23–October 22: Libra is the cardinal air sign that has a creative polarity. It is ruled by Venus or Juno. Libra is the true lover of symmetry, harmony, beauty, and everything that particular sentiment entails. Those born under the sign of Libra are thus diplomats, peacemakers, and the patrons of high culture and social decorum. They are socially adept and easily establish close and intimate relationships, often with many different people. Libras are counselors and keen advisers, since they understand what moves and motivates individuals and groups. They love to socialize and enjoy public entertainment (theater), and they are personally charming and socially attractive. Libra represents the gentle interaction of people, maintaining good manners, courtesy, and cooperation. Libra represents refinement, social charm, and gentle persuasion, but they can also be too appeasing, indecisive, fickle, superficial, and conflict-averse at all costs. The magic of Libra helps to refine those who have rough edges, giving eloquence and social poise to the otherwise socially clumsy or awkward. Libra magic is a social magic that gives social charms and attractiveness to one, allowing them to easily fit into any social situation.

Scorpio—Scorpion: October 23–November 21: Scorpio is the fixed water sign that has a receptive polarity. It is ruled by Pluto or Mars. Scorpio symbolizes autumn, where nature dies, hibernates, or migrates. Scorpio is therefore concerned with death and transformation. Scorpio represents the emotional merging of two people that brings on the little death of ego and physical immersion. Scorpio symbolizes the great heights (as the eagle) and great lows (as the dung beetle) of one's emotions; it represents extremes and also great emotional intensity. People born under the sign of Scorpio experience very deep feelings that they often cannot share, making them secretive and distrustful of others. They live in a powerful inner emotional world, experiencing both pleasure and pain in an intense manner. Scorpios love mysteries, since they can identify with their own inexplicable desires; they are self-absorbed, brooding, and vengeful, but also magical and capable of resolving any crisis they experience or helping others do the same. Scorpios can be obsessive, pursing their objectives relentlessly. They can become addicted to experiencing pleasure and can thus be prone to excessive drug use, alcoholism, and sexual activity. However, they are capable of self-discipline and can materialize their highest ideas for all to share. The magic of Scorpio is emotionally very potent, and it can be used to either materialize one's highest ideals or to cause others to fall and be subdued. Scorpio magic is also sex magic, and it can be used as a two-edged sword when applied to a specific targeted individual. It is a two-edged sword because it can inflict sexual desires on the target but also cause the operator to become obsessed and ensorcelled— Scorpio sex magic is therefore quite risky.

Sagittarius—Archer: November 22–December 21: Sagittarius is the mutable fire sign that has a creative polarity. It is ruled by Jupiter. Sagittarius represents personal freedom and self-expression, taking upon itself many of Jupiter's good and bad attributes. Those born under the sign of Sagittarius are idealistic reformers who also seek social agreement. They are typically engaged in education, sciences, philosophy, and religion. Sagittarius has the qualities of being visionary, legal-minded, optimistic, and the ability to see the big picture amid the minutiae of concerns and issues. Sagittarians have a love of travel, sports competitions, and outdoor activities. Sagittarians are humorous, typically straightforward, athletic, and broadminded, but they can also be procrastinating, gamblers, impatient, argumentative, and prone to exaggeration. The magic of Sagittarius assists the operator in acquiring a high-minded approach to life and its difficulties, helping to empower and embolden them and understand their role and purpose in life. Sagittarian magic frees the soul from worries and fears and bolsters confidence to face troubles with an optimistic and upbeat perspective.

Capricorn—Goat: December 21–January 20: Capricorn is the cardinal earth sign that has a receptive polarity. It is ruled by Saturn. Capricorn represents adherence to the status-quo, caution, and a conservative nature; it is materialistic and focused on practical objectives. Those born under the sign of Capricorn believe and trust in authority figures, institutions, and laws. They seek financial independence, status, and security, and they understand the limitations of ambition and the need for hard work and self-reliance. Capricorns are good in business because they are highly organized and self-disciplined. They are principled, traditional, and responsible with workaholic tendencies, often self-denying for the overall good. Capricorns have an inherent respect for posterity and precedence, but they can also be cold, stingy, close-minded, inflexible, stubborn, and unforgiving. The magic of Capricorn greatly aids in business pursuits and completing long-term projects. Capricorn magic helps the operator with legal issues, overcoming bankruptcy, and finding and building a long-term career.

Aquarius—Water Bearer: January 21–February 18: Aquarius is the fixed air sign that has a creative polarity. It is ruled by Uranus or Saturn. Aquarius represents the great social consciousness, acutely aware of injustice and inequality, since it is the socialized ego. Those born under the sign of Aquarius are gregarious, outwardly friendly, socially interactive, identifying with the group or generation. They are capable of innovative thinking, and they seek to promote social justice and freedom. Aquarians believe strongly in democracy and the rights of the individual. They are humanitarians who aspire to utopian social visions. Aquarius symbolizes inventiveness, love of change, and social idealism. Aquarius can foster revolutions for the sake of social reform and material equity. Aquarians zealously commit themselves to a cause or ideal. They can be tolerant, open minded, and altruistic, but they can also be temperamental, radical, coldly impersonal, and rebellious toward authority. The magic of Aquarius is that it promotes the overthrow of tyranny and oppression, whether on a personal or societal level. Aquarian magic can greatly aid one in seeking social justice or to right a wrong.

Pisces—Joined Fishes: February 19–March 20: Pisces is the mutable water sign that has a receptive polarity. It is ruled by Neptune or Jupiter. Pisces represents the transcendence of the self, subordination of the self to a higher principle, and rebirth to a higher level. Pisces represents deep sensitivity, psychic perception, and self-sacrifice. Those born under the sign of Pisces are dreamers and prone to fantasy. They are empathic and very compassionate. Pisces are very mystical, agoraphobic, introspective, and pessimistic about outcomes. Pisces tend to see the best in people and situations, they are romantic and very charitable, but they are also inhibited, socially timid, naïve, impractical, and indolent. The magic of Pisces assists the operator to transcend themselves, to gain visions of the highest nature of being, and to spiritually evolve. Piscean magic makes the projection of illusions, dreams, and fantasies into a unique art form, allowing for an inexhaustible resource of creative expression.

Practical Zodiacal Correspondences

Zodiacal correspondences, like planetary correspondences, assist the mind in connecting with the archetypal intelligence and powers associated with the signs of the zodiac. While planetary correspondences are more important than zodiacal ones, it is the element quality of the sign that allows the talismanic equation to be completed.

A basic talisman is produced through the combination of a planet and an element, yet a planet in combination with a zodiacal sign gives it a greater overall field due to a sign's quadruplicity and polarity. A planet and sign combination represents a dynamic attribute within natal, transit, and elective charts similar to a functional personality trait. A full series of all seven or ten planets within a chart (along with the angular relationships of the aspects and their location in the geography-based houses) represents a fully dynamic personality with all their potential assets and deficits represented in a chart. It is the dynamic intelligence and conscious energy produced from a planet and a sign that we seek to project into a consecrated metallic talisman.

Therefore, even though the planet in the talismanic equation has the greater emphasis, the zodiacal sign is also important and, in some cases (such as in the thirty-six decans), even has precedence over the associated planet. We will need to examine the basic qualities of the twelve signs of the zodiac in terms of color, gemstone, incense, and the presiding deities and spirits representing and governing them. The following tables have a practical use in zodiacal workings, although there are many more correspondences that can be found or attributed to them. These attributes are the ones I have collected and used over the years.

As in the case of the correspondences for the planets, you can look over the various tables of correspondences available in Crowley's *777*, Stephen Skinner's *Complete Magician's Tables*, and Bill Whitcomb's *Magician's Companion* to see all of the correspondences for the twelve signs. You will find some of these correspondences common to these authors, some not; they don't agree in every case, so there are some variances, hence it being necessary for me to determine my own correspondences.

The first table contains the basic zodiacal qualities distilled from the paragraphs outlining the qualities of the signs as detailed earlier in this chapter. I have added the color to this table to give you an idea of the full range of zodiacal correspondences. Note that although colors are included, I don't really "use" them in the rituals; I believe the color associated with the planet is more important than the color associated with the sign.

Basic Zodiacal Qualities

Zodiacal Name	Image	Planetary Ruler	Element Quality	Color
Aries	Ram	Mars	Cardinal Air	Scarlet
Taurus	Bull	Venus	Fixed Earth	Pink, brown ocher
Gemini	Twin children	Mercury	Mutable Air	Rainbow
Cancer	Crab	Moon	Cardinal Water	Bright green
Leo	Lion	Sun	Fixed Fire	Yellow orange
Virgo	Virgin with sheaf	Mercury, Ceres/Vesta	Mutable Earth	Navy blue
Libra	Scales	Venus, Juno	Cardinal Air	Pale azure
Scorpio	Scorpion	Pluto, Mars	Fixed Water	Maroon
Sagittarius	Centaur archer	Jupiter	Mutable Fire	Indigo
Capricorn	Sea goat	Saturn	Cardinal Earth	Dark brown
Aquarius	Water bearer	Uranus, Saturn	Fixed Air	Cerulean blue
Pisces	Twin joined fish	Neptune, Jupiter	Mutable Water	Sea green

The next table contains the magical correspondences for the twelve signs. While the gemstone could be used in an exclusive zodiacal working (same as the color association) or to embellish a piece of talismanic jewelry, the planetary correspondences would take precedence in the talismanic working. However, the listing of Archangel, Angel, and Angelic House/Sign Ruler are used in the talismanic workings where the zodiacal sign is represented in the working, such as the decan working. I also omitted the correspondence for incense because it is not used in any of the workings.

The archangel and angel are associated specifically with the astrological sign, while the angelic ruler is associated with the house that also has the quality of the sign. These three angels are used as representatives of the triangular gateway used in the decan and the septan workings as found in chapters 14 and 15.

Magical Zodiacal Qualities—Gemstones, Archangelic and Angelic Spirits

Zodiac Sign	Gemstone	Archangel	Angel	Angelic House Ruler
Aries	Diamond	Malchidael	Sharhiel	Aiel
Taurus	Star Sapphire	Asmodel	Araziel	Tual
Gemini	Agate	Ambriel	Sarayel	Niel
Cancer	Pearl	Muriel	Pakiel	Kael
Leo	Ruby	Verchiel	Shavatiel	Auel
Virgo	Sardonyx	Hamaliel	Shelathiel	Ziel
Libra	Sapphire	Zuriel	Chedeqiel	Yahel
Scorpio	Opal	Barchiel	Saitziel	Savasaval
Sagittarius	Topaz	Advachiel	Saritiel	Saviasal
Capricorn	Turquoise	Hanael	Sameqiel	Kasuyoiah
Aquarius	Amethyst	Cambriel	Tzakmiqiel	Ansuel
Pisces	Moonstone	Amnixiel	Vekabiel	Pasiel

The table of zodiacal deities are used as comparative reference points in continuity with the correspondences for the planets. They are not used in the magical workings described in this book, but I decided to include them for the sake of having a reference to zodiacal deities. You could use them if you wanted to work with the rich archetypal symbolism for the zodiacal signs—and there is a ritual to invoke just the zodiacal sign—but the talismanic rituals exclusively use the planetary correspondences for deity. As for the Babylonian names for constellations, I felt that examining and comparing these to what we have today would be useful. Some of the images are identical and others have since changed over time.

Zodiacal Deities—Roman, Greek, Egyptian, and Babylonian Names

Zodiacal Name	Roman Deity	Greek Deity	Egyptian Deity	Babylonian Name
Aries	Minerva	Athena	Sekhmet	Luhunga: Hired Laborer
Taurus	Venus	Aphrodite	Hathor	Gud-Annu: Heavenly Bull
Gemini	Janus, Mercury	Hermes	Thoth	Mashab-Bal-Galgal: Great Twins
Cancer	Juno	Hera	Isis as Mother	Allu: Crab
Leo	Jupiter	Zeus	Ra	Urgula: Great Dog (Lion)
Virgo	Ceres	Demeter	Osiris	Abshim: Spikes of Corn
Libra	Pax	Eirene	Maat	Zibanetum: Scales
Scorpio	Mars	Ares, Dionysus	Horus the Elder	Girtab: Scorpion
Sagittarius	Diana	Artemis	Nephthys	Pa-Bil-Sag: Overseer
Capricorn	Saturn, Vesta	Kronos	Geb, Hapi	Sukhuyar-Mashu: Goat Fish
Aquarius	Justitia	Themis	Nuit	Gula: Giant
Pisces	Neptune	Poseidon	Anubis	Shimmah: Great Swallow

To contact the intelligence of the zodiacal sign, I have used a combination of deity and/or archangel/angel to call them. Using any of these will help you to make contact with the intelligence behind the zodiacal sign so you can use its powers and wisdom. The color and gemstone will give this kind of operation an added boost, although the gemstone is more costly than for planets, usually made into jewelry worn by the operator. The need for making this kind of contact will be infrequent; the focus will be on the planetary ruler and its associated correspondences for talismanic workings.

Sectional Divisions of the Twelve Signs of the Zodiac

Each of the twelve zodiac signs consists of thirty degrees of the whole 360. So far, we have been considering the twelve signs individually, but each sign can be further broken into segments or parts, each having its own attributes and definitions. There are two traditional methods of division: decans and lunar mansions. Both systems are important because they represent the very heart of the talismanic equation, where a planet and an element symbolize the material energy and intelligence associated with a talismanic projection, and where a talisman is charged and fixed with its planetary and element qualities. In my research, I have discovered and use a third method, explained below.

Just as there are groupings of three signs for a given element, a single sign can be broken into three 10-degree segments. In total, there would be thirty-six of these segments, and because they contain only ten degrees, they are called decans or faces. These decans have a wide set of correspondences and are used in talismanic magic, advanced energy magic, and even spirit conjuration.

Zodiacal decans have a very ancient pedigree, having come down to us from ancient Egypt. For the Egyptian astronomer, there were not twelve distinct constellations, there were thirty-six distinct divisions of the heavens later called the decans. To the Egyptians, these were the star deities who were part of the mythology of the night sky and took part in the nightly struggle where the sun god Ra was transformed and reborn through the twelve hours of the night. The decans were also part of the Egyptian calendar of ten-day weeks to total thirty-six weeks with five extra days at the end of the year. The Egyptians also used the decans to tell the passage of time at night, as the night sky and its decan divisions circled around the sky.

It was Ptolemy who included the decans in his writings and astrological observations, and later Arabic astrologers developed the concept of the decans so they could be used specifically for magical purposes. The decans and their magical uses and images appear in the Arabic *Picatrix*, along with the lunar mansions.

An individual decan consists of a ruling planet and a 10-degree part or segment of its associated sign. The first ten degrees symbolizes the beginning of the zodiacal sign, its transition into the full representation of the qualities associated with the sign. The next ten degrees symbolizes the medial part of zodiacal sign signifying the static and fixed nature of the zodiacal qualities. The last ten degrees symbolizes the dissolution and transition of the sign into the next sign in the sequence. In many respects, these three phases of a single zodiacal sign emulate the quadruplicity of cardinal, fixed, and mutable qualities associated with the signs as a whole. Although there are correspondences for the decans, including a ruling angel and Egyptian godhead, those will be later covered in chapter 7 when we examine decan-based talismanic magic.

The twenty-eight lunar mansions represent the passage of the Moon through the zodiac for each 24-hour period. It creates a kind of uneven distribution because the passage of the Moon through the signs is variable. The Moon travels at a variable speed around 12 to 15 degrees per twenty-four-hour period and takes around forty-eight to sixty hours to travel through a sign. Accordingly, some of the divisions of the lunar mansions occupy two or three segments of a zodiacal sign. There are no planetary rulers for the lunar mansions because they are determined exclusively by the Moon, their sole and only ruler. Lunar mansions along with their associated correspondences are covered in more detail in chapter 6.

A third method for dividing the zodiac uses the four elements to make four distinct segments for each of the twelve signs of the zodiac. While not a traditional method, it is one that does appear to fit with the traditional approach to adding determinants to the zodiacal signs. Dividing each sign into four segments produces forty-eight parts, which have a significant set of correspondences already available within various occult associations.

The ruling planet for each segment would be the ruling planet for the whole sign, but the *quality* of the element segment of the sign would alter and qualify that planet's nature. We would look at the element qualities of Mars and Aries for the element quadrant of the sign. Each segment would consist of 7 degrees and 30 minutes, and each segment would last approximately a week.

I have proposed that the sequence of elements be based on the sequence of cardinal signs of fire (Aries), water (Cancer), air (Libra), and then earth (Capricorn), symbolizing the lifespan of a sign as the Sun passes through it, where fire is the birth and ascendancy, water as youth into adulthood, air to be full adulthood to decline, and earth as decline and transition from life into death.

Each element segment would qualify a sign's symbols like a colored lens, representing the full arch of ascendancy and decline associated with that sign. I call these segments *septans* because they are close to seven degrees, making them similar to the decans. These types of talisman structures are covered in chapter 8; I have likened them to planetary sub-elements (planet and an element qualifying an element base) and have found them very useful in celestial magic.

We have covered all the topics associated with the zodiac in this chapter. Let us next examine each of the three methods of dividing the zodiac and their correspondences so that we can apply the lunar mansions, decans, or septans to a talismanic working. These three mechanisms outlined in this treatise on celestial magic will be used to charm a magical talisman and capture the associated celestial components within it.

Chapter Six

LUNAR MANSIONS: TALISMANIC ELEMENTALS

"Let the magical night sky with beautiful music be your backdrop. Make the moon and stars your friends because they know your secrets."

—Hiral Nagda

The Lunar Mansions (*manzil al-qamar*) were an Arabic discovery developed and added to the astrological lore in the late tenth century CE.[22] Whether it was developed from previous speculations before the period of Arabic astrologers or invented by them is unknown at the present time. Lunar mansions of some form have been found in both Indian and Chinese astrology, but the ultimate source for these methods has been lost. We do find descriptions and depictions of it in the writings of Al Biruni and other Arabic astrologers, as well as in the *Pictatrix*.

While it may have originally been an astronomical tool developed to qualify sightings of the moon as it made its passage through the signs and fixed stars of the zodiac, it ultimately became a significant mechanism for generating talismans. The method of magic associated with the lunar mansions involved

---

22 Ryan Butler, "The Mansions of the Moon" at *Medieval Astrology Guide*, accessed January 1, 2022: *https://www.medievalastrologyguide.com/lunar-mansions*.

creating and exposing a talisman during a specific lunar mansion period while using the mansion name and imagery associated with it as a method for summoning and projecting it.

Thus, the twenty-eight lunar mansions are used today specifically for talismanic magic, and they represent some of the most effective magic one might want to perform. The mansions are represented by specific zodiacal qualities associated with a segment of the zodiac approximately 12 degrees and 51 minutes in length. The method for determining the lunar mansion event is astrological, based on lunar positions calculated from an ephemeris. In order for a mansion to be active, the Moon should be in that specific zodiacal sign and degree period when the magical operation is to be performed.

Waxing and waning moons have an important effect on the quality of the lunar mansion. A waxing Moon is where the outcome is typically considered positive, constructive, or a blessing, while a waning Moon outcome is generally negative or even considered a curse. The period for performing positive magic based on the lunar mansion is always when the Moon is waxing, from the point immediately following the new Moon to just prior to the full Moon.

Western magical use and qualifications of the lunar mansions are originally adapted from the *Picatrix*, but they became part of the lore of Western magic when they appeared in Agrippa's *Occult Philosophy*. The lunar mansions are used to charge and empower magical talismans. A talisman is blessed and charged at some point during the period of the lunar mansion, thus allowing the mansion to passively influence and affect the talisman.

Since the Moon travels through the zodiac at 14 degrees per day, it will only reside in a specific lunar mansion for slightly less than a day. In order to take advantage of a lunar mansion, the Moon should be waxing within its lunation cycle; any lunation type, from crescent to just before full Moon, can be employed. This short period of less than two weeks will limit the number of possible elective lunar mansions that can be employed during a specific seasonal period of the year.

While the lunar mansions represent a traditional and powerful system of magic by itself, I did not incorporate them into my basic talismanic workings at first. Instead, I approached it with the idea that there were seven planets and four elements, and that combining them into a matrix would produce a total of 28 planetary elements. While this might seem very different from the lunar mansions, it allowed me to quickly develop a system of talismanic magic, since I was using the basic components of planet and element to generate a talismanic field.

I discovered many years later that there was a match between the 28 talismanic elementals and the corresponding lunar mansions. What I propose here is to match the talismanic elemental with the lunar mansion to give it a more powerful overall field. This is not the traditional approach, since traditional lunar mansions do not have associated planetary rulers. The traditional mansions would not lend themselves to my requirement of having a planet and an element for the talismanic equation.

There is a tale to be told here about how I came up with my original approach and how the lore of lunar mansions fits in with this mechanism. I believe it makes for a larger approach, despite not being traditional.

Talismanic Elementals

Many years ago, when I was first putting together my system of planetary magic, I sought to work out a system of magic that incorporated a matrix of planets and elements similar to what I had developed with the four elements and the sixteen elementals. I saw that qualifying a base element with a planet would produce an array of 28 specific elements. Since I was keen on developing such an arrangement, I looked to the Enochian system of magic for something to use to specifically identify these particular entities. As fate would have it, there were spirits that consisted of a planet and an element in the Enochian spirit lists.

These planetary attributes were associated with spirit names derived from planetary associations in each of the four Enochian elemental tablets. It was where the sixteen god-name pairs that I used to name the sixteen elementals came from. These spirits were the 24 seniors or elders associated with six planets, excluding the Sun—matching them to the points of the magic hexagram. These names were obtained from the Enochian Great Watchtowers in the center rows of the grand crosses.

There were spirit names for the planets Saturn, Venus, Mars, Jupiter, the Moon, and Mercury. The four great kings were associated with the four elements of the Sun. The 24 seniors and the four great kings were combined together to produce a succinct method for naming the combination of planet and element. I called these spirits "talismanic elementals" and used them in a system of talismanic magic long before I was aware that this same structure might apply to the 28 lunar mansions.

The following is a cross reference of the 28 talismanic elementals arranged in order with each of the four elements. I have included a short description of the type of influence each produces. I am including this list so you can get an idea of how I developed my system of planetary and element magic. When we examine the lunar mansions, the correspondences for these talismanic attributes will become clearer.

Fire

Sun of Fire: Self-expression, generosity, nobility, pride.

Moon of Fire: Emotional dominance, self-dramatization, overcoming insecurities, and the need to be appreciated.

Mars of Fire: Positive initiative, leadership, power, competitiveness, an athlete.

Mercury of Fire: Fixed purpose, focused concentration, willpower, positive solutions.

Jupiter of Fire: Benevolence, ostentatiousness, grandeur, dignity, kingship.

Saturn of Fire: Desire for self-control, insightful, self-management, self-directed.

Venus of Fire: Romanticism, loyalty in love, love of life, musical talents, theatrical expressions.

Water

Sun of Water: Fundamental transformation, emotional healing, emotional insights, and wisdom.

Moon of Water: Healing powers, revealing hidden motives and unrevealed passions, hidden lovers, causing retribution to others.

Mars of Water: Courage, thoroughness, resourceful, uncompromising, death defying.

Mercury of Water: Visionary, powerful intuition, critical insight, self-determination.

Jupiter of Water: Inheritances, legacies, affairs with religious institutions, spiritual grace.

Saturn of Water: Perfectionism, responsibility, persistence, efficiency.

Venus of Water: Passion expressed, pleasure motives, lustful, intense emotions released, occult sensitivities.

Air

Sun of Air: Humanitarianism, social conscience, self-determination, friendship, foreknowledge.

Moon of Air: Sympathy, intuitive insight, promotes equality, good fortune, and freedom from bondage.

Mars of Air: Passionate communication, oratorical skills, seeking reformation, social activism, libertinism, activating anti-authority sentiment, revolutions.

Mercury of Air: Achieves openness in others, truthfulness, unbiased perceptions, mental objectivity, intellectual creativity.

Jupiter of Air: Promotes socially inspired ideals, democracy, social justice, tolerance, and universal solidarity.

Saturn of Air: Mental organization, clarity, concentration, science, objective truth.

Venus of Air: Friendship, unselfish principles, diplomacy, care for others, intellectual and aesthetic appreciation of beauty.

Earth

Sun of Earth: Purposeful determination, mastery over matter, love of luxury, green thumb.

Moon of Earth: Desire for domestic security, creativity, fertility, health, establishment of wealth.

Mars of Earth: Monetary ambitions, achieving material results, perseverance, craftsmanship.

Mercury of Earth: Practical and material application of intellectual pursuits, building, engineering, resourcefulness, ability to resolve limitations or restrictions.

Jupiter of Earth: Wise usage of resources, cautious generosity, investment, banking, financial partnerships.

Saturn of Earth: Patience, steadfastness, stability, reliability, centeredness.

Venus of Earth: Emotional stability, physical sensuality, personal beauty, art in all its forms.

These are the twenty-eight talismanic elementals as I determined them many years ago. The manner that I determined the definitions of each of these qualities was to simply imagine them combined together. However, a more sophisticated approach would be to examine each planet and its qualities as they would be interpreted when placing a planet in one of the signs associated with that element.

For instance, you could look at Venus of Earth (emotional stability) and examine the descriptions of the qualities of Venus in the three earth signs of Taurus, Virgo, and Capricorn, and the quality of the talismanic elemental would share in a synthesis of all three.

Lunar Mansions and Talismanic Elementals

When I became aware of the lunar mansions, I found it strangely coincidental that the talismanic elementals also had 28 attributes. These two systems were not the same, of course, but I wondered if perhaps they might be matched up in some manner. I was doubtful that it could be done but decided to try it anyway, just to see if they were indeed the same kind of attribute. So, I reviewed the meanings of the talismanic elementals and compared them with the meanings of the lunar mansions to see if they matched.

Lunar mansions are based on the Moon and its orbit through the zodiac; there are no planetary rulers. Assigning a planet and an element to these attributes would be completely contrary to astrological and magical traditions. However, the lunar mansions as defined would not fit into my talismanic equation.

While I am certain the lunar mansions would be quite effective using traditional magical methods, I saw an opportunity to join these two systems together and thereby make them fit within my magical definitions for talismanic magic. I had thought that matching them would produce something that was awkward, but to my surprise the two systems fit together as if they were made to be joined into a single system. I found that a few of the talismanic elementals vary somewhat from the magical uses as described for the mansions, but most do appear to match. I happily added the correspondences of the talismanic elementals to the lunar mansions and have been working with this system for many years now.

One glaring exception was the apparent mismatch between Mars of Air and Mansion 6, Brand or Mark, associated with 4 degrees of Gemini. The magic associated with the mansion is the classic one of love magic—the image is of a man and woman embracing. The qualities of the talismanic elemental Mars of Air do not lend themselves in any way to the idea of love magic. I would define this quality of planet and element as representing forceful or inspired communication (Mars and Air), or the gift of oration and the ability to reach a crowd of people through speech and activate them for reform. I think the sign of Gemini would reinforce this kind ability; to my knowledge, I would never see love magic between individuals as a part of the qualities associated with that sign.

While the rest of the talismanic qualities and mansion attributes seem to match in some manner (except for three others that are a little off),[23] this one particular mansion doesn't appear to match in any fashion whatsoever. What I would recommend is to use this talisman and mansion combination as two approaches to a similar end: use either the talismanic qualities or the mansion qualities in your magic, or just ignore the mansion qualities established by tradition and use just the talismanic quality. What I have done is consider the traditional magic associated with this mansion to be possibly erroneous (and perhaps dated).

---

23 These mansions and talismanic elementals are a bit off: Venus of Water, Moon of Air, and Saturn of Earth.

The following are the correspondences of the 28 talismanic elementals arranged in element order rather than zodiacal order, the way they are customarily ordered when associated with the mansions of the Moon. The correspondences consist of the planet and element combination, the name of the lunar mansion and its qualities and correspondences (mansion name and quality, angelic ruler, color, and waxing (+) and waning (-) lunar qualities). I decided to omit the image and the instructions for constructing a talisman, since these are not used in the magical workings incorporating the lunar mansion. You can consult any of the listed sources in the bibliography if you are interested or curious about these additional attributes.

You will also see short descriptions of the type of influence each talismanic elemental produces when used; these attributes appear to more or less fit with the lunar mansion. This is placed at the end of the list of correspondences for the mansions.

I recommend using the colors, incense or perfumes, and metals associated with the ruling planet. The seal of the Olympian spirit and the symbol for the element would ideally be engraved on a metallic talisman along with the planetary symbol. To summon the specific talismanic elemental lunar mansion, you can use the Arabic mansion name and the angelic ruler.

The collection of correspondences for the 28 lunar mansions below were distilled from four sources and a comparative compilation website.[24]

Fire (Mansions of Aries, Leo, and Sagittarius)

Sun of Fire: Mansion: *Al Zubrah* (#11 The Lion's Mane) Leo 8 degrees, 34 minutes; Angelic Ruler: **Neciel;** Color: Golden saffron; Mansion Qualities: (+) Attracts fear, reverence, and worship to the bearer; promotes loyalty, generosity, inspired leadership, and charismatic and awe-inspiring qualities; regains lost affections, establishes prosperity, and produces a powerful

24 Butler, "Mansions of the Moon" *https://www.medievalastrologyguide.com/lunar-mansions;* Christopher Warnock, *The Mansions of the Moon: A Lunar Zodiac for Astrology and Magic* (Self-published, 2010), 8–126; Skinner, *Complete Magician's Tables*, 111–119; Dan Attrell and David Porreca, *Picatrix: A Medieval Treatise on Astral Magic* (University Park, PA: University of Pennsylvania Press, 2019), 45–51; Alexander Kolesnikov, "The Mansions of the Moon" at *Lunarium* website, accessed January 1, 2022: https://www.lunarium.co/articles/lunar-mansions/.

optimism. (-) Causes hubris, recklessness, and a loss of faith and self-belief. Talismanic Qualities: Dignified self-expression, generosity, nobility, pride.

Moon of Fire: Mansion: *Al Nava'am* (#20 The Beam, The Ostriches) Sagittarius 4 degrees, 17 minutes; Angelic Ruler: **Kyriel;** Color: Cerulean azure Mansion Qualities: (+) Fortunate in hunting, efficacious for taming wild and vicious beasts (aggressive forces in nature), creates benign alliances and coalitions and can be used to magically summon an individual. (-) Used to bind or imprison individuals or inimical forces, causes the implementation of justice and redresses wrongs. Talismanic Qualities: Emotional dominance, self-dramatization, and overcoming insecurities and the need to be appreciated.

Mars of Fire: Mansion: *Al Sharatain* (#1 Horns of Aries) Aries 0 degrees; Angelic Ruler: **Gehiel;** Color: Infrared crimson; Mansion Qualities: (+) Promotes personal safety and protection during travel. Assists in making medicines and raising great powers. (-) Causes discord and destruction of opposing forces. Talismanic Qualities: Positive initiative, leadership, power, competitiveness, great physical strength.

Mercury of Fire: Mansion: *Al Baldah* (#21 The City or District) Sagittarius 17 degrees, 9 minutes; Angelic Ruler: **Bethnael;** Color: Azure ultramarine; Mansion Qualities: (+) Promotes protection for travelers, increases crops, house protection, geomancy (earth divination), insights into the cause of things, allowing one to capitalize on material and financial gain. (-) Complete destruction of an enemy. Talismanic Qualities: Fixed purpose, focused concentration, willpower, positive solutions.

Jupiter of Fire: Mansion: *Al Butain* (#2 The Belly of Aries) Aries 12 degrees, 51 minutes; Angelic Ruler: **Enediel;** Color: Scarlet crimson; Mansion Qualities: (+) Discovers hidden treasures (material or intellectual), protects one from the anger of powerful men or organizations, causes reconciliation and calms negatives energies, attracts material abundance and good returns (on investments). (-) Binding and restraining adverse forces (overturns negative magic). Talismanic Qualities: Benevolence, ostentatiousness, grandeur, dignity, kingship.

Saturn of Fire: Mansion: *Al Sarfah* (#12 The Lion's Tail) Leo 21 degrees, 16 minutes; Angelic Ruler: **Abdizuel;** Color: Greenish gold; Mansion Qualities: (+) Promotes an optimistic improvement of circumstances, brings help and benevolence, and generates prosperity and good profits. (-) Brings discord and disrupts friendships, causes material hardship. Talismanic Qualities: Desire for self-control, insightful, self-management, self-directed.

Venus of Fire: Mansion: *Al Thurayya* (#3 The Many Little Ones–Pleiades) Aries 25 degrees, 43 minutes; Angelic Ruler: **Anixiel;** Color: Vermilion red; Mansion Qualities: (+) Attracts wellbeing, happiness, felicity, contains all negative forces and protects those individuals navigating dangerous environments. Assists all types of love spells. (-) Causes relationship disruptions, used to seduce one against their will. Talismanic Qualities: Romanticism, loyalty in love, love of life, musical talents, theatrical expressions.

Water (Mansions of Cancer, Scorpio, and Pisces)

Sun of Water: Mansion: *Al Jabhah* (#10 The Lion's Forehead—the Brow of Leo) Cancer 25 degrees, 43 minutes; Angelic Ruler: **Ardesiel;** Color: Golden yellow; Mansion Qualities: (+) Facilitates birthing, promotes healing, convalescence and health, is a bringer of consolidation and strength. Promotes House protection, aids against adversity and enemies. (-) Causes sickness, dissolution, the fall of one's house, and death. Talismanic Qualities: Fundamental transformation, emotional healing, emotional insights, wisdom.

Moon of Water: Mansion: *Al Shaula* (#19 The Tail of the Scorpion, the Sting) Scorpio 21 degrees, 6 minutes; Angelic Ruler: **Amutiel;** Color: Viridian turquoise; Mansion Qualities: (+) Facilitates birthing in all forms, curative magic for feminine health problems and treating menstrual disorders. (-) Deploys the "Scorpion Sting" for besieging and driving forth enemies and bringing destruction upon their heads, and strongly binding inimical forces. Can also protect and preserve one from venomous or dangerous creatures or energies. Talismanic Qualities: Healing powers, reveals hidden motives and unrevealed passions, hidden lovers, brings retribution.

Mars of Water: Mansion: *Al Batn Al Hut* (#28 The Belly of the Fish) Pisces 17 degrees, 9 minutes; Angelic Ruler: **Amnixiel** Color: Ultraviolet purple; Mansion Qualities: (+) If cast into the sea, causes a good catch for fishermen. Effective for attracting a "shoal" of opportunities and a good "catch" in material affairs. Also is good for love charms, brings conjugal bliss, generates romantic sentiments. Also reputed as a powerful protective amulet for practicing magicians—bestows invulnerability and safety to travelers in perilous locations, binds inimical forces. (-) Causes weaknesses, drives away opportunities, brings disharmony; produces violent storms. Talismanic Qualities: Courage, thoroughness, resourceful, uncompromising, death defying.

Mercury of Water: Mansion: *Al Faragh Al Thani* (#27 Lower Spout, Second Drawing) Pisces 4 degrees, 17 minutes; Angelic Ruler: **Tagniel;** Color: Mauve-violet; Mansion Qualities: (+) Increases prosperity and financial gains, promotes good health and healing, forges bonds of alliance and cheerful friendship. Also assists operations of foreknowledge and prophecy. (-) Inflicts mischief on enemies, imprisons energies, and if image holds a broken vessel, then said to destroy fountains when buried near them. Talismanic Qualities: Visionary, powerful intuitions, deeply spiritual; a dreamer, at times extremely self-absorbed and inarticulate.

Jupiter of Water: Mansion: *Al Nathrah* (#8 The Gap or Crib, Misty, Cloudy) Cancer 0 degrees; Angelic Ruler: **Amnediel;** Color: Amber yellow; Mansion Qualities: (+) Increases protective forces, grants victory in contests, effective in war magic, and can drive away any kind of infestation and restrain negative forces. (-) Promotes defeat in war and contests, disrupts and destroys target's home base. Talismanic Qualities: Inheritances, legacies, love of home, patriotism, upholding traditions.

Saturn of Water: Mansion: *Al Tarf* (#9 Glance of the Lion's Eye) Cancer 12 degrees, 51 minutes; Angelic Ruler: **Barbiel;** Color: Golden amber; Mansion Qualities: (+) Protects against the schemes of rivals and claims made against one. (-) Causes infirmities, failure, weakness, and discord upon an enemy. Talismanic Qualities: Perfectionism, responsibility, persistence, efficiency.

Venus of Water: Mansion: *Al Qalib* (#18 The Heart of the Scorpion) Scorpio 8 degrees, 34 minutes; Angelic Ruler: **Egibiel;** Color: Green turquoise; Mansion Qualities: (+) Aids geomantic construction and house protection magic. Healing magic for stomach disorders and fevers. (-) Used to inflict quarrels and discord, to foment treachery and conspiracy against enemies. Talismanic Qualities: Passion expressed, pleasure motives, lustful, intense emotions released, occult sensitivities.

Air (Mansions of Libra, Aquarius, and Gemini)

Sun of Air: Mansion: *Al Farch Al Mukdim* (#26 Fore-spout, First Drawing) Aquarius 21 degrees, 43 minutes; Angelic Ruler: **Tagriel;** Color: Mauve-violet; Mansion Qualities: (+) Promote friendly relations and attract a life partner: it is a harbinger of good fortune, for it promotes love, benevolence, and favor. Also promotes safety for travelers, geomantic house magic, and containing and imprisoning negative forces. (-) Causes one's enemies to be deserted by their allies and all fortune to disappear, to be replaced by great misfortune. Talismanic Qualities: Humanitarianism, social conscience, friendship, self-determination, foreknowledge.

Moon of Air: Mansion: *Al Sad Al Ahbiya* (#25 The Butterfly–Lucky Star of Hidden Things) Aquarius 8 degrees, 34 minutes; Angelic Ruler: **Aziel;** Color: Violet; Mansion Qualities: (+) Improves and strengthens buildings and is potent for house protection. Promotes geomantic fertility and preserves trees and causes good harvests, especially if hung in a fruit tree. (-) Causes impotence when used with ligature spells, weakens buildings, and allows for unobserved access and burglary. Talismanic Qualities: Sympathy, intuitive insight, promotes equality, good fortune, and freedom from bondage.

Mars of Air: Mansion: *Al Hanah* (#6 Brand or Mark, Little Star of Great Light) Gemini 4 degrees, 17 minutes; Angelic Ruler: **Dirachiel;** Color: Burnt orange; Mansion Qualities: (+) Establishes bonds of affection, and is effective for love spells, since it causes love to occur between a man and woman. (-) Breaks down resistance to sieges, binds and imprisons the will of one's enemies, allowing vengeance to be wreaked upon them and destroying their resources. Talismanic Qualities: Passionate communication, oratorical skills, seeking reformation, social activism, libertinism, activating anti-authority sentiment, revolutions.

Mercury of Air: Mansion: *Al Jubana* (#16 The Horns of the Scorpion) Libra 12 degrees, 51 minutes; Angelic Ruler: **Azaruel;** Color: Blue-green verdigris Mansion Qualities: (+) Brings about strong financial success and wealth and can release and liberate bound energies. Can also assist in operations of sciomancy and necromancy. (-) Inflicts hindrances, disrupted travel, problematic relations, and failed expectations to enemies. Talismanic Qualities: Achieves openness in others, truthfulness, unbiased perceptions, mental objectivity, intellectual uniqueness.

Jupiter of Air: Mansion: *Al Dhira* (#7 The Fore Arm of Gemini) Gemini 17 degrees, 9 minutes; Angelic Ruler: **Scheliel;** Color: Bright orange; Mansion Qualities: (+) Promotes friendship; is potent for winning favor and help from others; generates wealth, gain, and a good harvest; attracts benign prosperity. (-) Assists in ridding oneself of annoying or distracting influences and destroying tyrannous power-structures. Talismanic Qualities: Promotes socially inspired ideals, democracy, social justice, tolerance, and universal solidarity.

Saturn of Air: Mansion: *Iklil Al Jabhah* (#17 The Crown of the Scorpion) Libra 25 degrees, 43 minutes; Angelic Ruler: **Adriel;** Color: Sea-green blue; Mansion Qualities: Works against thievery and robbers. (+) Improves and makes better a bad situation or ill fortune; promotes friendship; good for love spells, seduction magic, and conjugal relations. Restores vision to the deceived, drives away parasites and emotional vampires. (-) Promotes losses by thievery or emotional vampirism, causes delusions and seeds distrust, and breaks up amorous relations. Talismanic Qualities: Mental organization, clarity, concentration, science, objective truth.

Venus of Air: Mansion: *Al Ghafr* (#15 The Covering) Libra 0 degrees; Angelic Ruler: **Ataliel;** Color: Emerald green; Mansion Qualities: (+) Attracts and generates tolerance, goodwill, friendship, harmony, and peaceful relations. Aids search for lost treasures, whether material or spiritual. (-) Inflicts discord, hindrance, and ruptures alliances amongst one's enemies. Talismanic Qualities: Friendship, unselfish principles, diplomacy, care for others, intellectual and aesthetic appreciation of beauty.

Earth (Mansions of Capricorn, Taurus, and Virgo)

Sun of Earth: Mansion: *Al Haqah* (#5 The White Spot) Taurus 21 degrees, 26 minutes; Angelic Ruler: **Gabriel;** Color: Tawny ocher; Mansion Qualities: (+) Instrumental in the instruction of scholars and intellectual pursuits. Potently used with lamp oracles and divinations, aids all memory, mental powers, and intellectual endeavors. Promotes good health, wellbeing, pleasure, and good will, also powerfully defends the bearer from harm, and helps to establish a power base. (-) Causes a cloud of unknowing and ignorance, obscures any divination, and promotes fears and insecurity. Talismanic Qualities: Purposeful determination, mastery over matter, love of luxury, green thumb.

Moon of Earth: Mansion: *Al Simak* (#14 Spike of Virgo, the Unarmed) Virgo 17 degrees, 9 minutes, Angelic Ruler: **Ergediel;** Color: Verdant green; Mansion Qualities: (+) Causes the love of married folk (good for conjugal relations). Promotes healing and medicinal power, and saves and protects when one is at sea, for it preserves amidst perilous conditions. Improves personal fortune and attracts the "Luck of Kings." Also aids bowl divination and scrying operations. (-) Incensed with the hair of a black dog and a black cat, causes a dispersal of inappropriate sexual desire or to cause a separation. Talismanic Qualities: Desire for domestic security, creativity, fertility, health, establishment of wealth.

Mars of Earth: Mansion: *Al Dabaran* (#4 Eye of Taurus, the Follower) Taurus 8 degrees, 34 minutes; Angelic Ruler: **Azariel;** Color: Rust red; Mansion Qualities: (+) Attracts honor and wealth to the magus, promoting irresistible endurance. Magically causes intimidation, fear, sub-

104

☉

mission, and uncertainty in others, and can be used to undermine and destabilize. (-) Can wreck and destroy buildings, mines, and wells. Used for vengeance to sow discord, enmity, and rupture upon one's enemies. Talismanic Qualities: Monetary ambitions, achieving material results, perseverance, craftsmanship.

Mercury of Earth: Mansion: *Al Sad Al Dhabih* (#22 Lucky One of the Slaughterers) Capricorn 0 degrees; Angelic Ruler: **Geliel;** Color: Cobalt blue; Mansion Qualities: (+) Assists one to escape and grants success in liberation from any kind of restrictive or limiting conditions. Enhances personal health, heals sickness, and empowers medical treatments. Can also help to forge good business relationships. (-) Causes one to be incarcerated or intensely restricted; also causes illness, poor health, and foils medical treatments. Talismanic Qualities: Practical and material application of intellectual pursuits, building, engineering, resourcefulness, ability to resolve limitations or restrictions.

Jupiter of Earth: Mansion: *Al Sad Al Su'ud* (#24 The Star of Fortune) Capricorn 21 degrees, 51 minutes; Angelic Ruler: **Abrinael;** Color: Violet-blue; Mansion Qualities: (+) Promotes fertility and abundance, wealth, and good material fortune. Can also aid in the realization of a wish or long sought-after thing, and grant victory in all endeavors. (-) Causes diminishment, impotence, defeat in all endeavors, and loss of property. Talismanic Qualities: Wise usage of resources, cautious generosity, investment, banking, financial partnerships.

Saturn of Earth: Mansion: *Al Sad Al Bulah* (#23 Good Fortune of the Swallower) Capricorn 12 degrees, 51 minutes; Angelic Ruler: **Requiel;** Color: Midnight blue; Mansion Qualities: (+) Aids in spells deigned to attract friendship, fellowship, and alliance. Promotes healing and cure of illnesses; liberates constricted forces from oppressive restriction. (-) Causes dread, fear, wasting, and destruction when buried near the intended victim. Talismanic Qualities: Patience, steadfastness, stability, reliability, centeredness.

Venus of Earth: Mansion: *Al Awwa* (#13 Wings of Virgo, the Barker) Virgo 4 degrees, 7 minutes; Angelic Ruler: **Jazariel;** Color: Leaf green; Mansion

Qualities: (+) Strengthens marital harmony, dissolves ligature spells, and destroys charms against copulation. Promotes a diversity of benign aims including obtaining one's desire, aiding material profits and interests; enhances all material pursuits and their harvest; promotes geomantic fertility. Promotes personal protection, freeing up of constricted energies, increase love in a relationship, banish sexual problems, and neutralize the malign spells causing such. (-) Causes impotence, protects chastity and virginity, and binds and imprisons one's enemies. Talismanic Qualities: Emotional stability, physical sensuality, personal beauty, artistic visual and physical expression.

An alternate list by mansion in the signs starting with Aries appears below. This list is important because sometimes one would need to know the progression of talismanic elementals by the zodiacal signs of the lunar mansions.

Al Sharatain (#1 Horns of Aries): 0° Aries–Mars of Fire

Al Butain (#2 The Belly of Aries): Aries 12° 51'–Jupiter of Fire

Al Thurayya (#3 The Many Little Ones - Pleiades): Aries 25° 43'–Venus of Fire

Al Dabaran (#4 Eye of Taurus, the Follower): Taurus 8° 34'– Mars of Earth

Al Haqah (#5 The White Spot): Taurus 21° 26'– Sun of Earth

Al Hanah (#6 Brand or Mark, Little Star of Great Light): Gemini 4° 17'– Mars of Air

Al Dhira (#7 The Force Arm of Gemini): Gemini 17° 9'–Jupiter of Air

Al Nathrah (#8 The Gap or Crib, Misty, Cloudy): Cancer 0°–Jupiter of Water

Al Tarf (#9 Glance of the Lion's Eye): Cancer 12° 51'–Saturn of Water

Al Jabhah (#10 The Lion's Forehead–the Brow of Leo): Cancer 25° 43'– Sun of Water

Al Zubrah (#11 The Lion's Mane): Leo 8° 34'–Sun of Fire

Al Sarfah (#12 The Lion's Tail): Leo 21° 26'–Saturn of Fire

Al Awwa (#13 Wings of Virgo, the Barker): Virgo 4° 17'–Venus of Earth

Al Simak (#14 Spike of Virgo, the Unarmed): Virgo 17° 9'–Moon of Earth

Al Ghafr (#15 The Covering): Libra 0°–Venus of Air

Al Jubana (#16 The Horns of the Scorpion): Libra 12° 51'–Mercury of Air

Iklil Al Jabhah (#17 The Crown of the Scorpion): Libra 25° 43'–Saturn of Air

Al Qalib (#18 The Heart of the Scorpion): Scorpio 8° 34'–Venus of Water

Al Shaula (#19 The Tail of the Scorpion, the Sting): Scorpio 21° 6'–Moon of Water

Al Nava'am (#20 The Beam, The Ostriches): Sagittarius 4° 17'–Moon of Fire

Al Baldah (#21 The City or District): Sagittarius 17° 9'–Mercury of Fire

Al Sad Al Dhabih (#22 Lucky One of the Slaughterers): Capricorn 0°–Mercury of Earth

Al Sad Al Bulah (#23 Good Fortune of the Swallower): Capricorn 12° 51'–Saturn of Earth

Al Sad Al Su'ud (#24 The Star of Fortune): Capricorn 25° 51'–Jupiter of Earth

Al Sad Al Ahbiya (#25 The Butterfly–Lucky Star of Hidden Things): Aquarius 8° 34'–Moon of Air

Al Farch Al Mukdim (#26 Fore-spout, First Drawing): Aquarius 21° 43'–Sun of Air

Al Faragh Al Thani (#27 Lower Spout, Second Drawing): Pisces 4° 17'–Mercury of Water

Al Batn Al Hut (#28 The Belly of the Fish): Pisces 17° 9'–Mars of Water

Chapter Seven

ASTROLOGICAL DECANS: TALISMANIC DOMAINS

"Only through the living Nefa
Can intellect reach the heart,
And beyond become the haven
For the upstream struggle."

—EGYPTIAN TEXT: REBEL IN THE SOUL
–BIKA REED (TRANSLATION)

The astrological decans, also called faces, were developed by the ancient Egyptians as a method of marking their calendar and determining the time at night. Unlike the Mesopotamians, the Egyptians did not develop an extensive astrological system determined by constellations as is understood today. Instead, they developed a grouping of stars into thirty-six equal divisions of the sky referred to as *bktw*, or "those that live." Their system was based on the helical rising of those star groups during the course of the night.[25] The belt of the

---

25 Theresa Ainsworth, "A Timeline of the Decans: From Egyptian Astronomical Timekeeping to Greco Roman Melothesia," 2, online PDF at Queens University, Canda, accessed January 1, 2022: https://qspace.library.queensu.ca/bitstream/handle/1974/24821/Ainsworth _Theresa_201809_MA.pdf?sequence=1&isAllowed=y.

decans was located slightly south of the ecliptic where they still reside today, more or less.

The ancient Egyptians used a kind of erected north-to-south diagonal plumb line attached to a surveying staff, called the Merkhet, to sight the rising of the decans in the east.[26] The last decan of the night, just before sunrise, was considered the decan of the day, and this decan would continue to be seen just before dawn for approximately ten days until another decan in the sequence would take its place. Thus, the decan hour and the decan day enabled the Egyptians to determine the time at night and determine the calendric day.

The Egyptian New Year began with the helical rising of the star Sirius, which heralded the start of the annual inundation of the Nile in July, and this was considered the first of the thirty-six decans.[27] The Egyptian godhead associated with the first decan would have the personification of the star Sirius, known variously as Sopdet or Sothis. Then, each day following that event, the Egyptians would note the passage of decans at the dawning of each day, assisting them in determining the calendric day based on the decan.[28]

Later, when the decans were assimilated into the Hellenized zodiac, the first decan of the calendar year would have been the first decan in the sign Cancer. Over time, the rising of Sirius occurred later in the summer due to precession of the equinoxes and the slow change in the stars' positions. At present, Sirius rises in Egypt in early August, nearly six weeks after the summer solstice when it originally was documented to occur in the Egyptian calendar in the Old Kingdom period.

The Egyptian calendar consisted of nine days of work with a day of rest, totaling a ten-day week. The decans represented a calendric cycle of 360 days with five epagomenal days added to it to make 365. The five days were a separate thirty-seventh half-decan called *sabwa*, symbolizing the five days just

---

26 Staff writers, "Merkhet–Ancient Egyptian Time Keeping Instrument" at *Quantum Gaze*, accessed January 1, 2022: http://www.quantumgaze.com/ancient-technology/merkhet-for-time-keeping-and-astronomical-observations/.

27 Ainsworth, "Timeline of the Decans," 2–3.

28 Gary D. Thompson, "Episodic Survey of the History of the Constellations - 18: The decan stars" at Westnet Australia, accessed January 1, 2021: http://members.westnet.com.au/gary-david-thompson/page11–18.html.

before the rising of Sirius.[29] Keeping in mind that the apparent motion of the Sun is slightly less than 1 degree per day, the decan week would also represent approximately ten degrees of movement for the Sun. Because it did not make allowances for the leap year, the decan calendar would eventually fall out of synch with the seasons. At various times it was necessary to add a short month to the calendar to get it back in synch with the three seasons, but this was done only a few times according to Egyptian records.

Use of the decans in ancient Egypt can be found in the Coffin Texts, in which they were displayed as star tables showing the decan calendar. It is likely that these tables were developed prior to the Middle Kingdom, perhaps as early as predynastic times. The decans were stellar deities associated with the natural cycle of time, both at night and through the days as a calendar, representing the predisposition of order and continuity (Ma'at), which were very important concepts to their religious beliefs. Seasonal calendric festivals and liturgical events that occurred during night were determined by the decan days and hours. However, the actual list of decan stars and how they related to their positions in the sky has been mostly lost, with the exception of a few (Sirius, Orion, Ox-leg).[30]

The idea of the decans found its way into the Babylonian zodiac during the early period of the Ptolemaic dynasty, where there was a fusion between Hellenistic astrology and astronomy as taken from Mesopotamia and the decan system of the Egyptians. By the time of Claudius Ptolemy, the decans had been defined as dividing the twelve signs of the zodiac into ten-degree parts or segments. The previous association with the fixed stars, now largely lost, retained the association with the lesser gods of Egypt and was used as a system of divination and magic.

There were two systems of decans in use: the Triplicity and the Chaldean, but they only diverged based upon the associated decan planetary ruler.[31] The

---

29 Sarah Symons, "A Star's Year: The Annual Cycle in the Ancient Egyptian Sky" 17, PDF accessed January 1, 2022: https://citeseerx.ist.psu.edu/viewdoc/download?doi=10.1.1.370.9383&rep=rep1&type=pdf.

30 Ainsworth, "Timeline of the Decans," 6.

31 This should not be confused with the triplicity associated with the four elements of the zodiacal signs.

astrological decans were used in a form of astrology called melotheisa, a system of determining sickness or potential illness through divination, including seeking good health and protection against harm from the talismans of the spirits or demigods associated with the decans.[32] Decans were associated with the parts of the body, the possible afflictions that might occur to that body part, and the magic associated with acquiring a healing and protecting influence to overcome the illness. These techniques of medical astrology and magic were very active among practitioners of traditional astrology but were ignored by modern astrologers until very recently.

The simplest way to determine the significance and meaning of a decan using the Triplicity method, is to represent them as the cardinal, fixed, and mutable energies of the base element of an element sign. For instance, when examining the sign Aries, which is cardinal fire, the three decans for Aries would have the corresponding associations of Aries, Leo, and Sagittarius. The first ten degrees of Aries would be qualified by Aries, making it more like the pure expression of Aries and ruled by Mars. The second decan, from 11 to 20 degrees, would be qualified by Leo and ruled by the Sun, representing a more dignified, sunny, and sustainable (fixed) energy of Aries. The third decan of Aries, from 21 to 30 degrees, would be qualified by Sagittarius and ruled by Jupiter to represent a milder, more flexible and dissolute (mutable) energy of Aries. Each planet is the traditional planetary ruler of the element sign that is used to divide the zodiacal sign into three segments.

The Chaldean method is based on a planetary order for the specific planetary rulers based on the geocentric speeds of the seven traditional planets.[33] From the slowest to fastest planet, the order was Saturn, Jupiter, Mars, Sun, Venus, Mercury, and the Moon. Since the first decan of Aries 0–10 degree was ascribed to Mars, the rest of the planets were determined in sequence from there, so the second decan of Aries was ascribed to the Sun, and the third to Venus. This sequence of planets was used from the first decan to the last.

---

32 Ainsworth, "Timeline of the Decans," 32.

33 "Decans" at *Astro* website, accessed January 1, 2022: https://www.astro.com/cgi/h.cgi?f=gch&h=gch_decans&lang=e.

The meanings for each decan would change slightly due to the planetary ruler when compared to the traditional method, but they were still seen as representing the cardinal, fixed, and mutable aspects of a given sign. In other words, only the order of the planetary rulers was changed.

The planetary rulers I am using to qualify the decans are from the Chaldean attributions, which are also used to qualify the tarot's numbered lesser arcana cards. Thus, I will use these attributions in examining the qualities of the decans.

Tarot Cards, Decan Domains, and Hierarchy of Spirits

To enrich the qualification for each of the thirty-six decans, I have employed the correspondences of the thirty-six pip cards in the lesser arcana of the tarot. This attribution was determined by the Golden Dawn, whose members employed the tarot in both their magical and Qabalistic methods and practices. In addition to greatly assisting me in visualizing the various qualities of the decans, the tarot cards have also helped in developing the idea of the talismanic domain.

The Chaldean attributions are particularly obvious when examining the illustrations of the Waite-Smith tarot deck. Each pip card has a vignette depicting some allegory of a dynamic life situation. I have found these vignettes to be useful in perceiving the tarot cards as part of an allegorical realm. The decan association with these colorful cards brings the astrological associations of the decan with the ruling planet and its qualities with the pip cards' illustrations and their allegorical associations into a singular expression. It would seem that you could imagine yourself walking through the borders of any of these cards and be in a special place where an allegorical theatrical act is played out. Indeed, since they are like a house containing a distinct spiritual hierarchy and astrological attributes defining a kind of conscious space, it would seem that referring to them as decan domains is appropriate as a short-hand term for the total collective of correspondences.

In my book, *Elemental Powers for Witches*, I used the attributes of the tarot to describe and qualify what I have named the 40 Qualified Powers.[34] I started by determining the archetypal meaning of the ten mystical numbers of these

---

34 Frater Barrabbas, chapter 8 of *Elemental Powers for Witches* (Woodbury, MN: Llewellyn Publications, 2022).

tarot cards, used them to qualify the four basic elements, and produce the correspondences and meaning for the 40 Qualified Powers. If we remove the four aces from this construction, we have the thirty-six decans defined and qualified with the remainder of tarot's thirty-six pip cards.

The 40 Qualified Powers are therefore somewhat similar to the thirty-six decans, minus the four element aces. The true difference between a decan and a Qualified Power is the emphasis on the planetary ruler for the former, since the decan would therefore meet the expectation for the talismanic equation. With the Qualified Power, we listed but then ignored the planetary attribution, since the combination of element and mystical number as an attribute of deity fully represented its elemental quality. In the decan domain, we emphasize the ruling planet and downplay the mystical number and its hierarchy since we are omitting the number 1 (the aces) from its structure.

Therefore, the decan domain will represent the combination of the base zodiacal sign, the qualities of the decan segment (ascendant, succedent, cadent), and the associated planetary ruler. Therefore, we have a matrix of planet, decan segment, and zodiacal sign to fully qualify the decan domain. Keep in mind that the decan segments are 0 to 10 degrees for ascendant, 10 to 20 degrees for succedent, and 20 to 30 degrees for cadent.

Additionally, there is a spiritual hierarchy associated with the decan domain. Each domain has the following spiritual correspondences that fully represent the spiritual correspondences for the decans. The division of the thirty-six decans is by the quadruplicity of the houses, represented by the ascendant (angular), succedent, and cadent houses, which is also true for the ha-shem angels and the Goetic demons by day and night. We won't list the ha-shem angels or the Goetic demons here because their provenance is better suited to magical conjuration rather than talismanic magic.

- Twelve archangels and angels of the zodiac signs
- Seven archangels (Olympians) of the seven planets
- Twelve angel lords of the triplicity by day
- Twelve angel lords of the triplicity by night

- Thirty-six angelic rulers of the decans (ascendant, cadent, succedent)— decan ruler
- Thirty-six ha-shem angels of the decans by day (ascendant, cadent, succedent)
- Thirty-six ha-shem angels of the decans by night (ascendant, cadent, succedent)
- Thirty-six Goetic demons of the decans by day (ascendant, cadent, succedent)
- Thirty-six Goetic demons of the decans by night (ascendant, cadent, succedent)

Each decan domain would house the archangel and angel of the zodiacal sign, the planetary archangel (Olympian) ruler, angel lord of the day and night, angelic ruler of the decan, ha-shem angel of day and night, and Goetic demon by day and night. The archangels and angels of the sign, planet, and angel lords by day and night of the sign would represent the authorities of the decan, but it is the *angelic ruler of the decan* that is truly the intelligence and power that would be called or summoned to open the decan domain. You can summon the angelic ruler or alternatively summon the Egyptian demigod of the decan to project the talismanic intelligence and power associated with the decan domain. I have used both approaches with great success.

The first part of the spiritual hierarchy listed above is determined by the angelic spirits, starting with the archangel of the zodiacal sign. Here is a table showing how that hierarchy looks and the relationship between the angelic spirits and the angelic ruler of the decans.[35]

---

35 Crowley, *777*, 26–30; Skinner, *Complete Magician's Tables*, 121–126.

Table of the Angelic Hierarchy of the Zodiacal Signs and Decans

Sign	Arch-angel	Angel	Lords Triplic-ity by Day	Lords Triplic-ity by Night	Decan Angels–Ascen-dant	Decan Angels–Succe-dent	Decan Angels–Cadent
Aries	Malchi-dael	Sharhiel	Sateraton	Sapatavi	Zezar	Behhemi	Setneder
Taurus	Asmodel	Araziel	Raydel	Totath	Kedamadi	Manach-erai	Yaksog-nox
Gemini	Ambriel	Sarayel	Sarash	Ogarmon	Sagaresh	Sahdani	Bithon
Cancer	Muriel	Pakiel	Raadar	Akel	Methraush	Rahdax	Alinkayer
Leo	Verchiel	Shavatiel	Sanahem	Zalbarhith	Lusnahar	Zacha'ai	Sahiber
Virgo	Hamaliel	Shelathiel	Lastara	Saisia	Ananaurah	Raidyah	Meshep-har
Libra	Zuriel	Chede-qiel	Thergebon	Achro-draon	Taresni	Saharnax	Shachdar
Scorpio	Barchiel	Saitziel	Bethchon	Sahaqnab	Kamox	Nindohar	Vathro-diel
Sagittar-ius	Advachiel	Saritiel	Ahoz	Lebarmim	Mesheret	Vaharin	Abuha
Capri-corn	Hanael	Sameqiel	Sandali	Aloyar	Masenin	Yasiseyah	Yasa-ndibero-diel
Aquar-ius	Cambriel	Tzak-miqiel	Athor	Polayon	Saspham	Abdaron	Garodiel
Pisces	Amnixiel	Vekabiel	Ramara	Nath-dorinel	Bahalmi	Auron	Sateriph

The ruling planets for the decans, listed in the table that follows, are quite important. The planetary correspondences are used to qualify the decans and, to a lesser degree, the signs of the zodiac and the quality of the triplicity. The Chaldean order of planets is used here.

Table of the Planetary
Rulers for the Decans

Sign	Decan Planetary Rulers Ascendant 0°–10°	Decan Planetary Rulers Succedent 10°–20°	Decan Planetary Rulers Cadent 20°–30°
Aries	Mars	Sun	Venus
Taurus	Mercury	Moon	Saturn
Gemini	Jupiter	Mars	Sun
Cancer	Venus	Mercury	Moon
Leo	Saturn	Jupiter	Mars
Virgo	Sun	Venus	Mercury
Libra	Moon	Saturn	Jupiter
Scorpio	Mars	Sun	Venus
Sagittarius	Mercury	Moon	Saturn
Capricorn	Jupiter	Mars	Sun
Aquarius	Venus	Mercury	Moon
Pisces	Saturn	Jupiter	Mars

If you are using the angelic hierarchy, you can use the archangel associated with the planet in order to summon the planetary part of the talismanic equation. However, if you wish to use the Egyptian demigods associated with the decans, the following table would be useful to you. It lists the god names as they would have been known in Ptolemaic times.[36]

---

36 E. A. Wallis Budge, *The Gods of the Egyptians Volume 2* (New York: Dover Publications, 1969), 304–308.

⊙

Table of the Egyptian Ptolemaic Decan Demigod Names

Sign	Decan Egyptian Demigods Ascendant 0°–10°	Decan Egyptian Demigods Succedent 10°–20°	Decan Egyptian Demigods Cadent 20°–30°
Aries	Tepa-Kenmut	Kenmut	Kher-Khept-Kenmut
Taurus	Ha-Tchat	Pehui-Tchat	Themat-Hert
Gemini	Themat-Khert	Ustha	Bekatha
Cancer	Tepa-Khentet	Khentet-Hert	Khentet-Khurt
Leo	Temes-Khemtet	Sapt-Khennu	Her-Ab-Uaa
Virgo	Shesmu	Kenmu	Semtet
Libra	Tepa-Sent	Sert	Sasa-Sert
Scorpio	Kher-Khept-Sert	Khukhu	Baba
Sagittarius	Khent-Heru	Her-Ab-Kentu	Khent-Kheru
Capricorn	Qet	Sasaqet	Art
Aquarius	Khau	Ramen-Heru-An-Sah	Metscher-Sah
Pisces	Ramen-Kher-Sa	A-Sah	Sah

You can imagine the Egyptian decan demigods as stellar deities or sky pharaohs standing in their solar boats, holding the staff of office and wearing crowns with a shining star placed upon it. A few are queens or goddesses; one is a young princeling; another, a sacred baboon. More details are available in a number of sources; I leave that pleasant task to you should you choose to embellish and further develop what is shown here.

We also need to list the planetary correspondences for the seven traditional planets, showing the Archangels, Angels, and the Olympian spirits, since these will need to be the primary focus for opening the decan domain. (These were taken from chapter 5.)

Table of Archangels, Angels, and Olympians

Planet	Archangels	Intelligences	Spiritual Powers	Olympian Spirits
Sun	Raphael	Graphiel	Serath	Och
Moon	Gabriel	Malkah b'Tarsh-ishim	Chasmodai	Phul
Mercury	Michael	Tiriel	Taphthar-tharath	Ophiel
Venus	Haniel	Hagiel	Kedemel	Hagith
Mars	Kamiel	Nakhiel	Bartzabel	Phalegh
Jupiter	Tzadkiel	Yophiel	Hismael	Bethor
Saturn	Tzaphkiel	Agiel	Zazel	Aratron

Finally, I needed to add the specific lesser arcana cards, numbered 2 through 10, of the four suits as they apply to the thirty-six decans. As I have said, the tarot works quite well as representations of the decans' qualities and images. What clued me in about this correspondence was in the writings of Aleister Crowley in his *Book of Thoth*—in the appendices, he shows how the tarot matches up with the planetary ruler of the decan. Prior to realizing this correspondence, I had seen the cards and the decans as completely separate things, not knowing that the foundational meaning of the pip cards in the lesser arcana (minus the four aces) very much aligned with the decans! I have found that these images work in any traditional tarot deck, but the table below is taken from Crowley's attributions. My experience has been that tarot card titles designed by Crowley mostly fit with what I would expect for the decans' meanings.[37]

---

37 Crowley, *The Book of Thoth* (York Beach, ME: Weiser Books, 1944), 282–283.

⊙

Table of Lesser Arcana
Pip Cards and Decans—Thoth Tarot

Sign	Lesser Arcana Ascendant 0°–10°	Lesser Arcana Succedent 10°–20°	Tarot Lesser Arcana–Cadent 20°–30°
Aries	2 of Wands: Dominion–Mars	3 of Wands: Virtue–Sun	4 of Wands: Completion–Venus
Taurus	5 of Disks: Worry–Mercury	6 of Disks: Success–Moon	7 of Disks: Failure–Saturn
Gemini	8 of Swords: Interference–Jupiter	9 of Swords: Cruelty–Mars	10 of Swords: Ruin–Sun
Cancer	2 of Cups: Love–Venus	3 of Cups: Abundance–Mercury	4 of Cups: Luxury–Moon
Leo	5 of Wands: Strife–Saturn	6 of Wands: Victory–Jupiter	7 of Wands: Valor–Mars
Virgo	8 of Disks: Prudence–Sun	9 of Disks: Gain–Venus	10 of Disks: Wealth–Mercury
Libra	2 of Swords: Peace–Moon	3 of Swords: Sorrow–Saturn	4 of Swords: Truce–Jupiter
Scorpio	5 of Cups: Disappointment–Mars	6 of Cups: Pleasure–Sun	7 of Cups: Debauch–Venus
Sagittarius	8 of Wands: Swiftness–Mercury	9 of Wands: Strength–Moon	10 of Wands: Oppression–Saturn
Capricorn	2 of Disks: Change–Jupiter	3 of Disks: Work–Mars	4 of Disks: Power–Sun
Aquarius	5 of Swords: Defeat–Venus	6 of Swords: Science–Mercury	7 of Swords: Futility–Moon
Pisces	8 of Cups: Indolence–Saturn	9 of Cups: Happiness–Jupiter	10 of Cups: Satiety–Mars

Armed with the above correspondences and knowing what we know about the decans, we can put together a list of magical qualities associated with each of the thirty-six decans. These qualities would complement and work with the 40 Qualified Powers, since the Power would represent the decan's energy base.

Decan Components for Summoning the Decan Domain

The following list contains the various components for opening the decan domain and summoning the principle ruling spirit, whether that be the decan's angelic ruler or its Egyptian demigod. Among those components are the relevant degrees of the zodiacal sign, quadruplicity of the zodiacal element, the tarot pip card, the ruling planet, the quality of house quadruplicity, and a description of the talismanic qualities of the decan.

While there are at least two sources for the magical images of decans as depicted in the *Picatrix* and Agrippa's *Occult Philosophy*, I have decided to use the vignettes of the tarot pip cards as depicted in the Waite-Smith imagery instead. I have consulted and embellished the magical uses of the decans using this deck's vignettes to refine the definitions of the thirty-six decans. The combination of these attributes (my own) determines the magical meaning and use of the decans.

Thirty-Six Decan Domains and Attributes

Here is the list of the spirits and the components of the decan domain.

Zezar/Tepa-Kenmut: 0°–10° of Aries–Cardinal Fire–2 of Wands–Mars–Ascendant

Image: A tall man looks from a battlemented roof over the sea and mountainous shore. He holds a globe in his right hand. In his left hand he holds a staff that rests on the battlement; another staff appears standing behind him fixed to a ring. Magical meaning: The ability to accomplish all objectives and achieve lasting renown.

Behhemi/Kenmut: 10°–20° of Aries–Cardinal Fire–3 of Wands–Sun–Succedent

Image: A serene, regal man richly adorned, with his back turned, is looking from a cliff's edge at ships passing on the sea. He holds two staves on his right; the third is planted on his left. Magical meaning: Ability to envision the future and to predetermine crises before they occur.

Setneder/Kher-Khept-Kenmut: 20°–30° of Aries–Cardinal Fire–4 of Wands–Venus–Cadent

Image: From the four great staves planted in the foreground is a great garland suspended. Two women hold up flowery bouquets, and people can be seen heading to a manor house in the background. Magical meaning: Ability to determine truth from falsehood, virtue from deception, and to retain one's integrity.

Kedamadi/Ha-Tchat: 0°–10° of Taurus–Fixed Earth–5 of Pentacles–Mercury–Ascendant

Image: Two beggars, one a young man on crutches and the other a woman, pass by a lighted casement window with five pentacles. Magical meaning: Material compassion, seemingly miraculous aid, and the spirit of giving and equality. This magic helps the needy and the desperate to achieve some degree of material security. This is the Winter Solstice magic that gives help to everyone in need.

Manacherai/Pehui_Tchat: 10°–20° of Taurus–Fixed Earth–6 of Pentacles–Moon–Succedent

Image: A merchant weighs money on a pair of scales and distributes the coins to two paupers. There are six pentacles around his head. Magical meaning: Ability to ensure material equality and fairness in all financial endeavors. This magic is helpful for combating the inequality and entrenched power of the rich and connected.

Yaksagnox/Themat-Hert: 20°–30° of Taurus–Fixed Earth–7 of Pentacles–Saturn–Cadent

Image: A young man leaning on his staff looks upon seven pentacles attached to a grapevine. Magical meaning: Protecting one's material achievements from the avarice of others. This magic gives one the insight to avoid material failure and adverse diminishment.

Sagaresh/Themat-Khert: 0°–10° of Gemini–Mutable Air–8 of Swords–Jupiter–Ascendant

Image: A woman standing, bound and blindfolded, with eight swords nearby. There are five on her left and three on her right side. They all stand erect, planted in a swampy ground. Magical meaning: Overcoming victimhood through the power of mental clarity, unbinding and uncrossing oneself, and upsetting the forces arrayed against one. This magic is ideal for dealing with legal issues or with self-imposed cross purposes.

Shahdani/Ustha: 10°–20° of Gemini–Mutable Air–9 of Swords–Mars–Succedent

Image: A man sitting up in bed with his hands to his face, crying, while suspended horizontally above him are nine swords. Magical meaning: Ability to overcome seemingly hopeless obstacles. This magic empowers and manifests the imagination and dreams to force circumstances to bend and to be resolved through the counter effect of positive stories, affirmations, and propaganda. When oppressed by others, tell wonderful tales about yourself and your abilities.

Bithon/Bekatha: 20°–30° of Gemini–Mutable Air–10 of Swords–Sun–Cadent

Image: A man lying prostrate with his face to the ground is partially covered by a red cape. His body is pierced by a line of ten swords. Magical meaning: Ability to accept failure, to recover, and reestablish belief in oneself. This magic is a manifestation of the will that helps one to start over again after surviving a disaster.

Methraush/Tepa-Khentet: 0°–10° of Cancer–Cardinal Water–2 of Cups–Venus–Ascendant

Image: A young couple facing each other, heads wreathed in garlands, hold two cups together. A winged lion head mounted on a caduceus staff is above them. Magical meaning: Ability to cause or enhance love between individuals, particularly of the high-minded and idealistic variety.

Rahdax/Khentet-Hert: 10°–20° of Cancer–Cardinal Water–3 of Cups–Mercury–Succedent

Image: Three young women stand facing each other with their arms intertwined, holding three golden goblets in a form of a salute. Magical meaning: Wisdom of the heart—knowing the hearts of others and being able to effectively communicate to people's emotions.

Alinkayer/Khentet-Khert: 20°–30° of Cancer–Cardinal Water–4 of Cups–Moon–Cadent

Image: A young man is seated under a tree looking upon three golden goblets. An arm issuing from a cloud to the side appears to be offering him a fourth goblet. Magical meaning: The gift of charisma as a divinely inspired compassion to behold the hearts of others.

Lusnahar/Temes-en-Khentet: 0°–10° of Leo–Fixed Fire–5 of Wands–Saturn–Ascendant

Image: A group of youths are facing each other, brandishing staves at different angles, although one is carrying his stave on his shoulders. They seem to be engaged aggressively with each other. Magical meaning: The ability to maintain balance and poise amongst chaotic and antagonistic wills and directives. Insight into the motivations of others help to determine the proper action.

Zacha'ai/Sapt-Khennu: 10°–20° of Leo–Fixed Fire–6 of Wands–Jupiter–Succedent

Image: A warrior mounted on a horse wears a laurel wreath upon his head, with another laurel wreath mounted on the stave that he holds. Five other foot solders accompany him, each holding a stave. Magical image: The insight to understand one's place in the world amid various challenges and to meet and exceed those challenges.

Sahiber/Her-Ab-Uaa: 20°–30° of Leo–Fixed Fire–7 of Wands–Mars–Cadent

Image: A man holds a stave across his body in a defensive pose while standing on a narrow precipice. Six staves, wielded by antagonists, arise from below. Magical meaning: Self-protection and acquiring insight into the motivations of others together will help turn enemies away and achieve peace.

Ananaurah/Shesmu: 0°–10° of Virgo–Mutable Earth–8 of Pentacles–Sun–Ascendant

Image: An engraver is engraving a pentacle with hammer and chisel, sitting on a bench. Under the bench is a finished pentacle, and six pentacles are arrayed vertically on a wall in front of him. Magical meaning: Ability to steadfastly and consistently build one's material accomplishments. This magic protects one against minor losses and ensures a degree of luck and good fortune.

Raidyah/Kenmu: 10°–20° of Virgo–Mutable Earth–9 of Pentacles–Venus–Succedent

Image: A richly adorned woman wearing a glove with a falcon on her wrist is standing before a rich vineyard. Six pentacles are stacked before her and three behind her. Magical meaning: Achieving success and material increase though good fortune.

Mashephar/Semtet: 20°–30° of Virgo–Mutable Earth–10 of Pentacles–Mercury–Cadent

Image: A man and woman stand under an arch with a child. In the foreground is a seated bearded man greeting two hunting dogs. In the background is a large manor house with a tower. The pentacles are arrayed in the foreground in the pattern of the Tree of Life. Magical meaning: Manifestation of material fulfillment in all aspects of life. This magic requires that one has built up a material foundation that can be used to achieve overall fulfillment.

Taresni/Tepa-Sent: 0°–10° of Libra–Cardinal Air–2 of Swords–Moon–Ascendant

Image: A blindfolded figure is seated, holding two swords balanced on either shoulder. In the background is a calm sea and a crescent moon in the sky. Magical meaning: Ability to completely balance objectives and moderate crossed purposes. This magic produces mental balance and internal clarity.

Saharnax/Sert: 10°–20° of Libra–Cardinal Air–3 of Swords–Saturn–Succedent

Image: Three swords pierce a heart suspended in the air, with their points downward. In the background are dark clouds and a rainstorm. Magical meaning: Achieving perseverance, steadfastness, and mental integrity despite personal setbacks and emotional betrayal.

Shachdar/Sasa-Sert: 20°–30° of Libra–Cardinal Air–4 of Swords–Jupiter–Cadent

Image: A effigy of a knight lies upon a sarcophagus with hands in the gesture of prayer in a tomb chapel with a stained-glass window. One sword is carved upon the base of the sarcophagus, and the other three are mounted side by side on the wall. Magical meaning: Establishing a mental refuge and sense of security within to deal with the conflicts and issues without one. This magic is the fulcrum of one's will and integral sense of self. Empowering it will make one indomitable.

Kamox/Kher-Khept-Sert: 0°–10° of Scorpio–Fixed Water–5 of Cups–Mars–Ascendent

Image: A dark cloaked man stands in despair before three spilled goblets on the ground before him. Behind him, two goblets are still standing. In the background is a road to a castle. Magical meaning: The ability to transform emotional hardships and personal sacrifice into overall long-term emotional gain. Learning the emotional lessons of life.

Nindohar/Khukhu: 10°–20° of Scorpio–Fixed Water–6 of Cups–Sun–Succedent

Image: A boy offers a girl a goblet filled with flowers in a castle garden. There is another goblet with flowers on a pedestal behind him, and four goblets with flowers in the foreground. Magical meaning: Ability to break down emotional barriers and to enable friendship, love, and harmony to innocently emerge.

Vathrodiel/Baba: 20°–30° of Scorpio–Fixed Water–7 of Cups–Venus–Cadent

Image: A man beholds a misty vision of seven chalices, each offering a different temptation: the head of a woman, a serpent, a veiled figured, a castle, rich jewelry, a wreath of victory, and a dragon. Magical meaning: Ability to clearly see emotional based opportunities and risks and dealing with the various offerings that one will meet on the path of life.

Mesheret/Khent-Heru: 0°–10° of Sagittarius–Mutable Fire–8 of Wands–Mercury–Ascendent

Image: Eight staves arch across the sky, as if in flight. They are grouped together in three groups. The highest consists of four staves, the lower two groups consist of two each. In the background, a river winds through a countryside with a castle in the distance. Magical meaning: Ability to communicate eloquently and efficiently, both in speech and writing. Ability to achieve mutual understanding and rapport.

Vaharin/Her-Ab-Khentu: 10°–20° of Sagittarius–Mutable Fire–9 of Wands–Moon–Succedent

Image: A man is holding a stave diagonally against his body with both hands. He is warily looking behind him, where eight staves are arrayed as if against him. Magical meaning: Ability to achieve a complete reversal in fortune, to overcome insurmountable obstacles.

Abuha/Khent-Kheru: 20°–30° of Sagittarius–Mutable Fire–10 of Wands–Saturn–Cadent

Image: A man is walking toward a distant town with a bent back, struggling to move forward with the weight of ten staves in his arms. Magical meaning: The ability to lighten nearly impossible loads and to wear one's responsibility with dignity, despite the difficulty and the importance of every action. Additionally, getting others to help distribute that weighty responsibility.

Masenin/Qet: 0°–10° degrees of Capricorn–Cardinal Earth–2 of Pentacles–Jupiter–Ascendent

Image: A man is holding two pentacles in either hand, apparently trying to balance them, and a ribbon making a lemniscate appears to connect them. He appears to be dancing, while behind him ships sail on a sea of large, rolling waves. Magical meaning: Ability to manifest material change where required, ensuring a successful outcome.

Yasiseyah/Sasaqet: 10°–20° of Capricorn–Cardinal Earth–3 of Pentacles–Mars–Succedent

Image: A sculptor standing on a bench with a mallet in his right hand is engaged in a discussion with an abbot and a cloaked architect who holds a plan. Above them are three pentacles engraved in a keystone arch. Magical meaning: Manifesting the fortitude and ambition to work toward material achievement. Sometimes it is difficult to start a project, and this magic will jump start any project, and help to inspire others to engage with the work.

Yasandiberodiel/Art: 20°–30° of Capricorn–Cardinal Earth–4 of Pentacles–Sun–Cadent

Image: A crowned king is seated upon a throne, holding a pentacle in his arms. His feet rest each on another two pentacles, and a fifth is resting above his crown. In the background is shown the buildings of a great town. Magical meaning: Building a magical and material fortress to protect oneself and one's material belongings. This magic protects against thieves, con artists, and deceitful contracts of all kinds.

Saspham/Khau: 0°–10° of Aquarius–Fixed Air–5 of Swords–Venus–Ascendant

Image: A victorious fighter smirks at two defeated men standing apart with their backs to him, heads bowed. He holds two swords balanced on his shoulder and one in his hand. Two swords lay at his feet, dropped by the defeated men. Magical meaning: Overcoming strategic defeat and humiliation. This magic is the power of dominance, which can be sought and acquired even in the midst of loss. Defeat can only be overcome through clever cunning and knowing and seeking the weakness of one's enemies.

Abdaron/Remen-Heru-An-Sah: 10°–20° of Aquarius–Fixed Air–6 of Swords–Mercury–Succedent

Image: A man is punting a boat on a river that contains a veiled woman and a child. There appear to be six swords mounted to the floor of the boat arrayed before them. Two swords are on the side of the boat, and four form a corridor before the woman and child. Magical meaning: Ability to assess oneself and to make internal changes so that one's outer objectives conform to one's internal perceptions and needs. This magic clarifies the will and unifies the self to become an instrument of strength and personal power.

Garodiel/Metscher-Sah: 20°–30° of Aquarius–Fixed Air–7 of Swords–Moon–Cadent

Image: A well-dressed man is sneaking away with two and three swords to either shoulder. Another two swords are planted in the ground just behind him. In the background are the tents of a tournament. Magical meaning: Ability to protect oneself from false allies and betrayal.

Bahalmi/Ramun-Kher-Sa: 0°–10° of Pisces–Mutable Water–8 of Cups–Saturn–Ascendent

Image: A man walks away, staff in his hand, along a rocky water course. He leaves behind him eight golden goblets, three stacked on five. A baleful moon shines low in the sky. Magical meaning: Ability to see the truth behind emotional happiness, to determine when complacency may blind one, and to know when love and friendship is based on deception and lies.

Auron/A-Sah: 10°–20° of Pisces–Mutable Water–9 of Cups–Jupiter–Succedent

Image: A proud merchant wearing a feathered cap sits arms crossed upon a bench. Behind him is an arched counter covered with cloth upon which nine golden goblets are arrayed. Magical meaning: Achievement of complete emotional happiness, harmony, and peace. This magic requires one's emotional relationships to be based on truth and integrity.

Sateriph/Sah: 20°–30° of Pisces–Mutable Water–10 of Cups–Mars–Cadent

Image: A happy man and woman stand together in a sideways embrace, their other arms held aloft to the sky. A boy and girl dance together at their side. Above them is an arched rainbow with ten golden goblets shining. In the background is a fertile farmland with a red gabled home. Magical meaning: Achievement of total emotional fulfillment. The archetypal expression of a happy and fulfilling life. This magic can overcome all adversity and emotional troubles, heal emotional pain, and right wrongs in relationships.

Chapter Eight
ASTROLOGICAL SEPTANS: TALISMANIC SUB-ELEMENTALS

I will love the light for it shows me the way; yet I will
love the darkness for it shows me the stars.

—Augustine Mandino

I developed the system of astrological septans in order to make use of the forty-eight Dukes of the grimoire named the *Theurgia-Goetia*. It seemed to me that dividing each of the twelve zodiacal signs into four segments (one for each of the four elements) was in line with various traditions of astrological structures. However, further analysis of this system has shown me that it is quite elegant and useful. Each sign is divided using a divisor of the four elements for its 30-degree segment. Therefore, the following structure is determined for each sign.

No.	Septan Degree	Element	Septan Quality
1	0–7.5 degrees	Fire	Activity, Energy, Ambition (Aries)
2	7.5–15 degrees	Water	Feelings, Emotions, Clarity (Cancer)
3	15–22.5 degrees	Air	Knowledge, Decision, Analysis (Libra)
4	22.5–30 degrees	Earth	Material, Practicality, Fortune (Capricorn)

The septans can have a cosmogonic symbolic quality that represents the rise and fall of the energies of a zodiacal sign. However, the four divisions are used for a more practical purpose, in particular allotting abilities to a set of spirits. From an astrological perspective, a septan would occur only once a year for approximately seven days when considering the movement of the Sun. The other planets (especially the slower ones) would take years to achieve that point in the zodiac and remain there for weeks or months. It is for this reason I am not inclined to use the positioning of a target planet in the zodiac to trigger use of the septan. I believe that following the planetary day of the week and the planetary hour should suffice for determining the timing for a rite to open the septan and summon the ducal spirit. The position of the Sun in the zodiac can also be used if it is practical to wait for a specific seasonal date when the septan would be active.

The characteristics of the septans is that they represent a combination or fusion of the planetary ruler of the sign, the element, and quadruplicity of the sign, and an additional element qualifying these three components. For this reason, I refer to the septans as talismanic sub-elementals—two elements are joined together producing an elemental connected to a planet. The extended correspondences for the septan are taken from the qualities of the ruling planet and applied to the working. That means that the color, incense or perfume, and metal would conform to the qualities of the planetary ruler.

Having developed the quality and definition of the septan, I was able to place one of the forty-eight Dukes with each septan. However, there is no traditional mechanism for doing this kind of allotment, so I had to perform some divination and deep meditative analysis in order to come up with a structure that would work. I believe that my magical research was successful because I have had successful outcomes when I have used the septan and Duke in combination. With the distribution of the spirits of the *Theurgia-Goetia* to the four elements, sixteen elementals, eleven modern planets, and the forty-eight zodiacal septans, all the spirits are integrated into three different magical systems, two of which are part of celestial magic.[38]

Let us now examine the qualities associated with each of the forty-eight Dukes in order to determine how they are to be employed and for what purpose they would be used in a working.

Forty-Eight Dukes and the Talismanic Sub-Elementals

The following list are the qualities of the forty-eight talismanic sub-elementals. I have used the traditional seven planets for the planetary rulers instead of the more modern attributions. I did this because I wanted to keep the planetary configurations simple and within the traditional structure as an aid in summoning them. The quadruplicity combined with an elemental component represents the base energy associated with the talismanic construct. This energy will be easy to express within the talismanic ritual, as you will see when we go through the ritual patterns. The operator should keep in mind that these spirits can be invoked to project or receive the qualities that they own and express. The quality can also be used to charge a specially made talisman, based on the ruling planetary correspondences.

The *Theurgia-Goetia* uses the four Emperors as the primary organizing principle for the rest of the spirits. These four Emperors represent the spirits associated with the four elements. The forty-eight Dukes are part of an underlying hierarchy of the sixteen Grand Dukes, but for the sake of fitting them into this talismanic structure, I have pulled them out of that hierarchy, although the four Emperors would still rule over them. The operator can first summon the emperor and then the associated duke residing in that element hierarchy. Additionally, the operator can use the seal associated with the duke.[39] These additional attributes will lend a certain aesthetic quality to the working, but

---

38 The eleven wandering Princes would represent the eleven planets in a modern system of celestial magic. We won't be covering that kind of working in this book, but the potential for development is there.

39 Skinner and Rankine, "Sixteen [Grand] Dukes," in *The Goetia of Dr. Rudd*, 223–277.

they are not needed. The operator can make a sigil based on the duke's name and employ that in the construction of a talisman.

Determination for the meaning of the forty-eight septans is based on the combination of the ruling planet of the sign and the base element of the sign, with the addition of a qualifying element that is determined by the segment. The combination of the ruling planet and the base element of the sign produces a talismanic elemental. The base element of the sign and the qualifying element of the septan segment combined together also produces an elemental. Therefore, the hybrid combination of a talismanic elemental and an elemental represents the potent combination of planet and energy that is a signature quality of the septan.

You can examine the qualities of the talismanic elementals in chapter 6, pages 98–107, and look at the qualities of the sixteen elementals in appendix 2 to see how these qualities are combined. Because there are only sixteen elementals, they are repeated in the 48 septans.

Fire Segments: Southern Quadrant–Activity, Energy, Ambition
Element Emperor: Caspiel

Ursiel: Aries–Mars–Cardinal Fire of Fire–courage, enthusiasm, leadership qualities (used for all kinds of battles)–Elemental Fire of Fire

Chariel: Taurus–Venus–Fixed Earth of Fire–material acquisitions, practical endeavors

Maras: Gemini–Mercury–Mutable Air of Fire–ingenuity, critical mind, linguistically able or articulate–Elemental Fire of Air

Femol: Cancer–Moon–Cardinal Water of Fire–protection of the home and loved ones against all harm–Elemental Fire of Water

Budarim: Leo–Sun–Fixed Fire of Fire–willpower, creativity, charisma, self-confidence–Elemental Fire of Fire

Camory: Virgo–Mercury–Mutable Earth of Fire–empowerment and focus used for work, extreme skillfulness, manual dexterity–Elemental Fire of Earth

Larmol: Libra–Venus–Cardinal Air of Fire–social motivator, justice, fairness, and equality–Elemental Fire of Air

Aridiel: Scorpio–Mars–Fixed Water of Fire–courage, tenacity, emotional empowerment–Elemental Fire of Water

Geriel: Sagittarius–Jupiter–Mutable Fire of Fire–warrior, crusader, military strategy, impassioned idealism–Elemental Fire of Fire

Ambri: Capricorn–Saturn–Cardinal Earth of Fire–social advancement, empowered ambition, attainment of status–Elemental Fire of Earth.

Camor: Aquarius–Saturn–Fixed Air of Fire–reformist, social freedom, overthrowing of authority and power figures–Elemental Fire of Air

Oriel: Pisces–Jupiter–Mutable Water of Fire–artistic, musical, powerful intuition, and deep sensibilities–Elemental Fire of Water

Air Segments: Eastern Quadrant—Knowledge, Decision, Analysis
Element Emperor: Carnesiel

Myrezyn: Aries–Mars–Cardinal Fire of Air–decisiveness, original thinking, winning competitive endeavors–Elemental Air of Fire

Ornich: Taurus–Venus–Fixed Earth of Air–financial common sense, shrewd judgment in money matters–Elemental Air of Earth

Zabriel: Gemini–Mercury–Mutable Air of Air–logical reasoning, insightful and perceptive, eloquence–Elemental Air of Air

Bucafas: Cancer–Moon–Cardinal Water of Air–unlocking lost memories, learning by absorption and feeling–Elemental Air of Water

Benoliam: Leo–Sun–Fixed Fire of Air–mental concentration, problem solving

Arifiel: Virgo–Mercury–Mutable Earth of Air–analytical skills, precision, mastery of foreign languages–Elemental Air of Earth

Curmeriel: Libra–Venus–Cardinal Air of Air–insight into others, revealing all hidden truth about others–Elemental Air of Air

Vadriel: Scorpio–Mars–Fixed Water of Air–profound insights, perceptive and shrewd judgments of others–Elemental Air of Water

Armany: Sagittarius–Jupiter–Mutable Fire of Air–knowledge of all social codes, social motivations–Elemental Air of Fire

Capriel: Capricorn–Saturn–Cardinal Earth of Air–organizational skills, shrewd ambition, material accomplishments–Elemental Air of Earth

Bedary: Aquarius–Saturn–Fixed Air of Air–perfect objectivity, deep social insight, realizing social transformations–Elemental Air of Air

Laphor: Pisces–Jupiter–Mutable Water of Air–photographic memory, power of visualization, poetic and imaginative–Elemental Air of Water

Water Segments: Western Quadrant—Feelings, Emotions, Clarity
Element Emperor: Amenadiel

Vadros: Aries–Mars–Cardinal Fire of Water–causes emotional volatility and impulsiveness, knowing emotional triggers–Elemental Water of Fire

Camiel: Taurus–Venus–Fixed Earth of Water–satiety, emotional fulfillment, peaceful coexistence, good friendship–Elemental Water of Earth

Luziel: Gemini–Mercury–Mutable Air of Water–ability to rationalize emotions and resolve emotional issues, clear thinking–Elemental Water of Air

Musiriel: Cancer–Moon–Cardinal Water of Water–emotional depth, psychic insights, nurturing, culinary arts–Elemental Water of Water

Rapsiel: Leo–Sun–Fixed Fire of Water–theatric arts, social and personal charm, charisma–Elemental Water of Fire

Lamael: Virgo–Mercury–Mutable Earth of Water–orderliness, practical health knowledge, good diet and health, healing–Elemental Water of Earth

Zoeniel: Libra–Venus–Cardinal Air of Water–personal charm, beauty and glamor, social elegance–Elemental Water of Air

Curifas: Scorpio–Mars–Fixed Water of Water–sexual domination, seduction, sexual empowerment–Elemental Water of Water

Almesiel: Sagittarius–Jupiter–Mutable Fire of Water–altruism, ideals, religious insights, celebrating traditional values–Elemental Water of Fire

Codriel: Capricorn–Saturn–Cardinal Earth of Water–establishing boundaries, moderating relationships, maintaining dignity–Elemental Water of Earth

Balsur: Aquarius–Saturn–Fixed Air of Water–establishing friendships, civic morality, public celebrations, social empathy–Elemental Water of Air

Nadroc: Pisces–Jupiter–Mutable Water of Water–psychic empathy, sympathy, emotional absorption, mediumistic powers–Elemental Water of Water

Earth Segments: Northern Quadrant—Material, Practicality, Fortune
Element Emperor: Demoriel

Arnibiel: Aries–Mars–Cardinal Fire of Earth–strength of character, resilience, implacable will–Elemental Earth of Fire

Cabarim: Taurus–Venus–Fixed Earth of Earth–enduring, patience, steadfast, good long-term investments–Elemental Earth of Earth

Menador: Gemini–Mercury–Mutable Air of Earth–mental discipline, logic, mathematical reasoning, scientific–Elemental Earth of Air

Burisiel: Cancer–Moon–Cardinal Water of Earth–responsible, family values, preserving family and relationships–Elemental Earth of Water

Doriel: Leo–Sun–Fixed Fire of Earth–establishing protective boundaries, thwarting the ill will of others–Elemental Earth of Fire

Mador: Virgo–Mercury–Mutable Earth of Earth–focusing on details, practical mental acuity, establishing service institutions–Elemental Earth of Earth

Carnol: Libra–Venus–Cardinal Air of Earth–obtaining consensus, acceptance, lasting social accomplishments–Elemental Earth of Air

Dubilon: Scorpio–Mars–Fixed Water of Earth–acquiring inheritances, revealing plots, financial resourcefulness–Elemental Earth of Water

Medar: Sagittarius–Jupiter–Mutable Fire of Earth–search for truth, intellectual discipline, concentration, achievements–Elemental Earth of Fire

Churibal: Capricorn–Saturn–Cardinal Earth of Earth–obtaining worldly power and status, material position and wealth–Elemental Earth of Earth

Dabrinos: Aquarius–Saturn–Fixed Air of Earth–organizational perfection, impartial truth, social justice and equality–Elemental Earth of Air

Chamiel: Pisces–Jupiter–Mutable Water of Earth–view into the past, understanding personal fate, charity, benevolence–Elemental Earth of Water

Chapter Nine

TALISMANIC TOOLS AND RITUAL ARTIFICES

"I am a child of the Moon being raised by the Sun in a world walked by stars and a sky drawn with flowers."

—Zara Ventris

We have now covered everything that you need to know to organize the spiritual and magical components of celestial magic. The previous eight chapters represent the foundation of celestial lore and information required so that you can understand all the attributes underlying celestial magic. It has been quite an amazing journey, but the real magic is where I show you how to put all this knowledge to work within a series of five magical ritual workings. It is time and we are ready to examine the actual tools and techniques needed to formulate these five ritual workings. These tools, ritual structures, and techniques have been uniquely fashioned to help you to effectively and succinctly work celestial magic and project these intelligences and powers into specially constructed receptors. Whether as elixirs, consecrated oils or balms, jewelry, or metallic talismans, these receptors will generate a field that will indelibly alter your material world. Some, such as magical jewelry or talismans, will maintain a perpetual field of magical effects nearly forever; others will hold this field temporarily so that it can be absorbed or ingested.

Though I present five different ritual workings here, there are many more kinds of workings the experienced practitioner could develop independently—the possibilities for applying celestial magic are nearly endless. The production of celestial magical receptors is this book's whole purpose and the raison d'être for the kind of magical workings it describes. We had to cover a lot of material to get to this point in order for these magical workings to make sense and for the techniques of establishing the magical auspices to be easily understood.

This chapter describes the ritual structures, tools, and liturgical components needed to build a magical system that will allow you to perform celestial magic and to produce talismanic receptors. Once we have defined all the elements needed to perform the five celestial magical workings, we then need to examine the method for determining when the magical operation should be performed. After that, we cover the five celestial ritual workings in three chapters, describing the ritual patterns and assembling a ritual example for each type.

Star Polygon Icons

The star polygon icon is the central tool used for invoking a planetary intelligence. The operator traces the lines of the star on the icon in a fashion similar to tracing the lines when drawing an invoking pentagram. Each point of the star is represented by one of the planetary intelligences that one would seek to invoke. The operator starts at the point of the star opposite the target point and traces the lines of the star to that point, continuing to trace the lines until it reaches the target point for the second time. Performing this tracing on a star polygon produces what I call the active planetary energy signature, just like tracing the lines of a pentagram produces an active element energy signature. The angular vectors on a star polygon icon are an important factor in the operator's ability to dynamically generate the planetary field whenever it is needed.

The talismanic workings here use a septagram painted or drawn on paper, tag board, or wood. What I have done personally is paint a septagram on a rectangular plywood board measuring 18" by 14.5". I crafted it so that each planetary point is shown with a different color (using the planetary colors), and that the background is black so that the star is easily seen.

You can spend a lot of time and effort building your own polygon star icon or draw it on paper or tag board, so long as it is clear and the points are marked with the appropriate planetary symbols for easy identification. A painted board will last a long time; paper and tag-board may need to be replaced every so often. To increase longevity, you could waterproof it with a polymer coating. After construction, consecrate this tool in a charged and properly set magic circle with incense and just a touch of sanctified saltwater while projecting the power generated in the circle into the icon tool.

The septagram icon is placed on a small altar that stands in the center of the magic circle in addition to the standard temple altar, where it can be worked on within an empowered inner circle. The whole reason for having such a tool centrally placed in your sacred space is that it facilitates the use of stars which have seven or more points. I have found that drawing the septagram in the air is awkward, cumbersome, and difficult. Drawing a nine-, eleven-, or twelve-pointed star in the air requires a level of mental focus and imagination that I seem to lack, particularly when I am in the semi-trance state required for working magic. It is just simpler to use a septagram icon than to imagine a septagram and drawing its invoking vectors in the air.

The operator traces the lines on the septagram icon using a wand, since what is being invoked is a spiritual intelligence, and the wand is a gentler tool used to invoke spirits. Using the same rules as drawing a pentagram, the operator performs cool breathing while drawing the lines of the star, starting in the point opposite the target point, and then tracing the lines past the target and following the line until reaching again the point opposite, and then exhaling the breath as the final line to target is drawn. The operator then draws an invoking spiral around the septagram, circling three times from the outer periphery of the figure to its center, and then projects a final burst of energy into the core of the star. This is the central ritual action for all the talismanic workings that require a dynamic invoking trigger of energy for a ruling planet or a sign.

Since four of the five talismanic ritual workings make use of the seven-planetary construct, the septagram icon would be used to generate the energy field from its angular vectors, thanks to the use of the seven traditional planetary archetypes in these workings, whether lunar mansion, decan, or septan.

I felt it was important to present the ritual workings based on the traditional set of planets to limit the scope of this work. I am continuing to work and develop a system of talismanic magic that would use additional planets as they are in astrology, but it is not something I could present without revising and rebuilding a lot of the traditional correspondences and their associated ritual structures. I may choose to present these revised ritual workings in another future work. For now, what follows is a good representation of the star polygons that would be used in this system of talismanic magic.

Figure 3 shows the magical septagram with planetary symbols for the seven points. The seven septagram points are divided by 360 degrees to get the number of degrees for each point, roughly 51 degrees (51.42 to be a bit more accurate). That would mean that the first point of the septagram is 0 degrees, the second 51, the third 102, the fourth 154, the fifth 205, the sixth 257, and the seventh 308. These points are approximate, of course, but when created with a protractor on a lightly drawn circle, it results in a nice looking septagram when all the lines are connected.

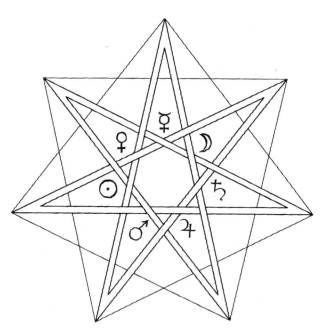

Figure 3: Septagram with Planetary Points

Notice that the planets associated with the points of the septagram have Mercury at the top point, followed by Venus on the left, the Moon on the right, and then the last four planets as the Sun on the left, Saturn on the right, Mars on the left, and Jupiter on the right. There are many variations of septagram attributions, and there doesn't appear to be any traditional order. Mercury is at the top in my configuration because it is neutral, Venus and Moon are next because they are receptive, and the remaining four planets—Sun (fastest) to Saturn (slowest)—are creative. That said, I don't believe that what I have chosen is the one true planetary association for the septagram.

Another star polygon is the twelve-pointed star called the dodecagram. This star polygon is used to invoke a zodiacal sign, which is an optional icon that you can build. While a dodecagram might have additional uses in celestial magical workings, in this book the only use that I would attribute it to is a magical working to invoke one of the twelve signs of the zodiac. You could use it in conjunction with the septagram to generate the field for a planet in a zodiacal sign, but you would have to fuse both operations into a single planetary-zodiacal quality in order to accomplish that task.

Figure 4 shows the dodecagram with its designated zodiacal sign points. Notice that the points start with Aries at about the same point (90 degrees) that the first house in an astrological chart would start. From there, circle around the points counterclockwise to fill in all twelve signs.

Figure 4: Duodecagram with Zodiacal Points

Additionally, I do use the four Lesser Hexagrams in the three talismanic workings of the lunar mansion, decan, and septan. These are used to denote the quadruplicities (cardinal, fixed, and mutable). I also use the hexagram to symbolize the union of opposites. I don't use the lesser hexagram devices to generate and invoke the planetary fields; the lesser hexagram of fire is used to denote the quality of cardinal signs, the hexagram of air the quality of fixed, the hexagram of water the quality of mutable, and the hexagram of earth is what I use to denote the quality of unity.

A zodiacal sign is defined by an element in combination with a quality, so the use of an invoking pentagram and one of the three lesser hexagrams gives me the devices needed to define a zodiacal sign within a working. I have invented and used this method in my celestial magical workings, so it does not fit with the traditional uses of the hexagram as defined in the Golden Dawn magical rituals of the hexagram.

Figure 5 shows the four Lesser Hexagrams and how they are drawn, in addition to both the traditional meanings and my own usage.

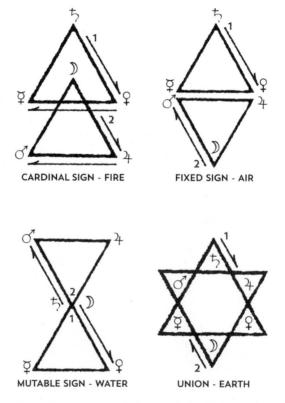

CARDINAL SIGN - FIRE

FIXED SIGN - AIR

MUTABLE SIGN - WATER

UNION - EARTH

Figure 5: Lesser Hexagrams and Their Drawing Method and Meanings

The four hexagrams of the Lesser Hexagram configuration are drawn in the air with the wand and therefore do not require the operator to paint them onto polygon icons. Building at least the septagram icon and maybe the dodecagram icon should be sufficient for all the workings that the practitioner might need to perform within the basic set of rituals for celestial magic. As with all of the tools, these can be made as simple or elaborate as needed to satisfy the practitioner's aesthetics.

Other Ritual Devices and Structures

Performing the ritual workings for celestial magic requires some additional ritual devices and structures: the pylon, the rose ankh, the inverted pentagrams (for the creative and receptive spirit configuration), obverse pentagrams, the rose ankh vortex, the pylon pyramid, the elemental octagon, and the western and eastern gateway structures.

Pylon

The pylon was covered in *Elemental Powers for Witches,* where it was used to bind the energy fields of two devices together.[40] The top point and bottom point of the imaginary pylon line are set with devices, such as an invoking pentagram, that are then fused with an invoking spiral that joins the top with the bottom points. The result is a pylon or pillar of magical energy set at the point or node in the magic circle.

Figure 6: Pylon with Two Points for Defining a Zodiacal Sign

---

40 Barrabbas, *Elemental Powers for Witches,* 50, 163.

In celestial magic, the pylon can be set with a base element to the bottom of the pylon plus one of the lesser hexagrams of fire, air, or water and then fused with an invoking spiral to denote the element and quality of the zodiacal sign. However, the decan and septan workings use a three-point pylon that incorporates the top, bottom, and mid-point on the device.

Figure 7: Pylon with Three Points Instead of Two

A three-point pylon uses the mid-point to place either another lesser hexagram structure or an invoking pentagram, therefore lending the quality of the decan segment or the element segment for a septan.

Pylon Pyramid

The pylon can be erected at the four watchtowers or the four angles; with the center of the circle also occupied by a pylon, the result is the energy structure of the pylon pyramid, the base for more complex celestial magical workings.[41]

---

41 Barrabbas, *Elemental Powers*, 51.

Rose Ankh and Rose Ankh Vortex

The rose ankh was covered in *Spirit Conjuring for Witches*, where it was used to fashion a powerful goddess-based and magnetic energy field that assisted the operator in building an invoking web to draw in the conjured spirit.[42] We use a similar construction in celestial magic, although in this case the magnetic invoking web is used to collect and coalesce the intelligence and energy field of the talismanic spirit that has been invoked. Coalescing and compressing this energy into a point in the center of the circle is how the talismanic energy field is collected and then projected into a talismanic receptor.

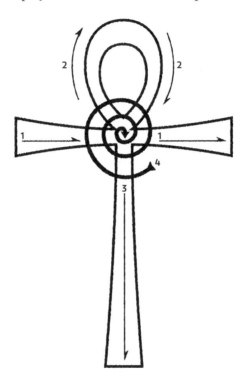

Figure 8-A: Rose Ankh Device

---

42 Barrabbas, *Spirit Conjuring for Witches*, 62–66.

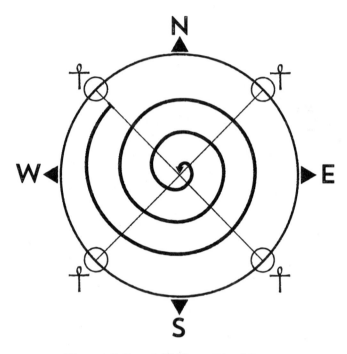

Figure 8-B: Rose Ankh Vortex Ritual Pattern

Invoking Pentagrams

The invoking Pentagram device has been covered in the book *Elemental Powers for Witches* and there is no need to review that information here.[43] We will be employing the invoking pentagrams to define the element base for the celestial workings, since all talismanic constructs require a union of element and planet to satisfy the talismanic equation.

Inverted Pentagrams

There is another ritual working that projects a talismanic field into a talismanic receptor; this one requires the use of the inverted pentagrams of creative spirit and receptive spirit. I had hinted in *Elemental Powers* that inverted pentagrams were quite acceptable magical devices; in this particular ritual we will have use for two of them.

---

43 Barrabbas, *Elemental Powers*, 67–73.

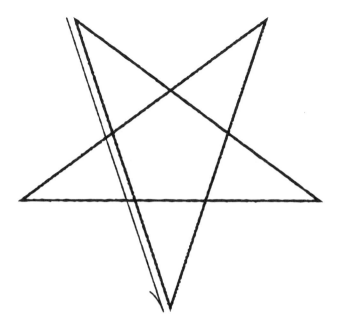

Figure 9-A: Inverted Pentagram of Creative Spirit

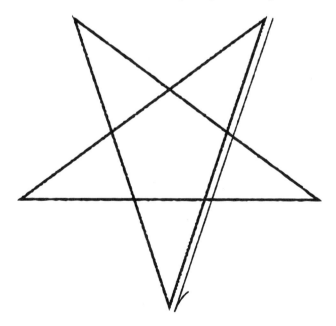

Figure 9-B: Inverted Pentagram of Receptive Spirit

As was stated in my previous book, the inverted pentagram signifies the drawing down of spirit into a consecrated and sacramental element—in this case, the active and passive attributes of spirit. Using these two devices will cause the talismanic field to coalesce and then to be focused and projected into the talismanic receptor, however it is constructed.

Western and Eastern Gateway

I described the use of the western and eastern gateway ritual structures in both *Spirit Conjuring for Witches* and *Elemental Powers for Witches*, so I will not get into too much detail about these structures in this work beyond a basic synopsis of these ritual structures.[44]

The basic gateway structure is a triangle that uses the western circle node or the eastern circle node as the focus of the magic, and the place where the opening portal gesture is made. The western gateway consists of the southeast and northeast angles joined to the western watchtower. This is the gateway to the west where the sun sets and represents the doorway to the underworld domain of the magic circle when the opening portal gesture is made facing it. The gateway's three nodes are symbolized by the three stages in the classic underworld passage where the hero as the operator is assisted by the guide (southeast), challenged by the guardian (northeast), and undergoes the ordeal of transformation at the doorway of the underworld (west). These themes, as they occur in the ritual format, can be made elaborate or simple, based on the tastes of the operator. However, the rite should be memorized with a few mental cues to trigger the ordeal of the gateway.

The eastern gateway is the mythic hero's return from the underworld, also represented by three stages. It uses the southwestern and northwestern angles joined to the eastern watchtower to form the triangle gateway structure. This gateway is to the east where the sun rises and represents the doorway out of the underworld domain and into the light of clarity and realization. The three stages are the guide (powers that assist—northeast), the guardian (powers that challenge—northwest) and the ordeal at the doorway of underworld exit (transformative process—east).

---

44 Barrabbas, *Spirit Conjuring*, 60–61; *Elemental Powers*, 54–55.

Each gateway has the same basic pattern: the operator stands in the east facing west, or the west facing east. The operator joins the nodes of the gate together into a triangle and slowly proceeds from east to west (or west to east). In front of the gateway central door, the operator makes the sign of the opening of the portal, takes one step into that watchtower, turns, and draws the powers down using their hands from their head to the floor. Then the operator proceeds either down to the center of the circle into the underworld plunging the world into the darkness of night, or up to the center of the circle exiting the underworld with the brilliant dawning of day.

The gateway ritual structure is used to enter the sacred domain of the talismanic energy field, uniting the previous levels of the ritual working and generating a new level where the planetary intelligence can be invoked as the head of the fused energy body. This means that the invocation of the planetary intelligence occurs in the highest ritual layer of the multi-layered vortex working. Like the rose ankh vortex, the western gateway is integral to this kind of magical ritual working just as it is in the conjuration of a spirit. The return eastern gateway helps to surface the talismanic field and bring it into manifestation.

Eight-Node Magic Circle, Inner Circle, and the Use of Spirals

The last three ritual structures I use in celestial magic are the basic eight-node or pointed circle, an inner circle that defines a more sacred perimeter, and the four basic spirals used in conjunction with vortex energy fields. These have been covered in my previous two books, so I only briefly touch on them here.[45]

The magic circle I employ for the rituals of celestial magic use an eight-pointed magic circle. These eight points are the four cardinal directions and the four angles or in-between points. The cardinal directions are the lines of the circle that travel east and west, and north and south; they function as the watchtowers. The angles are between the cardinal points, being the directions of northeast, southeast, southwest, and northwest. Depending on the vector of the circle (whether the nodes are set using a deosil arc or a widdershins arc), the four angles will take on the qualities of the watchtower either to the right (deosil) or left (widdershins). The middle of the magic circle has three points:

---

45 Barrabbas, *Elemental Powers*, 52.

the nadir, zenith, and midpoint. Altogether, there are eleven points to this circle: eight in the periphery, three in the center.

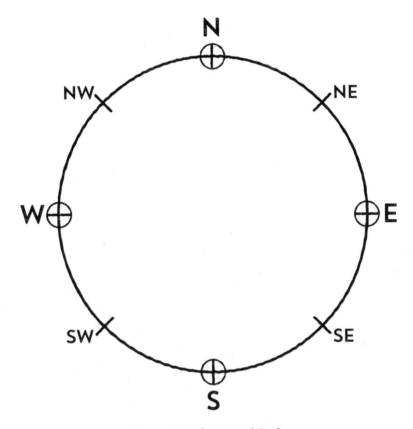

Figure 10: Eight–pointed Circle

I will set a circle within the magic circle to surround its middle and to create a higher level of a sacred domain. The outer magic circle is set during the
circle consecration rite, and additional inner circle structures are constructed
and established within the sacred domain. Setting another magic circle within
the basic boundary of the first defines a kind of holy of holies or ultra-sacred
place. In the rituals of celestial magic, this inner circle is drawn around the central altar to make it an ultra-sacred domain set-off from the regular magical circle. In that domain, the archetypal planetary intelligence is generated through
the artifice of the septagram and the associated spiritual hierarchy is invoked.
This part of the talismanic ritual symbolizes the god-work associated with the

operation, where the element body is joined to the mind of a living deity who is exteriorized as a demigod and projected into a talismanic receptor. The inner circle represents a critical part of that work.

The four spirals are used to generate and manipulate vortex energies.[46] The combination of direction (deosil, widdershins) and vector (inward and outward) are the two dimensions of a spiral. Typically, the wand is used to draw spirals, but hybrid devices can be used as well such as a crystal tipped transmuter wand that can replace both a wand and a dagger.

The four spirals are defined in the following way: When an operator uses their wand to draw a deosil arc that travels from outside to inside, that spiral is an invoking spiral. When an operator uses their wand to draw a widdershins arc traveling from inside to outside, that spiral is a banishing spiral. When an operator uses their wand to draw a widdershins arc traveling from outside to inside, that spiral is a sealing spiral. When an operator uses his wand to draw a deosil arc traveling from inside to outside then that spiral is an unsealing spiral.

Because a vortex magical working cannot be banished effectively, the operator will use a sealing spiral to seal the vortex in place; later, when they wish to resume the magical working, they will deploy an unsealing spiral. This peculiar quality of the vortex was discussed in detail in *Elemental Powers for Witches*.[47] The sealing and unsealing spirals are drawn to the nodes in the magic circle that were used in the ritual at every layer. My instructions include the use of sealing spirals to still a vortex or resume it, if required. Keep in mind that invoking and banishing spirals have a very specific use to wind up and exteriorize the energy. Because a vortex cannot be banished, you wouldn't use a banishing spiral to somehow banish it. I discuss the use and quality of the four spirals in my book *Elemental Powers for Witches*, so you can examine that writing to fully realize the use of the four spirals.[48]

---

46 Barrabbas, *Spirit Conjuring*, 53–57.

47 Barrabbas, *Elemental Powers for Witches*, 47–49.

48 Ibid., 161–163.

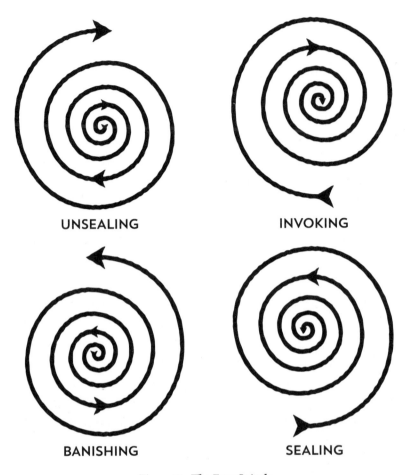

Figure 11: The Four Spirals

Celestial Magic Tools and Paraphernalia

We have already covered the need for a polygon icon painted on wood, paper, or tagboard, and a small portable table to act as a central altar. These two elements are critically important to the talismanic ritual workings as detailed in this system of celestial magic; they must be built or acquired in some manner before attempting to perform this work.

The next item important to celestial workings is a colored scarf or liturgical stole. The color is important, but this piece of apparel can be customized to include embroidered or drawn symbols of the planet or other such decorative markings. Wearing this apparel will signal your intention to summon a planetary intelligence. Because it becomes liturgical, the garment should be consecrated and charged in a separate ritual for that purpose. You can also add jewelry to your ceremonial adornment that has been consecrated or even charged with the talismanic field of the target planet. Once you don this garment, you are acting as a priest of that planetary deity; train your mind to assume that role and the associated spiritual alignment to the planetary archetype.

Incense and perfumes are also a very important part of this kind of working because they will help the operator connect with the planetary associations and correspondences merely by wearing the colored vestment, smelling the incense smoke, and wearing a perfumed oil upon their forehead.

Celestial magic works with a spiritual hierarchy and spirits who are the intelligent representations of the talismanic field. As with all types of magic that work with spirits, you will need to create a consecrated sigil to summon the spirit. Included with the sigil of the talismanic spirit should be the sigils of the spirits that are part of its spiritual hierarchy. And once the talismanic receptor is charged, the consecrate sigil can be burned after three days, since it will no longer be needed.

The target for talismanic magic is the talismanic receptor. This is the receiver of the energy and intelligence of the talismanic spirit that enters into the receptor and resides there. There are two kinds of talismans: perishable and imperishable. Perishable receptors are typically some kind of perfumed oil, a balm, elixir (medicine or potion), libation, or food, such as wine and unleavened bread. These perishable receptors receive the blessings and empowerment of the talismanic spirit so that they might be applied to the skin or consumed as a powerful sacrament.

Imperishable talismanic receptors are metallic objects, jewels, or jewelry. An imperishable talisman should have some kind of markings on it to represent the talismanic field it contains, although if markings are missing, it doesn't diminish the efficacy of the talisman. Imperishable talismans should be blessed and consecrated before being charged by the talismanic field. Perishable talismans are not blessed in this way because the act of charging and transforming them sufficiently ensures that they are sacraments.

Crafting a metallic or wooden talisman requires some tools, metal or wood stock, and other items, not to mention skill to use the tools to fashion an imperishable talisman. I have already listed a good online source in the introduction that also includes the supplies needed to craft a talisman. Keep in mind that the end result of such work doesn't need to look like a professionally done artifact.

I have made my talismans from a sheet of metal stock and cut out a three-inch diameter disk using some heavy-duty craft scissors. I drew the disk with a pencil on the sheet metal using a circle template in the right size and lined up the circle on the edge of the metal sheet. After cutting out the disk, I carefully filed down the edges. I used a Dremel with a fine etching tip to etch the seal and spirit sigils on it. Once done with that, I used a buffing wheel attached to a drill to remove any scratches and to give it a smooth surface. It might not look like a fine piece of jewelry, but it is functional and it works.

Finally, the operator will have in their possession the typical working tools of a wand, dagger, sword, staff, chalice, and a pentacle dish. A space should be cleared for the magical working or they should have access to a permanent temple. The working space features a basic altar and small table used as a shrine, and some way of marking the watchtowers and angles. I would recommend using battery-operated luminaries for establishing the periphery of the magic circle. As stated previously, you will need to set up a central altar and place the consecrated septagram icon upon it. Containers of water, wine, salt, bread, and incense should also be stocked and at hand.

The shrine will hold the statues or markers of the operator's personal aligned family of deities, to include the seven markers for the planetary deities. The operator will function as priest or priestess and make certain that periodic rites consisting of votive offerings of candles, incense, food, and drink are dispensed for these deities. The operator will also perform services where hymns of praise, invocations, godhead assumption, and communion are performed at strategic times of the lunar cycle, particularly full and new moon periods. The operator will perform several of these services for the specific planetary deity before the planned talismanic working.

Choosing a talismanic working with a specific talismanic spirit as the target requires some research and analysis. The more information you can collect about yourself and what you want to accomplish, the more precise and appropriate the choice of the talismanic spirit, resulting in a greater guarantee of the magical operation's outcome.

Now that we have covered the ritual patterns, technique, and tools needed to perform celestial workings, we will next go over in detail how to plan a working and determine when it should be performed. All these considerations are crucial to an effective and successful outcome. You can approach these kinds of workings with the minimum of work as long as all of the elements are present or get very deep and detailed about the analysis, selection, timing, preparation, and performance of the working—either approach produces good results.

However, to make great and dramatic changes in your or your client's life, you are advised to approach this magic with depth, tenacity, and skill. You may certainly begin working this kind of magic with the idea that you will become more proficient, experienced, and adept over time, since learning and mastering this kind of magic is very challenging...and very rewarding.

Chapter Ten

ASTROLOGICAL AUSPICES

"The best way of handling astrological transits is to go with the flow. If the Universe is leading you to a certain place by hook or by crook, there's probably a reason."

—CATE EAST

Now that we have covered the background and tools associated with celestial magic, we should examine the core basis to any celestial magical working. That core basis is, of course, your natal horoscope. You should know your natal chart intimately and thoroughly. Once you have that understanding developed to a point of obvious self-knowledge, you can consider some of the other techniques and methods to fully realize the auspices affecting the event of any magical working.

Self-knowledge also helps you know exactly which kind of working will suffice and determine the exact talismanic spiritual intelligence to use in your working. Without some kind of self-knowledge, a talismanic working may be enhancing or strengthening psychic or causal attributes that aren't necessary. I learned this lesson the hard way, when I performed workings that had little or no effect on my situation.

I recommend purchasing some astrological software for your home computer and generating your natal chart. Next, get a few good books and spend some time studying your chart to help you understand yourself by noting your strengths and weaknesses. By finding weak points in your chart, you will begin to figure out the parts of yourself that need strength and empowerment after comparing what the chart describes and your experiences in life. Start by producing a list of your strengths and virtues, then list things that you are not good at or where you are lacking in abilities, opportunities, and good fortune. After that, apply these lists when studying your natal chart. If you study hard enough and get deep into an analysis of yourself, you will discover that your lists match up with the attributes of your natal chart.

The task of learning astrology and applying that knowledge to yourself might be a bit daunting; another option is hiring an astrologer to guide you or purchasing a completed natal chart report. You could also take a class on astrology, in person with a local astrologer or an online course. I found that a combination of receiving personal instruction, attending online classes, examining a completed natal chart analysis, and owning software that can produce charts on demand really helped me master the rudiments of astrology. I believe that having a basic understanding of astrology will greatly aid you in mastering the basics of celestial magic too.

It is true that you can work celestial magic without knowing much about astrology, or paying any attention to your natal chart, daily transits, or your deficits as astrology might describe them. You can simply and intuitively choose a talismanic working and perform it using the guidelines of the cycle of the moon, the planetary day and planetary hour, or not. If the magical working is just a simple way to gain an opportunity and not strategic or life-changing, making the operation more complex is probably not a good idea.

However, the goal of celestial magic is the production of an artifact that will have long-term effects on you or your client. I believe that a deeper background analysis will help you in determining if that artifact you created will really help, be neutralized by other psychic or situational circumstances, or actually work against your purposes. In this kind of magic, knowledge is power and, I might add, a necessity.

Additionally, you should be aware that an astrological natal chart shows the querent a snapshot of where the planets were at their birth. It may determine specific psychological potentials and predict, in a broad manner, the events of one's life. However, astrology is not deterministic; fate as we know it in these modern times is not fixed. Fate and destiny are flexible, and at the beginning of life they represent a large field of possibilities that narrow as a person grows older.

I can also argue that self-knowledge will help you avoid some of the pitfalls of life and steer your life's path in a more optimal direction. If you think of the astrological chart as a clock face that is changing every hour and every day, you can understand your natal chart is just a slice of an ever-changing continuum and that astrological factors will affect and influence that natal chart as time marches on. To understand the dynamics of our natal chart, we must also factor in the transits happening every day.

To determine what talismanic spirit to choose for a working, when to perform it, and what preparations are required are the most important considerations you will make when seeking to perform celestial magic to change some aspect of your life. This chapter will help you find the answers to these questions of what, when, and how so you can be prepared to effectively perform a talismanic working. Let us start by first attempting to answer the question of what talismanic spirit you should choose.

Selecting Talismanic Spirits and Workings

The choice for which talismanic spirits to use for a given working is tied to your knowledge of yourself. If you can easily identify your weaknesses and needs, it should not be difficult to identify the specific talisman you will want to produce. However, a clue to areas of deficiency in your personality (and we all have them) can be easily determined by looking at the element sort table for your given natal chart. This table has three columns: Cardinal, Fixed, and Mutable, and rows for the four elements.[49] This sort table shows the number for element and quality in your chart. The highest number for each element and quality gives you a predominate trait. For instance, in my chart, looking at the sort table, I have a count of five planets for the water element row, while

---

49 If you don't have a sort table, you can make one: Make a table with columns for the four elements and rows for the quadruplicity of Cardinal, Fixed, and Mutable. Count the sign qualities of the basic ten planets and put a number associated with that value, e.g., Sun in Capricorn would be a count of 1 for Cardinal and a 1 for Earth.

adding them for cardinal, fixed, and mutable. Adding the rows in the cardinal column equals 5, indicating that my quality is cardinal. That means that my strengths are cardinal water or Cancer. My weakness in the same sort table is not as easily determined because I have at least all four elements covered, though I do lack in the area of fire, specifically cardinal fire and mutable fire (Aries and Sagittarius respectively). Since I only have one planet in Leo, it would mean that the power of initiative associated with Aries and the competitive confidence associated with Sagittarius would be lacking in my chart. Knowing myself, I can say that this is true.

Another quick method is examining the occurrence of planets in houses and looking at the four quadrants. This diagram is a circle divided into four parts with a number in each quadrant.[50] Looking at my chart, I can see that once again that I have planets in every single quadrant, but a few more in the first and second quadrants and slightly fewer in the third and fourth quadrant. There are no really glaring weaknesses in my chart according to the element and quality sort table and the chart quadrant distribution diagram. To find the weakness in my chart, I have to examine the chart in greater detail. However, if you examine these two diagrams in your chart, perhaps you will see a lacking in terms of an element, quality, or chart quadrant distribution. For example, someone who has a lot of fire signs but doesn't have any earth signs could have a weakness related to material pursuits and practicality. For such a person, developing earth-sign based talismans would be a good approach, depending on how the rest of the chart is populated and what the aspects between planets determine.

One more way to determine strengths and weaknesses in the natal chart is to check the qualities of the planets in the houses and signs. Planets that are exalted or in the zodiacal sign that they rule makes them stronger and more effective, while planets that are fallen or detrimental in their zodiacal sign will make for weaker or even problematic attributes. In my chart, I have Jupiter in Cancer, which is exalted, but I have Venus in Scorpio, which is detrimental.

The balance of positive versus negative planetary attributes will help you determine your strengths and weaknesses and define your planetary profile. You determine the quality of the planets in your natal chart by consulting a

---

50 If your chart doesn't have a quadrant diagram on it, add up the number of the standard ten planets located in the four quadrants.

good introductory book on astrology. If you are going to analyze and interpret your natal chart, you will have to begin by defining the quality of the planets in your chart.

Approaching a chart interpretation and from there determining which talismans to produce to enhance and empower you from a standpoint of inherent natal chart weakness is beyond the scope of this work. You will need to spend some time analyzing yourself to determine what talisman would be appropriate. However, approaching this as a puzzle and answering some easy questions might also determine where you should start.

Think about your needs: What do you need right now in your life? Do you need help with your career, e.g., finding a job or starting a new career? Do you need help finding a lover or a long-term relationship? Do you need help with your health, attracting the right kind of friends, successfully completing a difficult course in school? Are you trying to get a degree or move to a new town?

I have already talked about how when I was a young man, I couldn't seem to find a woman anywhere I lived who wanted to have a long-term relationship with me. I worked a number of spells to try to overcome this issue, but they all failed. Had I examined my natal chart, I would have seen that my Venus is in Scorpio in the sixth house, my Saturn in Scorpio in the fifth house, and my Part of Fortune is positioned in between the two planets, causing them to be conjunct—I would never have used Venus in my talismanic workings for this reason.[51] What I should have done is focus on Jupiter (which is very well aspected in my chart) being in the first house, in the sign of Cancer. All those operations I performed using Venus were wasted because I didn't truly know myself as much as I should. Of course, this conjunction between my Saturn, Part of Fortune, and Venus was not intended as a permanent obstacle. I was able to resolve this issue, although it did take many decades to resolve; I didn't start living with my partner until I was in my late fifties. Knowing and understanding the nature of that simple yet troubling aspect would have made me realize many years in the past that I would either figure out my problem perhaps by using magic or that it would take decades for the issue to resolve itself. In the end, I just outgrew it and was able to have a normal relationship.

---

51 I don't expect the reader to know astrology to this depth but suffice it to say that Venus was not a good target for me to use in helping me find a long-term relationship. Analyzing my natal chart helped me to understand this fact about myself, although it was decades later.

If even after extensive self-analysis you are still having difficulties determining a talismanic working to perform, perhaps I can suggest one for you as your first attempt. I would recommend trying Jupiter of Earth, a benign talismanic elemental that, once projected into a talisman, can only help you to materialize good fortune in all of your pursuits. You are also free to invoke any of the planetary spirits you choose just to experience their energies and intelligences without having to project them into a talismanic receptor, an approach I also recommend. Many years ago, I invoked all twenty-eight talismanic elementals in order to experience and commune with them. Later on, I chose a few to forge into talismanic receptors.

Here are five different types of celestial magical workings to consider and how to use them. I have already discussed that there are five different workings but only three will produce some kind of talismanic artifact. All are quite useful.

1. Simple planetary working: This is does not have an elemental base and does not produce a talisman. This working is used to immerse oneself within the field of a planetary intelligence. I perform this kind of rite for divination purposes, asking the planetary intelligence for advice and counsel.

2. Simple zodiacal working: This does not produce a talisman. This working is used to immerse oneself within the field of a zodiacal intelligence. I perform this kind of rite for understanding myself and knowing the times and occurrences I am living within.

3. Talismanic element with associated lunar mansion: This ritual working produces a basic talismanic artifact. It is simply the combination of a planet and element that is fused with the angelic ruler of the lunar mansion, giving it a timing factor tied to the lunar cycle.

4. Talismanic domain with associated astrological decan: This ritual working produces a complex talismanic artifact that consists of the combination of planetary ruler, zodiacal sign, and a decan quality. The resultant talismanic artifact has greater potency than a basic talisman. Thirty-six decans are more diverse than twenty-eight mansions, resulting in greater precision.

5. Talismanic sub-elemental with associated astrological septan: This ritual working produces a complex talismanic artifact. It consists of three qualities combined: the planetary ruler, zodiacal sign, and the element of the septan division. The two elements (sign and segment) combine together to produce an elemental energy field that greatly boosts the power of the talismanic artifact. The forty-eight septans are even more diverse than thirty-six decans and twenty-eight mansions, resulting in even greater precision.

Depending on your need, the amount of energized intelligence, and the precision of the application you want your talisman to possess, you would use one of the three talismanic workings, numbered three to five in the above list. The other two (items one and two) are very helpful for divination and gaining insights and good counsel.

Lunation Cycle

The full eight-node cycle of the moon is called the lunation cycle. It is symbolized on a personal level as the struggle for conscious evolution, beginning first with awakening into individual self-consciousness and egoic awareness. The moon also has two qualities expressed by the lunation cycle: the zodiacal positions it occupies as it moves across the celestial equator in a single month, and the four lunar phases it makes as it crosses the path of the sun and the earth.

The elemental quality of the four lunar phases are:

- New moon—Earth
- First quarter—Air
- Full moon—Fire
- Last quarter—Water

Four phases of the moon are defined in astrology as the specific angular relationships that occur between the Moon and the Sun. These angular relationships are broken into 90-degree quadrants. The qualities of the phases are symbolized by the aspects of *conjunction, ascending square, opposition, descending square*, arriving again at *conjunction*.

New Moon to First Quarter (0–90 degrees): individualism and impulsiveness

First Quarter to Full Moon (91–180 degrees): maturation and fulfillment

Full Moon to Last Quarter (181–270 degrees): formulation and objectification

Last Quarter to New Moon (271–360 degrees): fruition and dissolution

Lunation cycles are actually an extension of the four well-known lunar phases, producing eight types that characterize the lunar qualities. Each lunation type has specific properties, and it is extremely useful for working earth-based or celestial magic that affects the material-based concerns and enterprises for people.

The lunation cycle is called the lesser cycle of transformation because it represents the variations of the reflected power of the Sun and is far more mutable and subtle in its effects on the life cycle of the individual human being when compared to the Sun. While the solar cycle symbolizes the greater cycle of transformation (representing seasonal milestones as well as annual and multi-year achievements), the lunation cycle is critical to the resolution of deep and internal issues and complexes, as the soul strives to become individuated and self-illuminated.

In the lunation cycle, the four lunar phases are broken into eight divisions (types) consisting of 45-degree segments. Each segment of the lunation cycle lasts approximately 3.5 days or eighty-four hours. Each of the phases and types of the lunation cycle are useful for a different kind of magic. They therefore represent a different mystery in the process of individual development. Lunation types include two states of the balsamic (healing) and two of the gibbous (swelling) moons, adding four more types to the regular four phases.

Balsamic phases are defined as the ascending and descending lunar crescent that occurs just before and just after the new moon. Gibbous phases are defined as nearly full, occurring just before and just after the full moon.

Here is the table of the eight phases of the lunation cycle.[52] Looking over it, you can get a pretty good idea how to use the lunation cycle in magic and Pagan

---

52 Dane Rudhyar, *The Lunation Cycle: A Key to the Understanding of Personality* (New York: Aurora Press, 1967), 50–56. I have used the text to distill the entries in this table.

liturgy. The entire lunation cycle is used for the application of many kinds of magical operations.

Lunation Type	Interval Degrees	Keyword	Description
New	0°–45°	Emergence	Subjective, impulsive, novelty
Crescent	45°–90°	Expansion	Self-assertion, self-confidence
First quarter	90°–135°	Action	Crisis in action, strong will
Gibbous	135°–180°	Overcoming	Clarification, revelation, illumination
Full	180°–225°	Fulfillment	Objectivity, formulation, manifestation
Disseminating	225°–270°	Demonstration	Disseminator of ideas, populist, teacher
Last quarter	270°–315°	Re-orientation	Crisis in consciousness, inflexibility
Balsamic	315°–360°	Release	Transition, seed state, germination

Examining the keywords in this table reveals a powerful bell curve wherein the latent powers of the internalized subjective mind emerge on or just after the new moon and then continue to grow as the moon waxes. From emergence, to expansion, to action, then to overcoming, the lunar energy reaches a climax with the full moon, whose forces are defined by the keywords: overcoming, clarification, revelation, and inner illumination. Although the energy begins to wane, a gibbous after full moon still has power and also an important role to play. At this point, the lunation type becomes objectified and capable of communicating what has been precipitating within the unconscious mind. Next is a critical reorientation or realignment, and finally, a release where the energy fully submerges and all is once again outwardly quiet.

New magical workings typically start during or just after the new moon phase, where a type of internalization is at its point of maximum effect. From there, the lunar cycle builds up the powers and magical structures until the full moon or just before, where the power is outwardly expressed as a climactic expression of force. The resolution one might be seeking through magic is either revealed or not. After the exteriorization of all that energy is the solace of self-reflection as the powers of the subjective internalized mind sink into its source. The waning moon, particularly at the point of the balsamic type is useful for healing and divination.

There are some things to remember about using the phases and types of the lunar cycle when you work magic. Not only should you consider the astrological and astronomical environment (Sun and Moon signs), you should also consider that magic is best served when performed at the most auspicious time—timing is important. The Sun and Moon serve as indicators of whether the time is right for a given magical action or not. To unleash the most effective magic, you must establish (in a symbolic manner) the temporal snapshot of your world to determine the time and location where the magic is to be applied. In celestial magic, this temporal snapshot is called the temporal link, since it establishes the all-important event of fateful magic and helps determine the operator's destiny. Although we have covered this topic previously when reviewing the temporal model of magic, it is mentioned again here to emphasize that the temporal link encapsulates all the celestial components active at a given moment and can be expressed by an elective horoscope.

Small-scale workings (such as elemental magic) don't really require a temporal link, but I have discovered—nearly by accident—that producing a temporal link for celestial magical workings helps accomplish two important things: (1) establishing a temporal signature that will be intelligible to spirits, intelligences, and magical forces; and (2) marking a spiritual milestone and giving it a focus in the present space-time continuum. Establishing a temporal link can also be useful in defining a time limit for a given magical working to produce intended results.

The temporal link can consist of the following six elements, listed below. At the very least, it should contain the combination of the seasonal, diurnal solar aspects and the lunar phase/type. These two elements produce a symbolic expression of time. Additionally, the place (space or location) is defined as the exact point where the magic is projected into the earth (through the temple or grove).

- Solar hour as planetary hour; solar day as planetary day
- Sun in zodiacal sign—in relation to nearest equinox or solstice
- Moon in zodiacal sign—seasonal moon in relation to the four phases
- Lunation type—eight phases of the moon
- Geological matrix—latitude, longitude, altitude, and even weather conditions
- Internal domain of the practitioner—natal chart and transit chart

Of these six items, the first four are the most critical and used to determine the magical equivalent of the temporal signature or link. In order to cause material manifestations and alterations, one must first determine the temporal signature.

Chapter Eleven

DETERMINING DATES, TIMES, AND PREPARATIONS

"Time unfolds beauty, wonder, and mystery to reveal the auspicious tapestry of life."

—A. D. Posey

Once you have selected a talismanic working to perform, you will need to determine when to perform it. That can be an elaborate or simple affair depending on how much astrological data you want to analyze and whether the working would be considered a strategic, life-changing event or a simple objective. Either approach requires you to determine the date of the event based on the cycle of the moon and the planetary hour and, if feasible, the planetary day. Other considerations are specific for the lunar mansion, the decan, and the septan. You will need to consult an ephemeris to determine the correct dates and times, since the positions of the Sun and Moon in the signs would also be a factor.

Celestial magic is best performed between the times when the moon is waxing, from just after the new moon to just before the full moon, the lunation cycle from the beginning of crescent to the end of gibbous. Since the waning Moon is subject to troubling and, at times, negative factors for talismanic magic, I would avoid that lunar phase altogether when planning a working. This advice applies to all three talismanic workings, even though the moon is less strategic for a decan or a septan.

Planning a working that incorporates a lunar mansion would have to be performed when that mansion is active; that is, when the Moon is in that mansion segment of the zodiac. Since the Moon will occupy the zodiacal segment for a lunar mansion for less than a day, it becomes very important to consult a special mansion ephemeris to determine the date and period of when the mansion will be active. I can provide you with a website that has such an ephemeris of the lunar mansions that you can consult, but the best source for such a query is to have astrology application software on your computer. A mansion ephemeris can be found in the footnoted link below.[53]

The times for the positions of the moon are in Universal Time or Greenwich Mean Time-based as it is on the prime meridian. If you live on the east coast of the United States, add four or five hours (depending on whether it is daylight saving time) to that time, and an hour more for every time zone to the west. The ephemeris shows the starting time for each mansion throughout the year. The period that you would want to set the magic circle and start the ritual is from that time right up to the starting time for the next lunar mansion. That period of time might occupy a very inconvenient day or time of day or night to perform the working. Luckily, the Moon passes through a specific mansion every month, but on a different day and at a different time. You might need to delay your working until you have the optimal day and planetary hour in which to perform the working.

Determining when to perform a working for a decan or a septan can be done in a simple manner or a complex one. The simplest way of performing either of these workings is to focus on the planetary ruler of the decan or septan. You would then perform the working on the planetary day and planetary hour of the ruling planet. If there are positive aspects (a trine, sextile, or in some cases a conjunction; negative aspects are squares or oppositions) between the Sun and the planetary ruler of the decan, that timing would be auspicious.

---

53 Peter Stockinger, "Lunar Mansions Ephemeris" at *Pete Stockinger's Traditional Astrology Weblog*, accessed January 1, 2022: https://starsandstones.wordpress.com/mansions-of-the-moon/lunar-mansions-ephemeris/.

Check the day's transit aspects in a daily astrological calendar to see aspects occurring during the target date and the time of the working.

Decan and septan elections can also be established using the position of the Sun within the zodiac signs. The election would as a result become seasonal due to the Sun's passage through a sign every thirty or so days. If you wanted to work with an Aries or Taurus decan or septan, you would have to wait until the Sun moved into that specific segment of the zodiac, in March, April, or May. Even when performing a seasonal election for a decan or septan working, you would still select the planetary day and planetary hour associated with the planetary ruler and perform the working when the moon is waxing.

A more complex or comprehensive analysis of the astrological auspices would involve more steps to determine the best date and time to perform a working. After using the above criteria for determining a date based on the kind of working you were going to perform, you would include the following steps and their associated tasks. Only use what follows if you have the astrological experience and knowledge, and if you believe the working is extremely critical.

1. Generate an elective astrological chart for the date you are considering to perform the working. The time can be variable, since it would only alter the ascendant and the house configuration. You might need to choose more than one date.

2. Analyze and interpret the elective chart and then compare features of it with your natal horoscope. Notice any unusually good aspects between the two charts as well as malefic aspects.

3. If there are some serious adverse effects associated with the elective date, it would be prudent to try an alternative date. Sometimes, delaying a working just a day or two can clear up any malefic aspect that might interfere with the successful outcome.

4. Examine the solar season, time of day or night, the weather prediction for that day. Note any unusual circumstances such as meteor showers, solar or lunar eclipses, spectacular or unusual storms, the appearance of a comet, and so on.

5. Once the date and time are set for a working, it is extremely important to keep it, if possible.

The planetary days are quite simple, since they are based on the conventional names for the days of the week. Pick the planetary day based on the planetary ruler of the working you are planning to do.

Monday—Moon

Tuesday—Mars

Wednesday—Mercury

Thursday—Jupiter

Friday—Venus

Saturday—Saturn

Sunday—Sun

If you have a regular job, chances are that you will be typically occupied during the weekdays. Weeknights are an alternative for performing a working, but the preparations would require that you are free of all distractions, clear-headed, calm, and ready to work magic. What I have found is that in order to work magic without any distraction, I had to perform my working on a weekend or plan for a day off from work. That limited what days I could choose for a working; though what I found was that the planetary hours were actually more important than the planetary days.

Decan and septan work may require you to perform a working on the planetary day, but I would recommend a Saturday or Sunday if you don't have an option to take a weekday off of work. If you can perform the working on the correct planetary day, that will no doubt add to your working, but if you can't, abiding by the planetary hour on a day where you are free should be sufficient for the working.

To determine the planetary hours requires two tables: one for the day and one for the night. We should examine the planetary hours in greater detail since all celestial magic will be performed in the appropriate planetary hour.

Planetary Hours Tables

The tables of planetary hours are traditionally separated into two tables, twelve hours for the day and twelve for the night. However, because there are only equal hours of day and night during the vernal and autumnal equinoxes, the tables must be adjusted in order to be useful, especially closer to the north and south poles, where the duration of day and night are greatly affected.

There are basically two methods for adjusting the tables conform to the duration of day and night. The first method calls for the shrinking or expanding of the planetary hour to accommodate the variable duration of day to night depending on the season. This method divides the period of daylight into twelve equal partitions for the day and divides the period of night into twelve equal partitions. In this manner, there are twenty-four hours for day and night. Using this method, the period around the summer solstice will see each planetary hour during the day will exceed sixty minutes; during the night, each hour will be less than sixty minutes due to the longer duration of daylight in summer. Correspondingly, in winter each planetary hour during the night exceeds sixty minutes and each planetary hour during the day amounts to less than sixty minutes for the opposite reason. Note that the planetary hours in these examples are not the length of a true hour (i.e., sixty minutes) but are a derivation based on dividing the period of day and night by twelve.

The second method is more simplistic and direct (in my opinion), since it is based on making the hour an immutable, basic unit and uses the exact time of sunrise to determine the beginning of the first hour. All that is required from there is to progressively divide the rest of the twenty-four-hour day into twenty-four planetary hours using the time of sunrise as the starting time and ignore the division of the table into day and night. In this fashion, the hour is always sixty minutes, and the day is divided into partitions from dawn of the present day to the advent of dawn of the next day. It appears that determining the time of sunset would not be relevant to the determination of the planetary hours, for this event may now occur in the middle of a planetary hour instead of beginning a new series of twelve planetary hours for night.

I developed this second method in the early 1980s, when there weren't any applications or simple calculators to determine a planetary hour. I still use this method today because it is how I automatically approach this problem. I can do this pretty much in my head when appraising a time to perform a working. However, applications you can download or even websites that make the whole process simple to follow take care of the first method. These applications and calculators make my way of calculating the planetary hours kind of idiosyncratic, but it is the system I have followed. For the sake of simplicity, I will use the application to calculate the planetary hours in my examples in the book instead of the method I have used previously. I encourage you to check out this online application and see what you think about it.[54] It makes the whole process ridiculously quick and easy, and yes, sometimes I am a dinosaur.

A day that has been targeted for a celestial working should be partitioned into its planetary hours, with the beginning time of each planetary hour and the astrological aspects contained therein; and these may be illustrated in a table drawn up for that purpose. I typically draw up a table, use the time of sunrise to set the beginning time of the first hour, and then calculate the time for each subsequent hour, noting the time of sunset in one of the planetary hours, and any planetary aspects that might occur. I also note the phase and zodiacal sign of the Moon and the Sun as additional considerations. Using the planetary hour calculator, you would make a two-part table of the day and night and copy the planetary hour, planet, the time of day, and any transits that occur during that period into the two tables.

Here are the tables of the planetary hours by day and night. You will note that the sequence of the hours uses the Chaldean planetary order, and that the first hour of each day has the same planet as the day of the week. This is the table that I developed years ago and still use today.

Planetary Hours of the 12-Hour Day

Hr.	Sun. Sol	Mon. Luna	Tues. Mars	Wed. Mercury	Thur. Jupiter	Fri. Venus	Sat. Saturn
1st	Sol	Luna	Mars	Mercury	Jupiter	Venus	Saturn
2nd	Venus	Saturn	Sol	Luna	Mars	Mercury	Jupiter
3rd	Mercury	Jupiter	Venus	Saturn	Sol	Luna	Mars
4th	Luna	Mars	Mercury	Jupiter	Venus	Saturn	Sol
5th	Saturn	Sol	Luna	Mars	Mercury	Jupiter	Venus
6th	Jupiter	Venus	Saturn	Sol	Luna	Mars	Mercury
7th	Mars	Mercury	Jupiter	Venus	Saturn	Sol	Luna

---

54 grant@planetaryhours, *Planetary Hours Calculator* site, accessed February 27, 2022, https://planetaryhours.net/.

Hr.	Sun. Sol	Mon. Luna	Tues. Mars	Wed. Mercury	Thur. Jupiter	Fri. Venus	Sat. Saturn
8th	Sol	Luna	Mars	Mercury	Jupiter	Venus	Saturn
9th	Venus	Saturn	Sol	Luna	Mars	Mercury	Jupiter
10th	Mercury	Jupiter	Venus	Saturn	Sol	Luna	Mars
11th	Luna	Mars	Mercury	Jupiter	Venus	Saturn	Sol
12th	Saturn	Sol	Luna	Mars	Mercury	Jupiter	Venus

Planetary Hours of the 12-Hour Night

Hr.	Sun. Sol	Mon. Luna	Tues. Mars	Wed. Mercury	Thur. Jupiter	Fri. Venus	Sat. Saturn
1st	Jupiter	Venus	Saturn	Sol	Luna	Mars	Mercury
2nd	Mars	Mercury	Jupiter	Venus	Saturn	Sol	Luna
3rd	Sol	Luna	Mars	Mercury	Jupiter	Venus	Saturn
4th	Venus	Saturn	Sol	Luna	Mars	Mercury	Jupiter
5th	Mercury	Jupiter	Venus	Saturn	Sol	Luna	Mars
6th	Luna	Mars	Mercury	Jupiter	Venus	Saturn	Sol
7th	Saturn	Sol	Luna	Mars	Mercury	Jupiter	Venus
8th	Jupiter	Venus	Saturn	Sol	Luna	Mars	Mercury
9th	Mars	Mercury	Jupiter	Venus	Saturn	Sol	Luna
10th	Sol	Luna	Mars	Mercury	Jupiter	Venus	Saturn
11th	Venus	Saturn	Sol	Luna	Mars	Mercury	Jupiter
12th	Mercury	Jupiter	Venus	Saturn	Sol	Luna	Mars

After choosing the day and the time, based on the appropriate planetary selection, you should then schedule that event and perform all the preparations necessary for this working to succeed. As pointed out above, the planetary hour is the most critical item in the criteria for considering when to perform a working. You should therefore choose the best kind of working at the most optimal day and time to ensure a successful outcome.

Preparing for Celestial Magical Workings

The day and time you have selected to perform a working should be considered a special, sacred day where you are the chief priest or priestess of the liturgical and magical rites. The focus of these liturgical rites should be on the deity associated with the planetary ruler of the specific talisman you are going to charge. The entire day should be free of any concerns or actual work. Everything needed for that working should have been prepared as early as the week prior to the date of the working. Again, consider this day a kind of special holy day in order to create the expectation that you will be sequestered from outside concerns or interference.

A celestial magical working, particularly a talismanic working, begins a week before the actual date and time of the working. During those seven days, you will craft the talismanic receptor, create and consecrate the sigil for the target talismanic spirit, and make any other preparations that might be needed. The purchasing of supplies and the cleaning and ordering of the working area or temple should all be completed before the day of the working. Be sure that the groceries are put away and the cooking is completed so that you can make proper votive offerings to the planetary deity and also have a small feast for yourself after the working is completed.

As I have indicated previously, you will need a shrine altar with either a small votive statue or some kind of marker or symbolic figurine of the planetary deity positioned prominently on the shrine. Prayers and meditations will be directed to this statue or marker as if it were a representation of the deity. I discuss how to employ a shrine in *Spirit Conjuring for Witches*.[55]

An important consideration in addition to the planetary deity is to focus on the planned working from the perspective of the deity of time, or Chronos. Every celestial working has a western gateway portal that has to be defined and developed. This portal is populated by the mythic guardian, guide, and ordeal for the working. As part of your devotions to the deity of time, you

---

55 Barrabbas, *Spirit Conjuring for Witches*, 86, 159.

should qualify the guide, guardian, and ordeal you are to encounter in your celestial working.

Taking some time to define and develop these personas and defining the ordeal that you are about to undergo is a critical and important part of a celestial working. You can define a specific kind of talismanic working regarding the gateway personas or even make every working unique regarding these entities. Knowing what you are about to encounter as an ordeal is one of the first steps you will take to properly define and prepare for a celestial working.

Liturgical tasks that you will need to follow each day of the seven days before the working would consist of the following actions.

1. Light candles and burn the appropriate planetary incense.
2. Meditation directed to the planetary deity.
3. Say hymns and invocations directed to the planetary deity.
4. On the third, fifth, and final day you will perform a planetary liturgy:

    A. Votive offerings to the planetary deity—food and drink,

    B. Invocations and exhortations to the planetary deity–a kind of summoning,

    C. Godhead assumption of the planetary deity (a kind of drawing down),

    D. Communion of wine and bread (or beer and bread), and

    E. Consecration of the talismanic sigil and receptor (day 5).

5. Giving a petition to the planetary deity for the objective of the working.

On the day of the working, you will perform a kind of sun salutation or special prayer meditation for the stations of the sun at dawn, noon, and sunset, and if possible, midnight. The focus of this meditation is on the sun and its endless cycle through the portals of day and night. You should keep a clearly printed copy of the planetary hours and note the times as you pass through them. You will be observing a light half-day fast. You will also perform the last of three planetary liturgies, making it the most intensive of them all, since this will be your last opportunity to commune with the Planetary Deity before you work the talismanic rituals.

Two hours before the time of the scheduled working, take a hot bath in scented water and perform any other ablutions (i.e., brushing your teeth), and then anoint and adorn yourself with your liturgical robes with the accompanied colored stole or scarf. Begin the rite by burning the planetary incense and begin a meditation session until the appointed planetary hour.

At the appointed time, consecrate the magic circle using the traditional ritual to which you are accustomed. This action sets the moment of the event of magic and actually stops the mundane clock until the work is completed. A consecrated magic circle produces an inner world that has a different time dimension (in our minds) from the outer mundane world. Once a consecrated magic circle is set for purposes of the work, the external time has stopped. I have adopted this idea because it explains how odd and peculiar our perception of time becomes when we are in a consecrated and empowered magic circle.

We have covered how to determine what kind of talisman working to perform and when to perform it. Now we need to examine the actual rituals for each of the five proposed kinds of workings.

PLANETARY AND ZODIACAL RITUAL WORKINGS

"The Planetary Spirits are the informing spirits of
the Stars in general, and of the Planets especially.
They rule the destinies of men who are all born
under one or other of their constellations."

—H. P. Blavatsky, *The Secret
Doctrine: Volume 1*

The simplest type of working an operator can perform among these five kinds of workings is a planetary or zodiacal working. Both of these workings do not generate the kind of talismanic field needed to charge a talisman. They are instead powerful invocative rituals that can immerse the operator within the archetypal intelligence and energies of the pure planet or the zodiacal sign. These two rituals will potently impact the practitioner and they can be a source of spiritual empowerment, self-knowledge, wisdom, and instruction. When working these two rituals, the practitioner can commune with the Planetary Deity and its materialized spiritual Angel or Demigod (daemon). Those who engage the Olympian spirits will learn all of their arts and wisdom and be blessed by their great reservoir of good will and compassion. In fact, outside of producing talismanic receptors and the importance of that kind of magical work, a person could engage with the spiritual intelligence of the planet or the zodiacal sign and be greatly enriched and blessed by the experience.

However, these kinds of workings produce only a temporary state of consciousness. If someone were to invoke these benefic spirits often and at length it is likely that a form of charmed enlightenment might be produced, but it only takes one of life's many tragedies to obscure or even break that enchantment permanently. In order to seek a charmed life and truly withstand all of the dark episodes and tragedies that seem to plague human existence, it takes an external talismanic artifact constantly sending out its energies and intelligence to help us to regain our poise and luck when something has snuffed it out. The talisman perseveres where the favor and fortune of the goddesses and gods can be capricious and at times distant and seemingly unconcerned.

Still, it is important to be able to perform these workings, and they represent the best place to start working celestial magic. If you want to truly understand the nature of this kind of magic and be inspired to learn much more than you do now, invoking one of the planetary or zodiacal intelligences will probably be an ideal starting point.

Even someone as widely experienced and crusty with age as myself will find a reason to invoke one of the planets or zodiacal signs on occasion. For me, invoking one of these intelligences is quite simple and easy, so it is something I can do without much preparation. I do these invocations particularly for insights, knowledge, and inspiration. They are a profound method for performing any kind of divination, particularly since these entities are close to the earth, tied as they are to the planets and the zodiac as perceived from the earth.

In summoning a planetary intelligence, I will work with the Olympian spirit or governors. The zodiac does not have anything like the Olympian spirits, so summoning the ruling archangel or angel through the zodiacal deity is the way to go. When I am in the magic circle working rituals, I never notice much difference between Pagan demigods and angels—they seem to operate in a very similar manner. Regardless, angels and demigods are all part of our spiritual and magical cultural heritage, and we can work with them as we see fit, or not.

Now that I have properly introduced the concept of this kind of work and stated how it is to be used, I should explore with you the structure of these rituals and how they actually work.

Ritual Patterns for Planetary and Zodiacal Invocations

The ritual patterns for invoking a planetary or zodiacal intelligence are quite similar in structure, although there are two different ways to invoke a zodiacal intelligence. We will examine all three of these different but similar rituals, since they represent the divinatory backbone to the art of celestial magic. Because it only has one method, the planetary invocation is explained first.

Planetary Intelligence Invocation Rite

The ritual pattern for invoking a planetary intelligence consists of just three simple stages. The first stage is the setting of a rose ankh invoking vortex to the four watchtowers. The second stage is where the operator performs the western gateway ritual and opens the gateway into the domain of the underworld. The third stage is where the operator draws an inner circle around the central altar that holds the septagram icon, draws the invoking septagram pattern, and performs the summoning of the planetary spirit.

This rite requires a sigil drawn on parchment and consecrated before the work. The sigil parchment should consist of a sigil bearing the spirit's name and a sigil for what the operator expects from the working. Both should be drawn on the single piece of parchment.

Here is the pattern for that ritual. This ritual is performed within a fully erected and charged magic circle.

1. Using the wand, proceed to the northern watchtower, and therein draw a rose ankh before it, projecting into it a deep violet color.

2. Proceed to the western watchtower and do the same operation.

3. Proceed to the southern watchtower and do the same operation.

4. Proceed to the eastern watchtower and do the same operation.

5. Proceed to the center of the circle and do the same operation.

6. Return the wand to the altar, take the sword and proceed to the northern watchtower. Using the sword, draw a line of force from the ankh in the watchtower to the ankh in the center of the circle at the nadir.

7. Proceed to the western watchtower and do the same operation.

8. Proceed to the southern watchtower and do the same operation.

9. Proceed to the eastern watchtower and do the same operation.

10. Return the sword to the altar, and pick up the wand. Proceed to the northern watchtower. Starting from there, proceed to walk in around the circle widdershins, and slowly arc into the center of the circle, passing the northern watchtower three times, holding the wand out to push the forces to the center of the circle. Once reaching the center, push the combined powers into the nadir. The invoking vortex is now set.

11. Return the wand to the altar. Proceed to the eastern watchtower, face the west.

12. Draw invoking spirals to the southeast, northeast, and western watchtower—these positions are the guide, guardian, and ordeal, respectively—address each when drawing the invoking spiral.

13. Draw lines of force with the right hand to the western watchtower, to the northeast angle, and then back again to the southeast angle. The gateway is established.

14. Proceed to walk slowly from the east to the west, and when arriving at the west, perform the pantomime of opening the veil or a curtain with a dramatic flourish. Step close into the western watchtower and turn to face the east, performing the descending wave of energy from above the head to the feet.

15. Proceed to walk slowly from west to east, imagining you are descending into a chamber. Stop at the center, where the central altar is located.

16. Draw an inner circle around the central altar starting in the north and proceeding widdershins around the circle until ending again at the north. Retrieve the wand and the sigil from altar and proceed to the central altar, standing on the western side. Place the sigil in the center of the septagram icon.

17. Using the wand, draw the invoking pattern for the target planet on the septagram icon. Start at the point opposite the target planetary point and draw a line toward it, then continue drawing following the lines of the septagram until you reach the point just before the tar-

get, then draw the last line projecting the energy of the wand to the action. Then point the wand at the sigil and draw an invoking spiral on the septagram icon, centering on the sigil and exhaling the breath. Set the wand on the icon.

18. Intone the prepared invocation of the target planetary intelligence three times,[56] and then call its name repeatedly using a dramatic voice. Let the voice diminish in volume until it is just a whisper.

19. Sit in meditation before the center altar and internally call to the planetary intelligence until a response is sensed. Use your imagination to help enhance the experience of the planetary intelligence.

20. When the meditative communion with the planetary intelligence is completed, stand before the septagram icon, take up the wand, and draw a banishing spiral over it while giving the planetary intelligence a warm farewell and thanks for visiting.

21. Place the wand on the septagram icon, then turn around and proceed to the west. Turn again to face east.

22. Draw invoking spirals to the northwest, southwest, and eastern watchtower—these positions are the guide, guardian, and ordeal respectively. Address each when drawing the invoking spiral.

23. Draw lines of force with the right hand, from the northwest angle, to the eastern watchtower, to the southwest angle, and then back again to the northwest angle. The gateway is established.

24. Proceed to walk slowly from the west to the east, and when arriving at the east, perform the pantomime of opening the veil or a curtain with a dramatic flourish. Step close into the eastern watchtower and turn to face west, performing the descending wave of energy from above the head to the feet.

25. Proceed to walk slowly from east to the west, imagining that you are ascending out of a chamber. Stop at the center, where the central altar is located.

---

56 An example of the prepared invocation and how to write it appears on page 202.

26. Take up the wand and proceed to the eastern watchtower, and draw therein a sealing spiral. Perform this same operation to the south, west, and north. Then return the wand to the altar.

27. The ritual is completed.

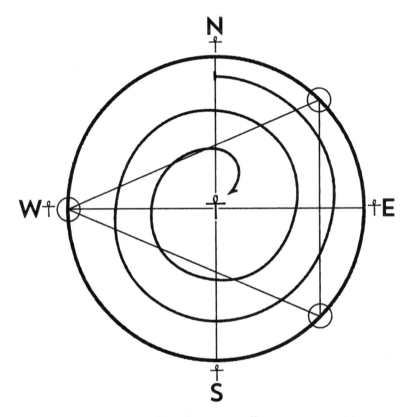

Figure 12: Diagram of the Planetary Intelligence Invocation Rite

If you have immersed yourself in the qualities and correspondences of the planetary archetype and visualized the archangel (based on the planetary colors and mythology) or the Olympian spirit, you should get some kind of response when performing this ritual. As stated in the ritual directions, let your imagination help you enhance and embellish the experience. I would also recommend using some appropriate music in the background to help set the mood.

If the experience you have is barely perceptible or nothing happens at all, I would examine all the steps you used to both prepare and perform this rite.

There might be something interfering with your ability to open up and be suggestible to the experience. The best approach is to perform this ritual often for each planet until the experience is quite intense and profound. This will be good practice for when you start considering to work with the more complex type of celestial workings. If you can successfully perform this rite, you will likely be successful with more complex workings.

Zodiacal Intelligence Invocation Rite

As has been already stated, the zodiacal intelligence invocation rite is very similar to the planetary invocation rite except for one variance based on whether you feel the need to construct a zodiacal dodecagram icon or believe such a tool is not necessary for your planned working. While the dodecagram icon can be handy and useful, it won't be used for the three talismanic workings. There are therefore two methods to invoke one of the signs of the zodiac: one uses the dodecagram icon and the other uses the pylon of base element and lesser hexagram of quality to define the zodiacal sign. Either approach produces the desired results.

Similar to the planetary intelligence invocation rite, the zodiacal intelligence invocation rite has three parts. The first part establishes the invoking vortex to the four watchtowers. The second part fashions a western gateway portal into the underworld domain of the magic circle, and the third part is where the operator sets an inner magic circle and uses the dodecagram to invoke the zodiacal intelligence *or* the operator erects a pylon pyramid to the four angles and the zenith point in the center of the circle. Setting an invoking pentagram at the base of the pylon, and a lesser hexagram of the quality of the sign (cardinal, fixed, or mutable) will appropriately define the zodiacal sign. These pylons are set within the magic circle in a deosil direction so that a positive energy field is established. Once the pylons are set and joined to form the pyramid, the operator will draw an inner circle, stand within it, and summon the zodiacal intelligence.

This rite requires a sigil drawn on parchment and consecrated before the work. The sigil parchment should bear a sigil of the spirit's name and a sigil for what the operator expects from the working.

Here is the ritual pattern that uses the dodecagram icon. This ritual is performed within a fully erected and charged magic circle.

1. Using the wand, proceed to the northern watchtower, and therein draw a rose ankh before it, projecting into it a deep violet color.

2. Proceed to the western watchtower and do the same operation.

3. Proceed to the southern watchtower and do the same operation.

4. Proceed to the eastern watchtower and do the same operation.

5. Proceed to the center of the circle and do the same operation.

6. Return the wand to the altar. Take the sword and proceed to the northern watchtower. Using the sword, draw a line of force from the ankh in the watchtower to the ankh in the center of the circle at the nadir.

7. Proceed to the western watchtower and do the same operation.

8. Proceed to the southern watchtower and do the same operation.

9. Proceed to the eastern watchtower and do the same operation

10. Return the sword to the altar, and pick up the wand. Proceed to the northern watchtower. Starting from there, proceed to walk around the circle widdershins, slowly arcing into the center of the circle, passing the northern watchtower three times, and holding the wand out to push the forces to the center of the circle. Once you have reached the center, push the combined powers into the nadir. The invoking vortex is now set.

11. Return the wand to the altar. Proceed to the eastern watchtower and face west.

12. Draw invoking spirals to the southeast, northeast, and western watchtower—these positions are the guide, guardian, and ordeal respectively. Address each when drawing the invoking spiral.

13. Draw lines of force with the right hand from the southeast angle, to the western watchtower, to the northeast angle, and then back again to the southeast angle. The gateway is established.

14. Proceed to walk slowly from the east to the west. Upon arriving at the west, perform the pantomime of opening the veil or a curtain with a dramatic flourish. Step close into the western watchtower and turn to face the east, performing the descending wave of energy from above the head to the feet.

15. Proceed to walk slowly from west to east, imagining you are descending into a chamber. Stop at the center, where the central altar is located.

16. Draw an inner circle around the central altar, starting in the north and proceeding widdershins around the circle until ending again at the north. Retrieve the wand and the sigil from the altar and proceed to the central altar, standing on the western side. Place the sigil in the center of the dodecagram icon.

17. Using the wand, draw the invoking pattern for the target sign on the dodecagram icon. Start at the point opposite the target zodiacal sign point and draw a line toward it, then continue drawing following the lines of the dodecagram until you reach the point just before the target, then draw the last line projecting the energy of the wand to the action. Next, point the wand at the sigil and then draw an invoking spiral on the dodecagram icon while centering on the sigil and exhaling. Set the wand on the icon.

18. Intone the prepared invocation of the target zodiacal intelligence three times[57], and then call its name repeatedly using a dramatic voice. Let the voice diminish in volume until it is just a whisper.

19. Sit in meditation before the center altar and internally call to the zodiacal intelligence until a response is sensed. Use your imagination to help enhance the experience of the planetary intelligence.

20. When the meditative communion with the zodiacal intelligence is completed, then stand before the dodecagram icon and take up the wand and draw a banishing spiral over it, and give the zodiacal intelligence a warm farewell and thanks for visiting.

21. Place the wand on the dodecagram icon, and then turn around and proceed to the west. Turn again to face east.

22. Draw invoking spirals to the northwest, southwest, and then the eastern watchtower—these positions are the guide, guardian, and ordeal respectively. Address each when drawing the invoking spiral.

---

57 An example of the prepared invocation and how to write it appears on page 202.

23. Draw lines of force with the right hand, from the northwest angle, to the eastern watchtower, to the southwest angle, and then back again to the northwest angle. The gateway is established.

24. Proceed to walk slowly from the west to the east. After arriving at the east, perform the pantomime of opening the veil or a curtain with a dramatic flourish. Step close into the eastern watchtower and turn to face west, performing the descending wave of energy from above the head to the feet.

25. Proceed to walk slowly from east to the west, imagining ascending out of a chamber—stop at the center, where the central altar is located.

26. Take up the wand and proceed to the eastern watchtower. Draw therein a sealing spiral. Perform this same operation to the south, west, and north. Return the wand to the altar.

27. The ritual is completed.

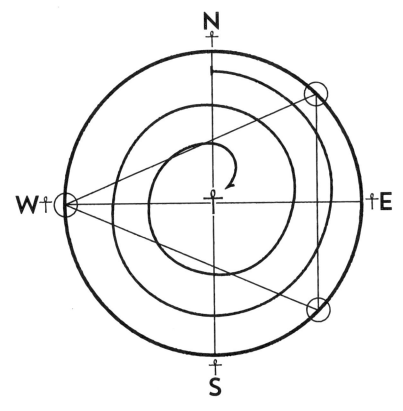

Figure 13: Diagram of the Zodiacal Intelligence Invocation Rite 1

Zodiacal Intelligence Invocation Rite 2

This ritual uses the Pylon Pyramid and is performed within a fully erected and charged magic circle.

1. Using the wand, proceed to the northern watchtower, and therein draw a rose ankh before it, projecting into it a deep violet color.

2. Proceed to the western watchtower and do the same operation.

3. Proceed to the southern watchtower and do the same operation.

4. Proceed to the eastern watchtower and do the same operation.

5. Proceed to the center of the circle and do the same operation.

6. Return the wand to the altar, take the sword and proceed to the northern watchtower. Using the sword, draw a line of force from the ankh in the watchtower to the ankh in the center of the circle at the nadir.

7. Proceed to the western watchtower and do the same operation.

8. Proceed to the southern watchtower and do the same operation.

9. Proceed to the eastern watchtower and do the same operation.

10. Return the sword to the altar, and pick up the wand. Proceed to the northern watchtower. Starting from there, proceed to walk in around the circle widdershins, and slowly arc into the center of the circle, passing the northern watchtower three times, and holding the wand out to push the forces to the center of the circle. Once reaching the center, push the combined powers into the nadir. The invoking vortex is now set.

11. Return the wand to the altar. Proceed to the eastern watchtower and face west.

12. Draw invoking spirals to the southeast, northeast, and western watchtower—these positions are the guide, guardian, and ordeal respectively. Address each when drawing the invoking spiral.

13. Draw lines of force with the right hand, from the southeast angle, to the western watchtower, to the northeast angle, and then back again to the southeast angle. The gateway is established.

14. Proceed to walk slowly from the east to west. After arriving at the west, perform the pantomime of opening the veil or a curtain with a dramatic flourish. Step close into the western watchtower and turn to face east, performing the descending wave of energy from above the head to the feet.

15. Proceed to walk slowly from west to the east, imagining descending into a chamber—stop at the center, where the central altar is located.

16. Proceed to the altar and take up the wand. Then proceed to the southeastern angle, bow before it and then draw an invoking pentagram of the element associated with the zodiacal sign at the base, and then well above it draw a lesser hexagram of the quality of the

sign. Then draw the two ends together with a narrow invoking spiral that creates the pylon. The pylon is now set at the angle.

17. Proceed to the southwestern angle, bow before it and then do the same operation. The pylon is now set at the angle.

18. Proceed to the northwestern angle, bow before it and then do the same operation. The pylon is now set at the angle.

19. Proceed to the northeastern angle, bow before it and then do the same operation. The pylon is now set at the angle.

20. Proceed to the center of the circle, bow before it, and then do the same operation. The pylon is now set at the center.

21. Proceed to the altar, return the wand, and take up the sword. Proceed to the southeastern angle and with the sword, draw a line from the pylon in the southeastern angle to the center of the circle at the zenith.

22. Draw a line with the sword from the pylon in the southwestern angle to the center of the circle at the zenith point of the pylon.

23. Draw a line with the sword from the pylon in the northwestern angle to the center of the circle at the zenith point of the pylon.

24. Draw a line with the sword from the pylon in the northeastern angle to the center of the circle at the zenith point of the pylon.

25. Draw a line with the sword from the southeastern angle to the southwestern angle.

26. Draw a line with the sword from the southwestern angle to the northwestern angle.

27. Draw a line with the sword from the northwestern angle to the northeastern angle.

28. Draw a line with the sword from the northeastern angle to the southeastern angle, then return the sword to the altar. The pyramid is now constructed.

29. Draw an inner circle around the central altar, starting in the north and proceeding widdershins around the circle until ending again at the north. Retrieve the wand and the sigil from altar and proceed to

the central altar, standing on the western side. Place the sigil in the center of the central altar. Then draw an invoking spiral around the sigil. Place the wand on the central altar. While standing before it, begin the invocation.

30. Intone the prepared invocation of the target zodiacal intelligence three times,[58] and then call its name repeatedly with a dramatic voice. Let your voice diminish in volume until it is just a whisper.

31. Sit in meditation before the center altar and internally call to the zodiacal intelligence until a response is sensed. Use your imagination to help enhance the experience of the planetary intelligence.

32. When the meditative communion with the zodiacal intelligence is completed, then stand before the central altar and take up the wand and draw a banishing spiral over it, and give the zodiacal intelligence a warm farewell and thanks for visiting.

33. Place the wand on the dodecagram icon. Turn around and proceed to the west, and turn again to face east.

34. Draw invoking spirals to the northwest, southwest, and eastern watchtower—these positions are the guide, guardian, and ordeal respectively. Address each when drawing the invoking spiral.

35. Draw lines of force with the right hand, from the northwest angle, to the eastern watchtower, to the southwest angle, and then back again to the northwest angle. The gateway is established.

36. Proceed to walk slowly from the west to the east, and when arriving at the east, perform the pantomime of opening the veil or a curtain with a dramatic flourish. Step close into the eastern watchtower and turn to face west, performing the descending wave of energy from above the head to the feet.

37. Proceed to walk slowly from east to west, imagining ascending out of a chamber. Stop at the center, where the central altar is located.

---

58 An example of the prepared invocation and how to write it will be shown in the example below.

38. Take up the wand and proceed to the eastern watchtower and draw therein a sealing spiral. Perform this same operation to the south, west, and north. Return the wand to the altar.

39. The ritual is completed.

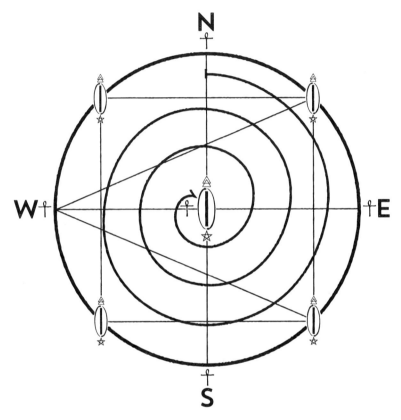

Figure 14: Diagram of the Zodiacal Intelligence Invocation Rite 2

Similar to the planetary intelligence invocation rite, the intensity of the experience will be based on the degree to which the operator is immersed into the correspondences and qualities of the zodiacal sign. Since there is nothing like the Olympian spirits associated with the signs of the zodiac, the operator will be calling and summoning the archangel and angel of the sign, perhaps with the corresponding ruling angel of the associated house anchoring the working in the material world.

Example: Invocation of the Planetary Intelligence of Jupiter

Now that we have gone over the ritual patterns for the planetary intelligence and the zodiacal intelligence invocation, I would be negligent if I didn't supply at least one example of how to apply the ritual pattern to a specific working.

Preparations for any working—but especially a celestial one—consist of the following five steps:

1. Determine the working's purpose and focus. It is a good idea to narrowly and succinctly define what it is you wish to accomplish. You should be able to clearly state what the objective of the working is going to be.

2. Select an appropriate date and time, working with the various restrictions associated with the particular celestial target that you wish to manifest. You will need to juggle the variables of date and time with the auspiciousness of the event, its strategic value, or importance to you, in addition to what is convenient versus what is optimal.

3. Create a sigil that properly and powerfully symbolizes the purpose of the operation. The sigil parchment should be consecrated in a magic circle before it can be used in a ritual.

4. Develop the ritual components needed to customize the working so you can readily perform it for a specific target intelligence. This would include the following tasks:

   A. Write up a short and succinct invocation for the target spiritual intelligence in which you name the hierarchy and the authority through whom you are able to summon it. That hierarchy, of course, starts with the archetypal planetary deity you will be worshiping on your shrine.

   B. Get the names of all of the spirits associated with the spiritual hierarchy. Using an alphabet wheel, construct a sigil for each one.[59] If any of the spirits already have a traditional seal or char-

---

59 Barrabbas, *Spirit Conjuring*, 116–123.

acter, use that. These sigils will be drawn on the parchment sigil used to invoke the target spirit.

5. Once the above tasks are completed, start the preparations for the working a week before it is scheduled (covered in chapter 11).

The example I have chosen invokes the planetary intelligence of Jupiter because it is the most benign, friendly, and helpful of the planetary intelligences. If you ever need fatherly advice, optimism, exuberance, and just plain good luck, Jupiter is the planet you can invoke for that and more.

Perhaps the least likely planetary intelligence to invoke would be Saturn, although when it comes to seeking justice and settling scores with your adversaries in a completely fair and karma-free manner, Saturn would be the logical choice. Yet for an introduction to this kind of magic, Jupiter is an excellent choice. That said, *all* the planetary intelligences are useful and important for some tasks.

Here is a hypothetical situation in which you might invoke Jupiter. Suppose you have a job you don't like but you keep doing because it pays the bills. You have put together a resume and have started to look for a new job but haven't gotten any return calls to the several job applications you have sent out. A few other things have happened to you recently that have made your job search seem hopeless and discouraging. You need something inspiring to change your life's equation at the present time; perhaps the planetary intelligence of Jupiter can help you.

What will make a big difference in your search is a change in your attitude—after all, no one will consider hiring you if you are discouraged and feeling negatively about yourself. For your first task, you will need to craft a sigil that encapsulates your desire.[60] After some considerations, you have come up with a short sentence that encapsulates what you need at the moment. That sentence would look something like this:

"I need exuberance and good luck to help me find a job."

---

60 Barrabbas, *Elemental Powers*, 121–131.

As part of the method for crafting a sigil, you just need to identify the key-words for this change and apply that to the reduction process in the making of a sigil. Eliminate all the words except for a few that get to the heart of the objective.

"Exuberance & good luck"

Then, through the process of redundant letter elimination, you would get the following letters.

EXUBRANC&GODLK

Using that collection of letters, reduce them down to the basic shapes—from that you will produce an effective sigil. Here is my example of the final two steps. You should also add the seal for the Olympian Spirit of Jupiter, whose name is Bethor, and the symbol for the planet of Jupiter. (The Olympian Spirit Seals are in chapter 4, page 69.)

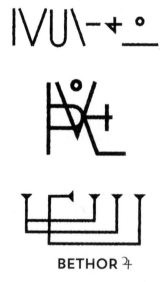

BETHOR ♃

Figure 15: Sigils of Jupiter

You now have a proper sigil and a clear objective for the working. The next thing you need to do is determine the date and time of the working.

For a planetary invocation, you will want to use both the planetary hour and planetary day to lock in the qualities of that planet. This invocation should be planned for a Thursday and for the third or tenth hour of the night, depending on how you divide up the planetary hours. That means that the working could be early or late in the evening depending on the time of the year. (The tables of Planetary Hours for Day and Night are found in chapter 11, pages 176–177.)

You can perform the working during the day if you wish for the first hour of dawn or the eighth hour in the early afternoon. Whatever time you choose, you will need some time for preparation, so be sure to incorporate it in your planning.

Although I might have spent a bit of time calculating the hours in my head, you can consult the online planetary calculator and come up with the exact planetary hours associated with the twelve hours of the day and the twelve of night. The calculator determines the time of dawn for the first hour based on geographic location and establishes the proportionate planetary hours. There is no estimation, and everything is exact. I wish I had this application when performing a lot of magical workings back in the 1980s and 90s. I will certainly use it in the future.

Here are the planetary hour tables by day and night for the date of December 9, 2021, in Richmond, Virginia.

Planetary Hours by Day for December 9, 2021— Proportionate Hour Calculation

Planetary Hour	Starting Time EST for 12/9	Planetary Ruler for Thursday	Celestial Event
1st	7:14 AM	Jupiter	Sunrise
2nd	8:02 AM	Mars	
3rd	8:50 AM	Sol	Moon enters Pisces
4th	9:38 AM	Venus	
5th	10:27 AM	Mercury	
6th	11:15 AM	Luna	
7th	12:03 PM	Saturn	
8th	12:51 PM	Jupiter	
9th	1:39 PM	Mars	
10th	2:27 PM	Sol	
11th	3:16 PM	Venus	
12th	4:04 PM	Mercury	Sunset 4:52 PM

Table of Planetary Hours by Night for December 9, 2021— Proportionate Hour Calculation

Planetary Hour	Starting Time EST for 12/9	Planetary Ruler for Thursday	Celestial Event
1st	4:52 PM	Luna	
2nd	6:04 PM	Saturn	
3rd	7:16 PM	Jupiter	Time of working
4th	8:28 PM	Mars	
5th	9:40 PM	Sol	
6th	10:51 PM	Venus	
7th	0:03 AM	Mercury	
8th	1:15 AM	Luna	
9th	2:27 AM	Saturn	
10th	3:29 AM	Jupiter	
11th	4:51 PM	Mars	
12th	6:042 PM	Sol	Sunrise 7:13 AM

If you wanted to perform the Jupiter invocation during the day then you would have the times of 7:14 a.m. and 12:51 p.m. in which to perform it. For the Jupiter planetary hours of night, the third hour of night would start at 7:16 p.m. and the tenth hour would start at 3:29 a.m. the next morning. Probably the best time would be to perform the rite at 7:16 p.m. during the third planetary hour of the night. The ritual doesn't take long to perform, so doing a ritual at that time would be quite feasible, even if you have to work the day of the rite and the next day, which would be Friday. You would have time after work to prepare for the ritual working, so that time would be feasible and also optimal, depending on the planetary transits occurring for that day.

Once you have chosen a time for the working, check your Daily Planetary Guide for any adverse transits affecting Jupiter. Considering how benevolent Jupiter is, it would have to be a very bad aspect to negatively impact the working. However, malefic aspects of Jupiter do exist, so you should check your guide and then look up the transit aspects to check on them. If you want to be really thorough, check the transit position of Jupiter against your own natal chart to see if there are any negative aspects lurking there. Use your best judgment, but it is my opinion that this kind of basic working is less affected by transit aspects than workings that produce a talisman artifact.

According to the Daily Planetary Guide, there is very little transit activity occurring for December 9, 2021. The Moon enters Pisces during the third planetary hour; the other two aspects occur before sunrise early in the morning. Moon in Pisces is auspicious for actions affecting the emotions, since during this period the emotions are easily contacted and open to inquiries. The Moon is also in the crescent lunation type, just a day before the first quarter, which will aid self-confidence for an undertaking.

There is a conjunction between the Moon and Jupiter at 3:53 a.m., and the Moon squares Mars in Scorpio at 5:00 a.m. According to Robert Hand, in his *Planets in Transit: Life Cycles for Living*, the Moon conjunct Jupiter in Aquarius would give you a boost in self-confidence that you might need for achieving the best results for this working, making it a positive indicator for doing this working.[61] The other aspect is Moon square Mars in Scorpio, which would advise you to beware of irritability or arguments during the day.[62] If you have to work that day then you should keep yourself calm and not allow yourself to react in a negative emotional way to any events that might occur.

Overall, it would seem that the auspices for working a Jupiter planetary invocation on this day are quite excellent, and there would be no need to have to look for another date and time. Now that you have the objective, a crafted sigil, and the date and time, what you need to do next is research the spiritual hierarchy for Jupiter, examining just the planetary intelligence. The only spirits in the hierarchy are your archetypal planetary deity and the Olympian spirit named Bethor. You have this covered on your parchment sigil, so you can move on to the next step which is to write a proper invocation.

What you want to do when writing an invocation is name the spirit, summon that spirit, give the authority through which you are doing this summoning, and give some of the qualities or image associated with that target spirit. You don't want to write a long and elaborate or overly flowery speech for your invocation. You want to write something that is brief, succinct, dramatic, and powerful. Here is a template that you can use to write an invocation:

---

61 Robert Hand, *Planets in Transit*, 113.

62 Ibid, 111.

I summon you to manifest and appear before me, O Spirit X, in the name of [planetary deity] whom I worship as my god[dess]. You are the spirit of [identify spirit type and function] whose qualities are [give a few qualities], and who answers to the spiritual authorities [list the spiritual hierarchy in descending order]. I call, summon, and invoke you, O Spirit X, on this date and planetary hour, to come before me and manifest your virtues, intelligence, and powers.

The invocation of Bethor for a planetary invocation would look like this:

I summon you to manifest and appear before me, O Spirit Bethor, in the name of Zeus whom I worship as my God. You are the spirit of the Olympians whose qualities are self-exaltation, provider of treasures earthly and spiritual, great healer, and who answers to the spiritual authorities Zeus, God of the planet of Jupiter. I call, summon, and invoke you, O Spirit Bethor, on this date and planetary hour, to come before me and manifest your virtues, intelligence, and powers.

The image of Bethor as a robust, dark, bearded man wearing white brocaded robes and golden turban would be something you would study and memorize, but you would not have to mention it unless you felt it prudent to do so. (See the table of the Olympian spirits and their qualities, in chapter 4, page 67.)

You now have the objective, the parchment sigil, and the date and time. You have determined that the auspices are good, researched the spiritual hierarchy, and written up a simple invocation for Bethor. You have covered all the tasks that you needed to perform, and a week before the working (or slightly less for just a planetary invocation and if you need to perform it quickly), you can perform the preparations for working. Finally, on the given date and time, do the working.

I would recommend taking the ritual pattern in this chapter for the planetary invocation and put it into a document and then embellish it by inserting the name of the Olympian Spirit. Print out a copy of the ritual, study it, and then practice it. You can write out the invocation on a piece of paper or even parchment and take it with you into the magic circle. I would keep it somewhere on or close to the central altar.

We have covered everything you would need to know to work a planetary or zodiacal invocation. While this might be the simplest type of celestial magic you could perform, it has all the elements needed to perform the more complicated rites for invoking the talismanic elemental, the decan and septan talismanic intelligences. Let us move forward and examine these rites, since they would be used to generate a talisman artifact or sacrament—the real reason for working celestial magic.

Chapter Thirteen

TALISMANIC MAGIC USING THE LUNAR MANSIONS

"All shadows of clouds the sun cannot hide
like the moon cannot stop oceanic tide;
but a hidden star can still be smiling
at night's black spell on darkness, beguiling"

—Munia Khan

The basic talismanic elemental, tied to its associated lunar mansion, is the real workhorse for talismanic magic. The rituals used to generate the field of the talismanic intelligence and to apply it to a talismanic receptor are easy to use and simplistic in their design. What makes this process more complex than a simple planetary or zodiacal invocation is the necessity of the timing and the requirements for a talismanic receptor.

The whole purpose to this ritual working is to produce the talismanic artifact, whether it is perishable or imperishable. It will take a bit of craft and some time to create the talisman, particularly if it is metal and unique to the magical objective. I have already discussed where you can get metal stock, tools, and other items in the introduction, in addition to how to construct a talisman in chapter 9, but the main point is that the artifact doesn't have to look pretty in order to work properly. I will discuss how to use a talisman in everyday magic in chapter 16.

The ritual working consists of two rituals: the first is used to invoke the planetary intelligence within the talismanic field, and the second is used to focus, charge, and bless the talisman receptor with that talismanic field. These two rituals are always performed together to produce the talismanic artifact.

In order to make use of the lunar mansion, the operator should deliberately perform the working during the time when the lunar mansion is active, and to make this part of their intention when forging the talisman. The other link to the mansion in this rite is the ruling planet.

Invocation of the Talismanic Elemental Ritual

Talismanic elementals are a fusion of an element and a planet, so there is a level in the ritual where each of these two actions are performed. Add in the invoking vortex, the western gateway, and the inner circle, and you have the four stages of this ritual working. Let me explain these four stages of the ritual in greater detail.

First, the operator erects a pylon pyramid to the four watchtowers and the center of the circle. This is accomplished through drawing an invoking pentagram of the target element in the base of the pylon and a lesser invoking hexagram of the quality of the zodiacal sign associated with the lunar mansion at the top of the pylon. This is done at all four watchtowers and the center of the circle with connecting lines to form the pyramid and a deosil circumambulation to wind up and compress the energy field. The energy field is imprinted with the zodiacal sign associated with the lunar mansion, helping to establish the temporal link for the working.

Second, the operator will erect an invoking vortex using the rose ankh device and set that to the four angles and the nadir. The rose ankh devices set in the angles are drawn to the center of the circle with a widdershins circumambulation to form the invoking vortex. The combination of element pylon pyramid and the rose ankh invoking vortex will function as the foundation for the working.

The third step is where the operator will establish a western gateway portal using the western watchtower and the southeast and southwest angles to form the gateway triangle. He or she will then descend down into the underworld domain of the magic circle and arrive at the central altar. This is the place or domain where the talismanic working will be performed.

The fourth and final step is where an inner circle is drawn around the central altar, after which the operator will stand before it where the septagram icon is set up and the talisman is placed along with the consecrated sigil in its center. Then the operator will draw the angular invoking pattern of the ruling planet on the septagram, draw an invoking spiral, and place the charge into the sigil talisman construct. Finally, the operator will intone the specially written invocation of the talismanic planetary intelligence three times and then summon the entity to appear.

Performed in sequence, these four steps will generate an element field imbued with the zodiacal signature and magnetized by an invoking vortex; the western gateway and the inner circle will fuse this foundation with the invocation of the planetary intelligence. The end product is a sentient energy field aligned with a specific lunar mansion thanks to the astrological attributes of the Moon at that moment, which will make the mansion fully active. This sentient field is quite powerful, and the operator will want to commune with it for a short time before moving on to the next phase of this ritual working.

Here is the pattern for the ritual to invoke a talismanic elemental with its associated lunar mansion. This ritual is performed within a fully erected and charged magic circle.

1. Take up the wand from the altar and proceed to the eastern watchtower. Facing east, draw an invoking pentagram of the target element to the base, and above it, a lesser hexagram of the zodiacal quality. Then join the two points together with a narrow invoking spiral, creating a pylon with the zodiacal sign signature.

2. Proceed to the southern watchtower. Facing the south, do the same operation.

3. Proceed to the western watchtower. Facing the west, do the same operation.

4. Proceed to the northern watchtower. Facing the north, do the same operation.

5. Proceed to the center of the circle. Facing the center, do the same operation.

6. Return the wand to the altar and pick up the sword. Proceed to the eastern watchtower. With the sword, draw the pylon residing there to the pylon in the center of the circle at the zenith point.

7. Proceed to the southern watchtower. With the sword, draw the pylon residing there to the pylon in the center of the circle at the zenith point.

8. Proceed to the western watchtower, and do the same operation.

9. Proceed to the northern watchtower, and do the same operation.

10. Proceed to the eastern watchtower and draw a line on the floor from the east to south, then the south to the west, then the west to the north, and then a line to the east.

11. Return the sword to the altar. Take up the staff and proceed to the eastern watchtower. Begin a circumambulation starting from the east and proceeding deosil around the circle with a spiral arc toward the center of the circle, passing the eastern watchtower three times and entering the center of the circle. Place the staff before the center altar and imagine the energy field fully activated within the circle. Then return the staff to the altar and pick up the wand.

12. Using the wand, proceed to the northwestern angle, and therein draw a rose ankh before it, projecting into it a deep violet color.

13. Proceed to the southwestern angle, and do the same operation.

14. Proceed to the southeastern angle, and do the same operation.

15. Proceed to the northeastern angle, and do the same operation.

16. Proceed to the center of the circle to the nadir, and do the same operation.

17. Return the wand to the altar, take the sword and proceed to the northwestern angle. Using the sword, draw a line of force from the ankh in the angle to the ankh in the center of the circle at the nadir.

18. Proceed to the southwestern angle, and do the same operation.

19. Proceed to the southeastern angle, and do the same operation.

20. Proceed to the northeastern angle, and do the same operation.

21. Return the sword to the altar. Pick up the wand and proceed to the northwestern angle. Starting from there, proceed to walk around the circle widdershins. Slowly arc into the center of the circle, passing the northwestern angle three times, holding the wand out to push the forces to the center of the circle. Once reaching the center, push the combined powers into the nadir. The invoking vortex is now set.

22. Return the wand to the altar. Proceed to the eastern watchtower, face the west.

23. Draw invoking spirals to the southeast, northeast, and western watchtower—these positions are the guide, guardian, and ordeal respectively[63]—address each when drawing the invoking spiral.

24. Draw lines of force with the right hand from the southeast angle, to the western watchtower, to the northeast angle, and then back again to the southeast angle. The gateway is established.

25. Proceed to walk slowly from east to west. When arriving at the west, pantomime opening the veil or a curtain with a dramatic flourish. Step close into the western watchtower and turn to face east, performing the descending wave of energy from above the head to the feet.

26. Proceed to walk slowly from west to the east, imagining descending into a chamber. Stop at the center, where the central altar is located.

27. Draw an inner circle around the central altar, starting in the north and proceeding widdershins around the circle until ending again at the north. Retrieve the wand, sigil, and talisman from the altar and proceed to the central altar, standing on the western side. Place the talisman with the sigil over it in the center of the septagram icon.

28. Using the wand, draw the invoking pattern for the target planet on the septagram icon. Start at the point opposite the target planetary point and draw a line toward it, then continue drawing following the

63 In chapter 5, I discussed the lintel god and the need to qualify the guardian, guide, and ordeal for a gateway passage as part of the liturgical preparations. I recommend that you think about the process that you are about to undergo and define these three attributes in your mind. Further explanation appears in the example that follows.

lines of the septagram until you reach the point just before the target, then draw the last line projecting the energy of the wand to the action. Then point the wand at the sigil, and then draw an invoking spiral on the septagram icon, centering on the sigil and exhaling the breath. Set the wand on the icon.

29. Intone the prepared invocation of the target talismanic intelligence three times, and then call its name repeatedly using a dramatic voice. Let the voice diminish in volume until it is just a whisper. State the hierarchical combination of zodiacal sign spirit (archangel), Olympic spirit, and mansion name as the authorities for summoning the zodiacal intelligence of the lunar mansion.

30. Sit in meditation before the center altar and internally call to the talismanic intelligence until a response is sensed. Use the imagination to help enhance the experience of the talismanic intelligence.

Perform the **Stellar Vortex for Talismanic Charging** rite as follows:

31. Standing at the central altar facing east with the wand in hand, draw a great inverted pentagram of creative spirit in the zenith point.

32. Then step one step away from the central altar, facing the southeast, with the wand draw a lesser hexagram of union (earth) to the southeastern angle. Draw a line of force with the wand from the hexagram to the sigil talisman in the center of the septagram icon.

33. Turn to face the southwest, do the same operation.

34. Turn to face the northwest, do the same operation.

35. Turn to fact the northeast, do the same operation.

36. Step toward the central altar and stand again before it. Draw an inverted invoking pentagram of receptive spirit upon the sigil talisman construct. Summon the name of the target spirit three times, and imagine it taking shape within the inverted pentagram in the zenith.

37. Take the wand and slowly draw a line of force from the great inverted pentagram in the zenith down to the inverted penta-

gram-charged sigil talisman construct, imagining the forceful descent of the intelligence and energy descending into the talisman. Exhale as this action is taken, then bow before the central altar. Remain kneeling before it for a few moments.

38. Once this action is completed, then stand again, and take a pouch placed nearby and take up the sigil and wrap the talisman with it and place both into a pouch and set it on the septagram icon.

Continue with the Talismanic Elemental Invocation rite

39. Sit in meditation for a short time before continuing with the next step of the talismanic invocation ritual

40. When the meditative communion with the talismanic intelligence is complete, stand before the septagram icon and take up the wand. Draw a banishing spiral over it and give the talismanic intelligence a warm farewell and thanks for visiting.

41. Place the wand on the septagram icon, and then turn around and proceed to the west then turn again to face east.

42. Draw invoking spirals to the northwest, southwest, and eastern watchtower—these positions are the guide, guardian, and ordeal respectively. Address each when drawing the invoking spiral.

43. Draw lines of force with the right hand, from the northwest angle, to the eastern watchtower, to the southwest angle, and then back again to the northwest angle. The gateway is established.

44. Walk slowly from west to east. After arriving at the east, perform the pantomime of opening the veil or a curtain with a dramatic flourish. Step close into the eastern watchtower and turn to face west, performing the descending wave of energy from above the head to the feet.

45. Proceed to walk slowly from east to the west, imagining ascending out of a chamber—stop at the center, where the central altar is located.

46. Take up the wand and proceed to the eastern watchtower and with the wand, draw therein a sealing spiral. Do the same to the southeast,

south, southwest, west, northwest, north, and northeast. Return the wand to the altar.

47. The vortex is sealed and the ritual is completed.

48. Take the charged and covered talisman and put it in a dark place for seventy-two hours.

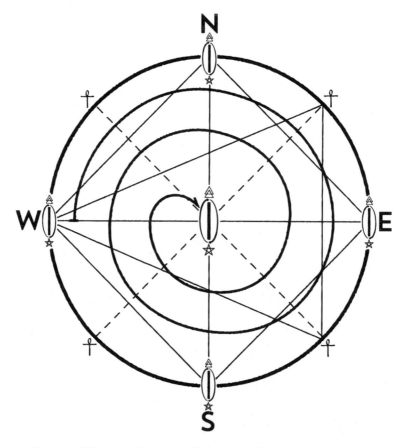

Figure 16: Diagram of the Invocation of the Talismanic Elemental Rite

Examining the many steps for this ritual might make it appear to be long and complicated, but once it is mastered, it doesn't really take very long to perform, and the stages flow from one into the other in a logical and graceful manner. Whenever you seek to learn a new ritual, especially one with a lot of steps, you will need to break it into parts that you practice and then reassemble. I could show you where you could add some verbiage to your own custom version of this ritual, but I believe it is essential to keep this ritual simple so it can be easily performed from memory.

Stellar Vortex for Talismanic Charging Ritual

A second ritual in this working is employed to project the sentient field generated through the talismanic elemental and focus it into the sigil talisman construct and thereby fully charge and bless it. The sentient field will enter the talisman and reside there forever. Its power and the radius of its effects will wax and wane based primarily on the mansions of the Moon in addition to the care and attention its owner gives it. A talisman can go dormant after a long period of neglect, but it is never completely extinguished and can always be brought back to full power by giving it votive offerings and focusing the mind on it for a period of a few hours.

I have included this ritual as part of the talismanic ritual above, but I wanted to discuss the ritual pattern separately to help clarify how it works. It is, in fact, the very step that takes the talismanic field and projects it into the talisman artifact. I felt that it should be included in the full ritual pattern because it is never performed separately without also performing the talismanic rite. It also has a specific ritual pattern I wanted to show in a diagram instead of including it in the talismanic ritual pattern diagram.

This ritual consists of three simple steps that are performed once the talismanic sentient field is fully active and can be felt by the operator. The first step is where the operator sets a great inverted pentagram of creative spirit in the zenith point above the central altar. Then, the operator will set the lesser hexagram of earth (as the sign of union) to the four angles in a deosil arc. They will draw these four hexagrams to the sigil-talisman construct.

Standing before the center altar, the operator will draw an inverted pentagram of receptive spirit on the sigil-talisman construct, and then draw the power of the inverted pentagram in the zenith to the inverted pentagram upon the construct. That last action will be done with all the energy that the operator possesses, and they will powerfully exhale all of their breath. The talisman is now fully charged. The operator will wrap the sigil around the talisman and place it in a cloth pouch where it will incubate for a full three days before it can be used.

Here is the ritual pattern used to charge and bless a talisman receptor.

1. Standing at the central altar, facing east with the wand in hand, draw a great inverted pentagram of creative spirit in the zenith point.

2. Take one step away from the central altar, face southeast, and with the wand draw a lesser hexagram of union (earth) to the southeastern angle. Draw a line of force with the wand from the hexagram to the sigil talisman in the center of the septagram icon.

3. Turn to face the southwest, do the same operation.

4. Turn to face the northwest, do the same operation.

5. Turn to fact the northeast, do the same operation.

6. Step toward the central altar, standing again before it. Draw an inverted invoking pentagram of receptive spirit upon the sigil talisman construct. Summon the name of the target spirit three times, and imagine it taking shape within the inverted pentagram in the zenith.

7. Take the wand and slowly draw a line of force from the great inverted pentagram in the zenith down to the inverted pentagram-charged sigil talisman construct, imagining the forceful descent of the intelligence and energy descending into the talisman. Exhale the breath as this action is taken, then bow before the central altar. Remain kneeling before it for a few moments.

8. Once this action is completed, stand again and take a pouch placed nearby. Take up the sigil and wrap the talisman with it and place both into a pouch and set it on the septagram icon.

9. Sit in meditation for a short time before continuing with the next step of the talismanic invocation ritual.

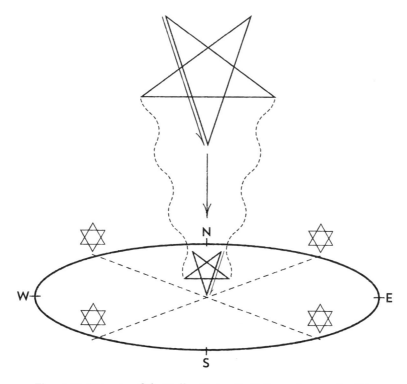

Figure 17: Diagram of the Stellar Vortex for Talismanic Charging Rite

As you can see, this is not an overly complex sequence of ritual actions. This is a ritual working that a nominally experienced Witch or Pagan will not have any difficulty mastering. It is important to actually see each step of this magical working in an outline, so I have presented it here as well as in the actual working.

Example: Talismanic Elemental Venus of Water

Now that we have covered the ritual patterns for performing the invocation of a talismanic elemental and the talismanic charging rite, I felt that it would be a good idea to present one example. I do not wish to overly embellish this ritual; it is performed as it is in the ritual pattern. The exception is the written invocation for the specific talismanic elemental and the timing. The ritual will have to be performed during the day or night of the month when the lunar mansion is active and also fit in with the planetary hours and day, if possible. A sigil and a talisman are required for this working.

We covered the five steps required for assembling the materials needed to perform a celestial magical working in the previous chapter. These steps are somewhat modified generating a talisman artifact, but the five steps are pretty much the same.

1. Determine the purpose and focus of the working. It is a good idea to narrowly and succinctly define what it is you wish to accomplish. You should be able to clearly answer the question about what the objective of the working is going to be.

2. Select an appropriate date and time, working with the various restrictions associated with the particular celestial target that you wish to manifest. You will need to juggle the variables of date and time with the auspiciousness of the event, its strategic value or importance to you, and what is convenient versus what is optimal. (This is more challenging for a lunar mansion.)

3. Create a sigil that properly and powerfully symbolizes the operation's purpose. If you are performing a rite to charge a talisman, you will need to craft a metallic talisman etched with some of the same symbols and signs that the parchment sigil possesses. The sigil parchment and the metallic talisman should be consecrated in a magic circle before they can be used in a ritual.

4. Develop the ritual components needed to customize the working so you can readily perform it for a specific target planetary talisman. This would include the following tasks:

   A. Write a short and succinct invocation for the target spiritual intelligence: Name the hierarchy and authority through whom you are able to summon it. That hierarchy, of course, starts with the archetypal planetary deity you will be worshiping on your shrine.

   B. Get the names of all of the spirits associated with the spiritual hierarchy. Using an alphabet wheel, construct a sigil for each one. If any of the spirits already have a traditional seal or character, use that. These sigils will be drawn on the parchment sigil used to invoke the target spirit.

5. Once the above tasks are completed then a week before the scheduled working, you should start the preparations for the working (covered in last section of chapter 12).

I have chosen the talismanic elemental, Venus of Water, because it characterizes that high-minded kind of love and mutual caring that is the basis for a long-term relationship. The talisman artifact may be chosen with a very specific objective in mind, but once set with a specific set of qualities, a talisman will continue to work and have its effect on the relationships of bearer. Where the pure planet and element combination does indicate passion and even sexual love, it is tempered by the lunar mansion, shifting it somewhat to a higher and more idealistic quality. Needless to say, this is the talisman to use if you want to draw people to you, especially lovers and long-term partners. It is the "Love Potion Number 9" of talismanic characteristics.

To state the obvious, a hypothetical use for this talisman artifact is to change a person's social equation and help to make them more popular and charming so as to draw people to them. It has the properties of fixing and healing a damaged relationship, drawing possible lovers and friends, or making a business relationship more stable. It does all of these things and more; once activated, it will continue to operate on the possessor of the artifact indefinitely. Even if things are going nicely now in your life as far as relationships are concerned, this talisman will help you keep them that way. As a talismanic jewel in your treasure box, it can always be useful to someone at some time.

We need to clearly define the purpose of this working and the talisman that it produces, and craft a sigil that we can use to perform the ritual and also brand the metallic talisman. Perhaps the most simple and iconic statement would be something like this:

"Help me to be loved."

You can omit the "me" because it is redundant, as is the verb determiner "to be" and you are left with: "Help loved."

To craft a sigil for this objective, you would go through this four-step process:

HELP LOVED

HELPOVD

In the final two steps, you reduce the form down to the non-repeating letter shapes and the final sigil formulation. Here is my example of how this sigil would look:

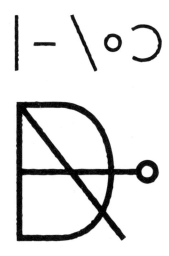

Figure 18: Diagram of Sigil Shapes and Sigil Form for "Help Loved"

So, now you have a basic sigil functioning as the intent and link for this working. You will need some other items to add to it in order for it to be fully representative of a talismanic elemental associated with a lunar mansion.

The components for the lunar mansion are the sign of the element and the seal of the Olympian spirit (the seals are found in chapter 4, on page 69). You also have the name of the mansion and the name of the ruling angel as found in chapter 6, pages 98–107, which can be expressed as a name-based sigil using one of the alphabetic wheels (found in appendix 1). These four components will be drawn on the parchment along with the sigil of the magical objective, totaling five in all.

You can include all five of the symbolic signs on the metallic talisman or omit the sigil of the objective since the talisman will, over the course of its long life, be used to fulfill many objectives. Although the talisman cannot function outside its basic definition, it does allow for a great deal of possibilities. If you include the sigil of the magical objective, you can always change it later (and I will show you how in chapter 16).

Olympian Spirit of Venus: Hagith

Element: Water

Mansion Angelic Ruler: Egibiel

Mansion Name: Al Qalib—the heart of the scorpion—Scorpio 8 degrees, 34 minutes

Here is the sigil objective and the four symbolic signs of the mansion qualities. I used the Hebrew alphabet wheel for both the angelic ruler and name of the mansion.

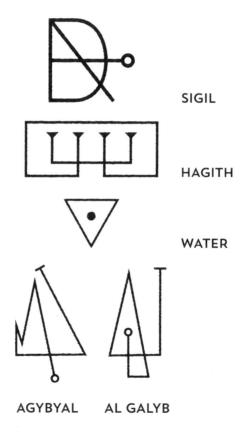

SIGIL

HAGITH

WATER

AGYBYAL   AL GALYB

Figure 19: Diagram of Sigil Objective and Four Components of the Talismanic Elemental

219

For this working, I would use a green-turquoise-colored ink to write the signs and sigils on the parchment. The metallic talisman should be made of copper to properly represent the metal associated with Venus, so etching it with the signs and sigils should not be difficult. You will need to consecrate both the sigil and the talisman before performing the working.

The gateway portal crossing will require some thought as to the ordeal that a talismanic field of Venus of Water will produce. I would say that the ordeal is learning to be lovable and having the ability to love someone with dignity and respect. The guide is there to teach you to listen and be compassionate, and the guardian is there to challenge your motivations. You would consider these attributes when making the gate crossing into the underworld and arising from the underworld into the daylight world. Upon your return, you would affirm that they are fully acknowledged.

The next thing that you will need to do is to pick a date and time to do this working. Since this talisman is basically a love spell, the optimal day would be a Friday and the optimal time would be the hour of Venus. The first thing that you need to do is to consult a lunar mansion ephemeris to determine when the mansion Al Qalib is active, and then when the moon is waxing. This will limit such an occurrence to a specific season. I had to look over the entire online lunar mansion ephemeris for 2021 to find a Friday when the moon was waxing and that specific lunar mansion was active. [64]

If I were going to perform this working on a Friday for the year 2021, I would have to do it in the month of September in order to capture when that lunar mansion is occurring during the waxing moon but before it is full. Checking the online ephemeris for September, I found the following entry for 8 degrees of Scorpio. Since this entry only shows the starting time of the lunar mansion, I will need the next one in sequence to know when the ending time would be. This will inform me about the duration of that specific lunar mansion.

Here is the entry I have found for September, both for the lunar mansion and the next one in sequence:

18 08 SC 34" 17' 10 Sep 2021 AD GC 8:29:02 PM
19 21 SC 25" 40' 11 Sep 2021 AD GC 6:06:47 PM

---

64 Stockinger, "Lunar Mansions Ephemeris," accessed January 1, 2022: https://starsandstones
.wordpress.com/mansions-of-the-moon/lunar-mansions-ephemeris/

These two entries indicate that the lunar mansion Al Qalib, or Scorpio 8 degrees, 34 minutes, starts at 4:29:02 p.m. EDT on September 10, and ends on September 11 at 2:06:47 p.m. The times are basically GMT (now called UTC), which is four hours ahead of my timezone in Richmond, factoring for Daylight Saving Time. The numbers eighteen and nineteen represent the eighteenth and nineteenth lunar mansions out of twenty-eight. That would indicate to me that if I want to generate this talisman in September on a Friday before the full Moon, it would have to be done on this date.

There would be plenty of time after 4:29 p.m. EDT to perform this ritual working during the evening. In order to determine the optimal date for this working, I have to check my Daily Planetary Guide and look for a date when the Moon is in Scorpio before the full Moon phase. For this lunar mansion and using the waxing Moon, the period of availability is limited to approximately six months. The other six months occurs during the waning Moon and would be subject to the inversion of the mansion properties, making it more like a curse than a benefit.

Building a table for the talismanic mansion working planetary hours based on the online planetary hour calculator, the sunrise on Friday, September 10 is at 6:49 a.m. EDT and the sunset at 7:27 p.m. EDT. The planetary hours governed by Venus for a Friday are the first and eighth hour of the day, in addition to the third and tenth hour of the night. The third hour of the night ruled by Venus would start at 9:20 p.m. EDT, making that the optimal time for the planned working.

Checking the auspices for September 10, there are a number of transit entries for this day. The most significant of these transits are Venus conjunct the Moon early in the morning in the sign of Libra, the Moon entering into the sign of Scorpio at 2:05 a.m., Venus entering Scorpio at 4:39 p.m., and the Moon squaring Saturn in Libra at 2:53 p.m. The rest of the aspects are not very significant. Venus entering into Scorpio is the sign of its detriment yet would give the talismanic intelligence of the lunar mansion a bit more of a sexual intensity that, because of the other factors in the working (particularly the lunar mansion qualities), would not cause the working to be malefic.

The Moon in Scorpio would also make the talisman more passionate and sexual, so it would seem that the talisman would be more likely to produce ardent lovers than business partners. The conjunction of Moon and Venus in

Libra occurs early in the morning, but it would have a positive impact on the working. The phase of the Moon is the crescent lunation type, which is symbolized by expansion and self-assertion, making it a positive lunar phase for this working.

Overall, this working will be quite successful based on the astrological determinants for the day of September 10. It will be performed during the day and hour of Venus, and will be aligned to the lunar mansion of Al Qalib. There are some possible negative transit aspects that could push this working in the direction of a more sexual quality, but if the intention of the operator as indicated by the sigil objective is above board, the talisman would be less likely to be used to seduce someone against their will. That said, the possibility and risk are there, and this is the only Friday that would feature this lunar mansion; the risk must be taken and care must be made such that the intention for the talisman and its powers is constructive and positive.

Now that we have the objective defined, the sigil parchment and metallic talisman constructed, and an elected date and time with overall good auspices, we need to determine the spiritual hierarchy and write up an invocation for the working for the planetary talisman of Venus of Water.

First of all, the hierarchy for a lunar mansion consists of just the name of the mansion, the zodiacal sign, and the angelic ruler. However, there is also the archetypal planetary deity for Venus, the Olympian spirit, and the basic element. Additionally, you could also use the archangel associated with the zodiacal sign to refine the definition of this entity. While I have also listed the Enochian seniors, I think I will stay away from using them in my workings because their use involves engaging with Enochian magic, which is not within the scope of this book.

Hierarchy for Al Qalib—Venus of Water—Heart of the Scorpion— In Descending Order

Archetypal Deity: Aphrodite—Goddess of Beauty and Love

Olympian Spirit: Hagith

Zodiacal Archangel: Barchiel (Scorpio—Fixed Water)

Mansion Name: Al Qalib

Mansion Angelic Ruler: Egibiel

The invocation would read something like this:

> I summon you to manifest and appear before me, O Spirit Egibiel, in the name of Aphrodite whom I worship as my goddess. You are the spirit of the lunar mansions whose qualities are passion, love, friendship, appreciation of beauty, diplomacy, and compassion, and who answers to the spiritual authorities of Aphrodite, goddess of the planet of Venus; Hagith, Olympian spirit of Venus; Barchiel, archangel of Scorpio; and the lunar mansion called Al Qalib. I summon, call, and invoke you, O Spirit Egibiel, on this date and planetary hour, to come before me and manifest your virtues, intelligence, and powers. I beseech you, O Spirit, to help me in the affairs of the heart between consenting adults so that I may love and be loved in return.

You will notice that I added the primary objective at the end of the invocation, telling Egibiel what I want it to help me accomplish. This sets the intention and the limits to the operation of the resultant talisman so its use will not violate the wills or desires of others. This statement represents the ethical use of the talisman, therefore ensuring that the more blatant sexuality of the auspices will be melded into good intentions and honorable decorum.

The image associated with the lunar mansion of Al Qalib is a blue-green serpent holding its tail about its head. You can readily memorize that image and visualize it when summoning the angelic ruler of the lunar mansion.

As you can see, we now have all of the components needed for the invocation of the talismanic elemental Venus of Water with the lunar mansion Al Qalib, the heart of the scorpion. The only thing left to do is write up the ritual using the pattern presented above and then develop it specifically for the talismanic elemental working. The invocation is written on a piece of paper or parchment and conveniently placed near the center altar. I would recommend studying and practicing the ritual with the few inserted names until it is committed to memory. A week before the scheduled date, begin the preparations as outlined in chapter 12.

Chapter Fourteen

TALISMANIC MAGIC USING THE DECANS

"All the heavenly Bodies, the Stars and Planets, are regulated with the utmost Wisdom! And can we suppose less Care to be taken in the Order of the moral than in the natural System?"

–Benjamin Franklin

The ritual used to invoke the angelic ruler of the decan is very similar to the basic talismanic elemental invocation. The exception is that the emphasis is more on the zodiacal sign and its particular segment rather than the ruling planet and the element. Facilitating the representation of the zodiacal sign and its decan segment uses the three-point pylon device. Additionally, one of the thirty-six tarot pip cards associated with the decan is chosen as its magical or telesmatic image.

A zodiacal sign consists of the element (the triplicity) as represented by the invoking pentagram, the quality of the sign as represented by the lesser hexagram (as cardinal, fixed, and mutable) and the decan segment represented also by the lesser hexagram (as ascendant, succedent, and cadent decan parts). Whereas the two-point pylon for a zodiacal sign has the invoking pentagram at

225

its base and a lesser hexagram at its top, the three-point pylon uses the middle point to define the decan segment part, which is where the second lesser hexagram is drawn. The three-part pylon defines the specific element and qualities of the decan segment of a zodiacal sign. Here is an example of the three-part pylon depicting the cadent decan of the sign of Virgo:

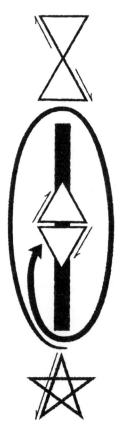

Figure 20: Diagram Showing the Three-Point Pylon

In addition to the three-part pylon, which would represent the energy field of the talismanic component, it is also necessary to represent the spiritual hierarchy of the zodiacal sign and the house associated with the sign. To integrate the spirits of the sign and house into this working, I will summon the archangel, the ruling angel of the sign, and the ruling angel of the house. This summoning will be done at the three points of the western gateway that is a basic and necessary part of all of the talismanic workings. The invocation consists of just calling the name of the angels. These angels will assume the guise of the symbolic guide (ruler of the house), guardian (ruler of the sign), and ordeal (archangel) of the gateway ritual structure in the working.

The reason I had to integrate the archangel and ruling angel of the zodiacal sign along with the associated angelic house ruler was to have three spirits associated with the three gateway points. If the decan occurs in the sign of Aries, then the archangel and ruling angel of Aries would be selected along with the ruling angel of the first house. There is no astrological necessity for including the ruling angel of the house except to fill out the number of angels used to qualify the gateway. I had crafted this ritual long before I knew as much about astrology as I do now, but it doesn't impinge on the ritual design to mix the sign with its associated house. You can find these angels listed in the zodiacal tables in chapter 5, in the table for Basic Zodiacal Qualities, on page 85.

These two additional ritual components are innovations that distinguish a talismanic working using the decan instead of the lunar mansion and talismanic elemental. The other difference is that the timing for a decan working is more generous than the narrow window of the lunar mansion. If you are seeking to perform a major strategic change in your life, waiting for the correct seasonal ten-day period for the astrological decan would be appropriate. Otherwise, you only need to plan for the working to coincide with the planetary hour and possibly the planetary day for the associated planetary ruler of the decan. Checking if that day and hour have positive or negative transit aspects would also be an important factor for validating the auspices for the date and time.

Like the invocation of the talismanic elemental, the invocation of the decan has four basic stages: erecting and setting an energy pyramid consisting of the three-part pylon that defines the decan segment of the zodiacal sign, the setting of a rose ankh invoking vortex, the opening of the western gateway portal, and the setting of an inner circle where a septagram is drawn for the planetary invocation and the invocation of the ruling angel of the decan is intoned. You could substitute an Egyptian decan godhead for the ruling angel if that is more to your liking. Similarly, the talismanic receptor and a parchment sigil are used together to define the function of the talisman, and the stellar vortex is used to charge and bless it, representing a common ritual action in all talismanic workings.

Since we have already discussed the structure and nature of the talismanic elemental invocation, we can go directly to showing the ritual structure for the decan talismanic invocation and then explain the notable differences.

Invocation of the Talismanic Decan Ritual

Here is the pattern for the ritual to invoke a talismanic decan. This ritual is performed within a fully erected and charged magic circle.

1. Take up the wand from the altar and proceed to the eastern watchtower. Facing the east, draw an invoking pentagram of the target element to the base, and above it, a lesser hexagram of the zodiacal quality. In the midpoint, draw a lesser hexagram for the quality of the decan. Join the three points together with a narrow invoking spiral, creating a pylon with the zodiacal sign and decan signature.[65]

2. Proceed to the southern watchtower. Facing the south, do the same operation.

3. Proceed to the western watchtower. Facing the west, do the same operation.

4. Proceed to the northern watchtower. Facing the north, do the same operation.

5. Proceed to the center of the circle. Facing the center, do the same operation.

6. Return the wand to the altar and pick up the sword. Proceed to the eastern watchtower, and with the sword draw the pylon residing there to the pylon in the center of the circle at the zenith point.

7. Proceed to the southern watchtower, and do the same operation.

8. Proceed to the western watchtower, and do the same operation.

9. Proceed to the northern watchtower, and do the same operation.

---

65 For the lesser hexagram associated with the sign quality and the decan quality, see chapter 9, page 144. The two qualities use the same lesser hexagram structure, but would likely be different when applied to a specific zodiacal sign and to a decan quality.

10. Proceed to the eastern watchtower and draw a line on the floor from the east to south, then the south to the west, then the west to the north, and then a line to the east.

11. Return the sword to the altar. Take up the staff and proceed to the eastern watchtower. Begin a circumambulation starting from the east and proceeding deosil around the circle with a spiral arc toward the center of the circle, passing the eastern watchtower three times and entering the center of the circle. Place the staff before the center altar and imagine the energy field fully activated within the circle. Return the staff to the altar and pick up the wand.

12. Using the wand, proceed to the northwestern angle, and therein draw a rose ankh before it, projecting into it a deep violet color.

13. Proceed to the southwestern angle, and do the same operation.

14. Proceed to the southeastern angle, and do the same operation.

15. Proceed to the northeastern angle, and do the same operation.

16. Proceed to the center of the circle at the nadir, and do the same operation.

17. Return the wand to the altar, take the sword and proceed to the northwestern angle. Using the sword, draw a line of force from the ankh in the watchtower to the ankh in the center of the circle at the nadir.

18. Proceed to the southwestern angle, and do the same operation.

19. Proceed to the southeastern angle, and do the same operation.

20. Proceed to the eastern watchtower, and do the same operation.

21. Return the sword to the altar, and pick up the wand. Proceed to the northwestern angle and, starting from there, proceed to walk in around the circle widdershins and slowly arc into the center of the circle, passing the northwestern angle three times and holding the wand out to push the forces to the center of the circle. Once reaching the center, push the combined powers into the nadir. The invoking vortex is now set.

22. Return the wand to the altar. Proceed to the eastern watchtower, face west.

23. Draw invoking spirals to the southeast, northeast, and then the western watchtower—these positions are the guide, guardian, and ordeal respectively. Address each when drawing the invoking spiral.

24. To the southeast, point the wand and call the name of the angelic ruler of the house, then point the wand to the northeast and call the name of the angelic ruler of the zodiacal sign, then point to west and call the name of the archangel of the zodiacal sign.

25. Draw lines of force with the right hand, from the southeast angle, to the western watchtower, to the northeast angle, and then back again to the southeast angle. The gateway is established.

26. Proceed to walk slowly from the east to the west, and when arriving at the west, perform the pantomime of opening the veil or a curtain with a dramatic flourish. Step close into the western watchtower and turn to face the east, performing the descending wave of energy from above the head to the feet.

27. Proceed to walk slowly from west to the east, imagining descending into a chamber—stop at the center, where the central altar is located.

28. Draw an inner circle around the central altar, starting in the north and proceeding widdershins around the circle until ending again at the north. Retrieve the wand, tarot card, sigil, and talisman from the altar and proceed to the central altar, standing on the western side. Place the talisman with the sigil over it in the center of the septagram icon. Place the tarot card to side where it is visible but not overlaying the icon.

29. Using the wand, draw the invoking pattern for the target ruling planet on the septagram icon. Start at the point opposite the target planetary point and draw a line toward it, then continue drawing following the lines of the septagram until you reach the point just before the target, then draw the last line projecting the energy of the wand to the action. Then point the wand at the sigil, and then draw an invoking spiral on the septagram icon, centering on the sigil and exhaling the breath. Then set the wand on the icon. Focus on the tarot card and briefly imagine oneself within it.

30. Intone the prepared invocation of the target decan ruler three times, and then call its name repeatedly, with a dramatic voice. Let the voice diminish in volume until it is just a whisper. State the hierarchical combination of zodiacal sign spirit (archangel), Olympic spirit, and decan ruler name as the authorities for summoning the zodiacal intelligence of the decan.

31. Sit in meditation before the center altar and internally call to the decan ruler until a response is sensed. Use the imagination to help enhance the experience of the decan intelligence.

Perform the **Stellar Vortex for Talismanic Charging** *rite in the following steps:*

32. Standing at the central altar, facing the east, with the wand in hand, draw a great inverted pentagram of creative spirit in the zenith point.

33. Then step one step away from the central altar, facing the southeast, with the wand draw a lesser hexagram of union (earth) to the southeastern angle. Draw a line of force with the wand from the hexagram to the sigil talisman in the center of the septagram icon.

34. Turn to face the southwest, with the wand do the same operation.

35. Turn to face the northwest, with the wand do the same operation.

36. Turn to fact the northeast, with the wand do the same operation.

37. Then step toward the central altar, standing again before it. Draw an inverted invoking pentagram of receptive spirit upon the sigil talisman construct. Summon the name of the decan ruler three times and imagine it taking shape within the inverted pentagram in the zenith.

38. Take the wand and slowly draw a line of force from the great inverted pentagram in the zenith down to the inverted pentagram-charged sigil talisman construct, imagining the forceful descent of intelligence and energy descending into the talisman. Exhale the breath as this action is taken, then bow before the central altar. Remain kneeling before it for a few moments.

39. Once this action is completed, stand again, take the pouch placed nearby and the sigil. Wrap the talisman and place both into a pouch and set it on the septagram icon.

40. Sit in meditation for a short time before continuing with the next step of the talismanic invocation ritual.

Continue with the decan talisman rite

41. When the meditative communion with the decan talismanic intelligence is completed, then stand before the septagram icon, take up the wand, and draw a banishing spiral over it, and give the decan talismanic intelligence a warm farewell and thanks for visiting.

42. Place the wand on the septagram icon, and then turn around and proceed to the west then turn again to fact the east.

43. Draw invoking spirals to the northwest, southwest, and then the eastern watchtower—these positions are the guide, guardian, and ordeal respectively. Address each when drawing the invoking spiral. (These will be the ordinary themes, not the angels.)[66]

44. Draw lines of force with the right hand from the northwest angle, to the eastern watchtower, to the southwest angle, and then back again to the northwest angle. The gateway is established.

45. Proceed to walk slowly from the west to the east, and when arriving at the east, perform the pantomime of opening the veil or a curtain with a dramatic flourish. Step close into the eastern watchtower and turn to face the west, performing the descending wave of energy from above the head to the feet.

46. Proceed to walk slowly from east to the west, imagining ascending out of a chamber. Stop at the center, where the central altar is located.

47. Take up the wand and proceed to the eastern watchtower and with the wand, draw therein a sealing spiral. Do the same to the southeast,

---

66 These themes will be represented by a resolution of the lesson learned, the challenge overcome and the ordeal accomplished.

south, southwest, west, northwest, north, and northeast. Return the wand to the altar.

48. The vortex is sealed and the ritual is completed.

49. Take the charged and covered talisman and put it in a dark place for seventy-two hours.

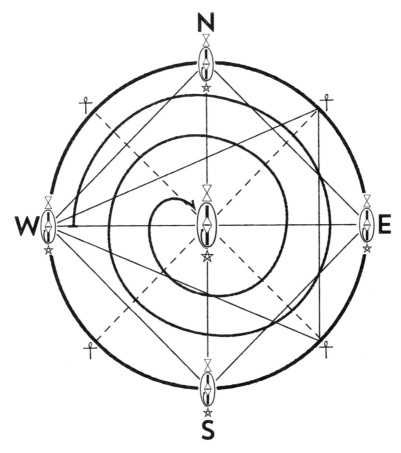

Figure 21: Diagram of the Invocation of the Talismanic Decan Rite

The invocation of the talismanic decan uses the three-point pylon to generate the proper energy field for the talismanic intelligence to manifest. In addition, adding the angels of the sign and house to the three nodes of the western gateway makes that portal a kind of stellar gateway, which is most auspicious for a decan working. The tarot pip card acts as the symbolic imagery of the decan and sets the ground or domain for the target spirit. Instead of just twenty-eight possibilities, the operator has thirty-six to work with, and the tarot card image sets the tone of the working.

The combination of the decan talismanic invocation rite and the stellar vortex talismanic charging rite will produce a fully charged, blessed, and imbued talisman artifact. So with only a few strategic modifications, the operator can invoke a decan talismanic intelligence and charge a talisman with its powers and spiritual wisdom. This is not an overly complex working, particularly since this working represents, along with the septan rite, the most complex ritual structure presented in the book. I found this ritual pattern easy to memorize and to work, after a little bit of practice. I don't doubt that the average experienced Witch or Pagan will have any difficulty working this and other rites in this book.

Example: Decan Invocation Rite for Mashephar/ Semtet 20°–30° of Virgo–10 of Pentacles

We have covered the ritual structures and pattern for invoking a decan ruler and charging a talisman, so now it is important to show an example of how such a working would be performed. Since we looked at an aspect of love for the talismanic elemental, I thought that presenting a decan invocation to assist with material wealth might be a good working that you would undoubtedly like to see. In my many years of teaching and working with students, I have found that love, money, and career achievements appear to trump everything else, so that would be what someone typically would want to see in a magical working—and who am I to disappoint the expectations of my readers?

Similar to the planetary invocation and the talismanic elemental invocation, the decan invocation requires five steps to identify and assemble the required components for performing this kind of working. We can follow them since they will guide us in determining what is needed to perform a talismanic working using one of the thirty-six decans. However, we don't need to repeat them since they are listed in full in chapters 12 and 13.

I have chosen a specific decan that would help you to gain a kind of comprehensive material fulfillment over time. That is the basic nature of the decan for 20°–30° of Virgo, and symbolized by the 10 of Pentacles. Just examining the image of this tarot card in the Smith-Waite tarot deck will readily show what it can do for the possessor of a talisman artifact charged and blessed with the power and intelligence of this decan. Pages 121–130 in chapter 7 feature the list of decans with the associated tarot images.

Now the first thing anyone would have to understand is that this is the kind of talisman that produces long-term material wealth and wellbeing. It is not used for short-term material gain, so it is better used by the possessor over decades than attempting to use it for anything short-term. I believe that what every Witch or Pagan could use is a powerful charm that will help steer and guide them to long-term success, wealth, and good health.

This talisman successfully manages those kinds of outcomes, but not immediately. It will also not prevent the possessor from doing stupid things with their money, or getting robbed, cheated, or deceived. However, it can help mitigate loss and misfortune over a period of years and decades. Having this talisman will ensure that you will ultimately be successful. That should make it a valuable talismanic jewel amongst one's collection of such jewels.

What I need to do is to define exactly what I intend to do with this decan talismanic artifact. Like the other workings, I will need to define my object in a clear and concise manner. Let me start this process out by writing a simple sentence that will fully encapsulate my intention. We will produce a sigil in four steps.

"I seek a long, productive and prosperous life, with good health and material wealth."

That is the long and comprehensive version, but it should be shortened down to just the essentials:

"Long Life, Good Health, Wealth."

Now we have just the words that describe the essence of the objective. The next step is to take that succinct statement and collect the nonrepeating letters, giving us this set of letters:

LONGIFEDHATW

In the final two steps, we reduce the form down to the nonrepeating letter shapes and use them to create the final sigil formulation. Here is my example of how this sigil would look:

Figure 22: Diagram of Sigil Shapes and Sigil Form for
"Long Life, Good Health, Wealth"

Now you have a basic sigil functioning as the intent and link for this working. You will need some other items to add to it in order for it to be fully representative of a talismanic intelligence associated with an astrological decan.

Defining a decan requires a few symbolic components and a hierarchy of spirits. The symbolic component consists of the base element of the sign, the quadruplicity of the sign, and the quadruplicity of the specific decan. The spiritual hierarchy would be the archetypal deity of the planetary ruler, the Olympian spirit of the ruling planet, the archangel of the zodiacal sign, the angelic ruler of the zodiacal sign, the angelic ruler of the house, and finally, the angelic ruler of the decan. You could use the Egyptian demigod of the decan, but using the angelic ruler fits better with the rest of the hierarchy. So, for the invocation of the 20°–30° decan of Virgo would contain the following specific spirits of the hierarchy.

Archetypal Deity: Hermes: God of Mercantile transactions, communication, and psychopomps

Olympian Spirit: Ophiel

Archangel of Virgo: Hamaliel

Ruling Angel of Virgo: Shelathiel

Ruling Angel of the VI House: Ziel

Ruling Angel of the Decan: Meshephar

The Olympian spirit attributes and seals are found in chapter 4, on pages 69–70; the zodiacal angels and decan ruling angel are found in chapter 5 on page 85, and in chapter 7 on pages 121–130, respectively. Since the sixth house is the house associated with Virgo, that is the ruling angel of the house we will select. With this, we have three angels associated with the underworld gateway.

In addition to the parchment sigil, you would also use the Hebrew alphabet wheel (located in appendix 1) to derive the name sigils for the four angelic names and use the seal for the Olympian spirit. These drawings should be added to the sigil parchment so that the objective is joined with the specific spirit-hierarchy definition of the decan. Here is what it would look like with the six components:

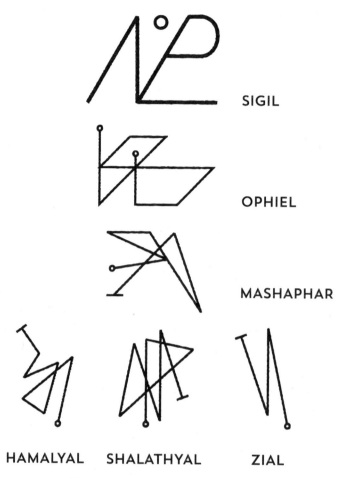

SIGIL

OPHIEL

MASHAPHAR

HAMALYAL   SHALATHYAL   ZIAL

Figure 23: Diagram of Sigil Objective and
Six Components of the Decan Talisman

When crafting the metallic talisman, you would use the same set of sigils and seals as used on the parchment sigil, perhaps with exception to the sigil of the objective. Since this is a working where Mercury is the ruling planet, the metal used to create the talisman would be aluminum, a suitable and much safer alternative to the metal mercury or the mineral cinnabar.

Now that we have the objective defined, the object sigil designed, the angelic name sigils designed, the six components assembled for the parchment sigil, and the metallic talisman, we will need to determine an auspicious date and time to perform this working.

Picking a date and time is not as difficult as it is with the lunar mansion. The best date for working the 20°–30° decan of Virgo would be when the Sun is in that particular decan, which falls in the middle of September. Since the planetary ruler is Mercury, we should choose a time that would be during the hour of Mercury. However, the day of Mercury is Wednesday, which would be a difficult date to arrange a working. Because we are working with a material wealth-based spell, we can perform the working on a Saturday, because Saturn is auspicious for the kind of objective that we are seeking. So, let us pick a date when the Sun is passing through the cadent decan of Virgo. According to our handy ephemeris in our Daily Planetary Guide, the days when the Sun is passing through 20° to 30° in Virgo are September 14 through September 23. The ideal date would be September 18, a Saturday. That day is just two days before the full Moon and just before the autumnal equinox.

We can check the date on the online planetary hour calculator for Richmond, Virginia, and come up with the following times. On September 18, the sun rises at 6:54 a.m. EDT and sets at 7:14 p.m. EDT. The planetary hour of Mercury occurs during the sixth hour of day, and the first and eighth hours of night. The starting time for the first hour of night is 7:14 p.m. EDT. Since the eighth hour of night would be 2:03 a.m. EDT the next day, I believe that the best time would be at 7:14 p.m. because it is the evening planetary hour of Mercury.

Checking the astrological events and transit aspects, we will find that there are not many occurring, and only a couple are significant: the Moon goes void of course during the early morning until 5:14 a.m. EDT, when it conjuncts Jupiter in the sign of Aquarius. The Moon enters Pisces at 4:22 p.m., and the remaining transit aspects are very minor. The Moon is in Pisces when it is gibbous and just two days before the full Moon psychically characterizes an emotional quality that is quiet and deep for the evening. The conjunction between the Moon and Jupiter symbolizes self-confidence, goodwill, and self-fulfillment when in Aquarius. Overall, these are positive auspices that should not in any way either deflect or distort the working. With that analysis complete, we can be assured that the date and time will be quite effective.

Now that we have the objective defined, the sigil parchment and metallic talisman constructed, an elected date and time with excellent auspices, we need to determine the spiritual hierarchy and write up an invocation for the working for the 20°–30° decan of Virgo. To craft the sigil, we have already covered the spiritual hierarchy, so let us just repeat here and move forward with crafting the invocation.

Here is the spiritual hierarchy we already determined above:

Archetypal Deity: Hermes: God of mercantile transactions, communication, and psychopomps

Olympian Spirit: Ophiel

Archangel of Virgo: Hamaliel

Ruling Angel of Virgo: Shelathiel

Ruling Angel of the VI House: Ziel

Ruling Angel of the Decan: Meshephar

The three angels of the zodiacal sign and house are invoked when the western gateway is being erected in the decan invocation ritual. You should insert these names into a copy of the ritual when you write up the custom version that you will use in this working.

Using this hierarchy, I would then produce the following invocation:

> I summon you to manifest and appear before me, O Spirit Meshephar, in the name of Hermes whom I worship as my god. You are the spirit of the decans whose qualities are wealth, health, abundance, and material happiness, and who answers to the spiritual authorities of Hermes, god of the planet of Mercury; Ophiel Olympian Spirit of Mercury; Hamaliel, archangel of Virgo; Shelathiel, angelic ruler of Virgo; Ziel, angelic ruler of the VI House and the cadent decan of Virgo. I summon, call, and invoke you, O Spirit Meshephar, on this date and planetary hour, to come before me and manifest your virtues, intelligence, and powers. I beseech you, O Spirit, to help me in the affairs of business, monetary transactions, and career moves. Grant me good health and earthly wisdom.

With all four tasks completed, the only thing left to do is to write up the ritual using the pattern presented above and then developing it specifically for the decan talismanic working. The invocation will be written on a piece of paper or parchment and conveniently placed near the center altar. I would recommend studying and practicing the ritual with the few inserted names until it is committed to memory. A week before the scheduled date, begin the preparations as outlined in chapter 11.

The three-point pylon used to build the pylon pyramid energy field for the 20°–30° decan of Virgo would position the invoking pentagram to earth at the base, the lesser hexagram of the quality of mutable (water) at the top, and the lesser hexagram of the quality of mutable/cadent (water) in the center of the pylon. These three qualifying nodes drawn on the pylon would aptly define the components of this decan.

Figure 24: Diagram of the Three-Point Pylon
for the 20°–30° Decan of Virgo

One more thing I would like to make clear to my readers: Even when a talisman is deployed after the seventy-two hours of incubation, it will take a few years for it to have an effect on your monetary and business affairs. However, you will notice a steady increase in your fortunes and your overall physical health. Things will go your way, and the momentum of your material affairs (although working slowly and steady) will eventually build you a happy and comfortable life.

Chapter Fifteen

TALISMANIC MAGIC USING THE SEPTANS

"I think the Earth and everything around it is connected—the sky and the planets and the stars and everything else we see as a mystery."

—Marion Cotillard

The zodiacal septan is an astrological segment I have invented to make use of the forty-eight Dukes listed in the *Theurgia-Goetia*. I have stepped outside of the traditional magic associated with lunar mansions and astrological decans to adopt this new method, but I believe it fits and extends that tradition to new heights.

Basically, if you have a matrix of spirits from a grimoire or other source and there isn't any known mechanism to characterize or invoke them *and* they just so happen to be numbered on one of the factors of seven or twelve, you could use them in a celestial magical working. I also liked the idea of having forty-eight possibilities for a targeted working since it would be even more advantageous and tailored to the particular needs of a working than having just twenty-eight or even thirty-six possibilities. That said, I will let you decide if you want to work with these entities. What I have done is organized their spiritual hierarchy, given it a functional meaning, and embodied with them rituals in which to invoke them, and through that talismanic field, to charge a talisman.

Similar to the other spirits of the *Theurgia-Goetia*, I have found the forty-eight Dukes to be empowering and quite capable of facilitating magical feats and material transformations. This, of course, only occurred after I figured out how to place these spirits within a matrix defined by the components of celestial magic, and in this case, the twelve zodiacal signs. Dividing the twelve signs into four segments, each one governed by one of the four elements, helped me to define the powers and intelligences associated with the forty-eight Dukes.

The ritual I used to invoke one of the forty-eight septans is nearly the same as the ritual used to invoke one of the thirty-six decans. The main and only difference is that instead of qualifying a zodiacal sign with a quality of ascendant, succedent, or cadent, the rite will use an invoking pentagram for a specific element. This will create a sub-element dimension to the zodiacal sign. To achieve this differentiation, I will employ the three-point pylon, but I will set an invoking pentagram to the mid-point. So, the three-point pylon will have an invoking pentagram of the element associated with the zodiacal sign set to the base, a lesser hexagram defining the quality of the sign set to the top, and the mid-point associated with the sub-element set with another invoking pentagram. The three-point pylon will have two pentagrams and a lesser hexagram to succinctly define the septan segment.

Here is what that three-part pylon would look like set to generate the energy qualities of the zodiacal septan:

Figure 25: Diagram of the Three-Part Pylon for a Septan

Since the pylon will have two invoking pentagrams (one at the base and one in the mid-point) you could consider treating them as a kind of elemental energy. In fact, I would recommend using the imagery of the sixteen court cards of the tarot to help you visualize the energy field associated with the septan. You won't need to invoke the elemental energy spirit since it will be subsumed into the quality of the zodiacal septan, but using the imagery will be a helpful boost to the working. We have already discussed in chapter 8 about the quality of the septan represented by the combination of a talismanic elemental with an elemental, and this should assist you in visualizing the planetary and energy qualities contained within each one. You can find the meanings of the sixteen elementals listed in appendix 2.

Similar to the decan invocation ritual, the septan invocation rite will use the astrological angels associated with the sign and house to qualify the three gateway points in the western gateway. This is done for the same reason: to emphasize the zodiacal quality of the working. The hierarchy of the septan includes the element spirit of the Emperor from the *Theurgia-Goetia* and the corresponding Duke ruled by that demigod, so these would be named when the invocation is performed.

The planetary component of this working is based on the planetary ruler and element associated with the zodiacal sign, so it would be augmented by the quality of the sub-element of the septan segment. The energy field for the septan does include an elemental and, interestingly enough, the combination of the sign element and the ruling planet would produce a talismanic elemental included within the septan intelligence. Let me give you an example:

The Duke Ornich of Taurus (fixed earth) of the quadrant segment of Air that is ruled by Venus would contain the elemental Air of Earth (Page of Pentacles) and the talismanic elemental of Venus of Earth. The elemental would represent the materialization of ambition and the talismanic elemental would symbolize emotional stability, sensuality, beauty, and aesthetic appreciation (art). The specific Taurean qualities of the septan are common sense (in material affairs), shrewdness, and good business judgment (based on a sense of orderliness and aesthetics). You can see how the elemental and the talismanic elemental work together to determine the qualities of the septan, and this is true for all forty-eight septans. The septans are therefore quite elegant and empowering, since they combine elementals and talismanic elementals together to formulate a unified power and intelligence.

Timing considerations for a septan working are similar to that of a decan, except a septan lasts around seven and a half days whereas a decan lasts around ten days. You have the option of performing the working when the Sun is in the degree span of the septan denoting a specific season or using the planetary hour along with the planetary day if feasible. You will also need to check the transits for that elected magical working event and determine if the transits for that day will either help or not impede the working.

The septan invoking rite has the same four stages as the other two previous workings, so I won't describe the function and structures of this working. We can proceed to the ritual pattern and point out differences in this working from the other workings. The talismanic receptor and a parchment sigil are used together to define the function of the talisman, and the stellar vortex is used to charge and bless it, just like in the previous two workings.

Invocation of the Talismanic Septan Ritual

Here is the pattern for the ritual to invoke a talismanic septan. This ritual is performed within a fully erected and charged magic circle.

1. Take up the wand from the altar and proceed to the eastern watchtower. Facing east, draw an invoking pentagram of the target element to the base, and above it, a lesser hexagram of the zodiacal quality. In the midpoint, draw an invoking pentagram of the sub-element of the septan. Join the three points together with a narrow invoking spiral, creating a pylon with the zodiacal sign and septan signature.[67]

2. Proceed to the southern watchtower. Facing the south, do the same operation.

3. Proceed to the western watchtower. Facing the west, do the same operation.

4. Proceed to the northern watchtower. Facing the north, do the same operation.

---

67 For the lesser hexagram associated with the sign quality, see chapter 9, page 144.

5. Proceed to the center of the circle. Facing the center, do the same operation.

6. Return the wand to the altar and pick up the sword. Proceed to the eastern watchtower and with the sword, draw the pylon there to the pylon in the center of the circle at the zenith point.

7. Proceed to the southern watchtower and with the sword, draw the pylon residing there to the pylon in the center of the circle at the zenith point.

8. Proceed to the western watchtower, and do the same operation.

9. Proceed to the northern watchtower, and do the same operation.

10. Proceed to the eastern watchtower and draw a line on the floor from the east to south, then the south to the west, then the west to the north, and then a line to the east.

11. Return the sword to the altar. Take up the staff and proceed to the eastern watchtower. Begin a circumambulation starting from the east and proceeding deosil around the circle with a spiral arc toward the center of the circle, passing the eastern watchtower three times and entering the center of the circle. Place the staff before the center altar and imagine the energy field fully activated within the circle. Return the staff to the altar and pick up the wand.

12. Using the wand, proceed to the northwestern angle, and therein draw a rose ankh before it, projecting into it a deep violet color.

13. Proceed to the southwestern angle, and do the same operation.

14. Proceed to the southeastern angle, and do the same operation.

15. Proceed to the northeastern angle, and do the same operation.

16. Proceed to the center of the circle at the nadir, and do the same operation.

17. Return the wand to the altar. Take the sword and proceed to the northwestern angle. Using the sword, draw a line of force from the ankh in the watchtower to the ankh in the center of the circle at the nadir.

18. Proceed to the southwestern angle, and do the same operation.

19. Proceed to the southeastern angle, and do the same operation.

20. Proceed to the northeastern angle, and do the same operation.

21. Return the sword to the altar, and pick up the wand. Proceed to the northwestern angle. Starting from there, proceed to walk in around the circle widdershins, and slowly arc into the center of the circle, passing the northwestern angle three times, and holding the wand out to push the forces to the center of the circle. Once reaching the center, push the combined powers into the nadir. The invoking vortex is now set.

22. Return the wand to the altar. Proceed to the eastern watchtower and face west.

23. Draw invoking spirals to the southeast, northeast, and then the western watchtower—these positions are the guide, guardian, and ordeal respectively. Address each when drawing the invoking spiral.

24. To the southeast, point the wand and invoke the angelic ruler of the house, then point the wand to the northeast and invoke the angelic ruler of the zodiacal sign, then point to west and invoke the archangel of the zodiacal sign.

25. Draw lines of force with the right hand, from the southeast angle, to the western watchtower, to the northeast angle, and then back again to the southeast angle. The gateway is established.

26. Proceed to walk slowly from the east to the west, and when arriving at the west, perform the pantomime of opening the veil or a curtain with a dramatic flourish. Step close into the western watchtower and turn to face the east, performing the descending wave of energy from above the head to the feet.

27. Proceed to walk slowly from west to the east, imagining descending into a chamber—stop at the center, where the central altar is located.

28. Draw an inner circle around the central altar, starting in the north and proceeding widdershins around the circle until ending again at the north. Retrieve the wand, tarot court card, sigil, and talisman from the altar and proceed to the central altar, standing on the western side. Place the talisman with the sigil over it in the center of the septagram icon. Place the tarot court card to the side where it can be viewed but not overlay the icon.

29. Using the wand, draw the invoking pattern for the target ruling planet on the septagram icon. Start at the point opposite the target planetary point and draw a line toward it, then continue drawing following the lines of the septagram until you reach the point just before the target, then draw the last line projecting the energy of the wand to the action. Then point the wand at the sigil, and then draw an invoking spiral on the septagram icon, centering on the sigil and exhaling the breath. Set the wand on the icon. Focus on the tarot court card and briefly imagine the energies it suggests.

30. Intone the prepared invocation of the target septan ruler (Duke) three times, and then call its name repeatedly with a dramatic voice. Let the voice diminish in volume until it is just a whisper. State the hierarchical combination of zodiacal sign spirit (archangel), Olympian spirit, and septan ruler name (Duke) as the authorities for summoning the zodiacal intelligence of the septan.

31. Sit in meditation before the center altar and internally call to the septan ruler until a response is sensed. Use the imagination to help enhance the experience of the decan intelligence.

Perform the **Stellar Vortex for Talismanic Charging** rite using the following steps:

32. Standing at the central altar facing east with the wand in hand, draw a great inverted pentagram of creative spirit in the zenith point.

33. Then step one step away from the central altar, facing the southeast. With the wand, draw a lesser hexagram of union (earth) to the southeastern angle. Draw a line of force with the wand from the hexagram to the sigil talisman in the center of the septagram icon.

34. Turn to face the southwest, with the wand do the same operation.

35. Turn to face the northwest, with the wand do the same operation.

36. Turn to face the northeast, with the wand do the same operation.

37. Then step toward the central altar, standing again before it. Draw an inverted invoking pentagram of receptive spirit upon the sigil talisman

construct. Summon the name of the septan ruler three times and imagine it taking shape within the inverted pentagram in the zenith.

38. Take the wand and slowly draw a line of force from the great inverted pentagram in the zenith down to the inverted pentagram-charged sigil talisman construct, imagining the forceful descent of intelligence and energy descending into the talisman. Exhale the breath as this action is taken, then bow before the central altar. Remaining kneeling before it for a few moments.

39. Once this action is completed, stand again, and take the pouch placed nearby and the sigil. Wrap the talisman and place both into a pouch and set it on the septagram icon.

40. Sit in meditation for a short time before continuing with the next step of the talismanic invocation ritual.

Continue with the Septan invocation rite

41. When the meditative communion with the septan talismanic intelligence is completed, stand before the septagram icon, take up the wand, and draw a banishing spiral over it. Give the septan talismanic intelligence a warm farewell and thanks for visiting.

42. Place the wand on the septagram icon. Then turn around and proceed west and turn again to face east.

43. Draw invoking spirals to the northwest, southwest, and the eastern watchtower—these positions are the guide, guardian, and ordeal respectively. Address each when drawing the invoking spiral. (These will be the ordinary themes, not the angels.)[68]

44. Draw lines of force with the right hand from the northwest angle to the eastern watchtower, to the southwest angle, and then back again to the northwest angle. The gateway is established.

45. Proceed to walk slowly from the west to the east, and when arriving at the east, perform the pantomime of opening the veil or a curtain

---

68 These themes will be represented by a resolution of the lesson learned, the challenge overcome and the ordeal accomplished.

with a dramatic flourish. Step close into the eastern watchtower and turn to face the west, performing the descending wave of energy from above the head to the feet.

46. Proceed to walk slowly from east to west, imagining ascending out of a chamber. Stop at the center, where the central altar is located.

47. Take up the wand and proceed to the eastern watchtower and with the wand, draw therein a sealing spiral. Do the same to the southeast, south, southwest, west, northwest, north, and northeast. Return the wand to the altar.

48. The vortex is sealed and the ritual is completed.

49. Take the charged and covered talisman and put it in dark place for seventy-two hours.

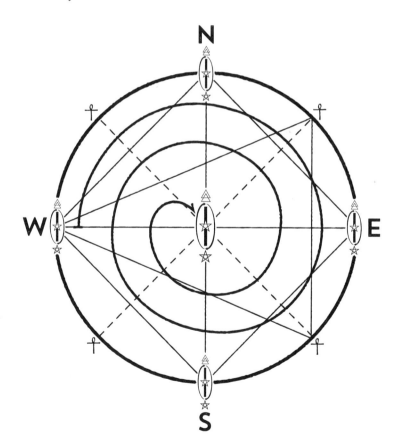

Figure 26: Diagram of the Invocation of the Talismanic Septan Rite

The invocation of the talismanic septan uses the three-point pylon to generate the proper energy field for the talismanic intelligence to occupy. The tarot court card acts as the symbolic imagery of the septan energy field and sets the ground or domain for the target spirit. Instead of just twenty-eight or thirty-six possibilities, the operator has forty-eight possibilities to work with, and the tarot court card image sets the elemental tone of the working.

Similar to the other two workings, the seamless combining of the septan invocation rite and the stellar vortex charging rite will produce the fully charged, blessed, and imbued talisman artifact. It is my opinion that the septan is more versatile and powerful than what either the talismanic elemental or the decan would produce.

The talismans produced through these two rituals using the septan will have an added quality of energy and intelligence operating within it, making it even more capable than the other two types of talismans.

Example: Septan Invocation Rite for Duke Ornich of Taurus of the Quadrant Segment of Air

Since I used Duke Ornich to show how the septan contains both an elemental and a talismanic elemental within its structure, I decided to choose that septan as an example. This is because nearly everyone could use the benefits of shrewdness and good business judgment. A septan talisman is my own unique contribution to celestial magic, so I would be greatly remiss if I did not supply a well-documented example to go with this chapter, too.

I have invoked several of these magical Dukes from the *Theurgia-Goetia*, but not this particular one. Still, invoking one or several of them will use the same ritual mechanisms and artifices, so I should be able to easily put together a working for you to examine and perhaps even use. As a Capricorn, I know and understand the utility of any kind of material-based magic that, as a talisman and magical field, would continue to aid and help the owner of the talisman long after the original desire has been satisfied.

As we did with the other working examples, we will use the five steps needed to flesh out a celestial magical working. I don't need to repeat them here since they are fully listed in chapters 12 and 13 for the purpose of generating a talismanic artifact.

Perhaps the most important guideline in any kind of material undertaking is to develop the skills of shrewdness and good judgment. Unfortunately, good judgment in one's business affairs is typically developed by making mistakes and learning from them. Depending on how egregious these mistakes might be, they will represent important lessons learned. Having some kind of intuition or insight into what might be a bad business decision or a poor investment choice might make the difference between having to deal with setbacks and engaging mitigation steps and being able to walk away from a bad deal unharmed. There is learning the hard way and then there is intuition, insight, and gut-level feelings that guide us to take the best path and avoid troubles.

What I am proposing to do in selecting this septan is to help enhance, empower, and strengthen the ability to see and choose the right path in business or investment strategies. The charged, blessed, and infused talisman artifact will help the owner to find the most profitable pathway and avoid the pitfalls that occur due to poor choices and bad decisions. A single deflection or insight from a considered choice or decision that turns out to be bad might make this talisman a very treasured jewel among one's collection of magical artifacts. That is what I am proposing to do with this last talismanic working, and I think it would be worthwhile and very helpful to nearly everyone.

What we need to do at this point is state very clearly and simplistically our intention for this working. We could all use some kind of intuitive, visionary, or sensual guidance to help us make good decisions and avoid costly mistakes. We are looking to activate our psychic sensibilities and focus them on our material affairs so that we can be directed to the right decision or the optimal path for material gain. Our objective would probably be encapsulated by the following sentences:

"Guide me in all business decisions. Help me to succeed and avoid costly mistakes."

We can break those sentences down to their fundamental words and come up with the following statement:

"Guide Business Success Avoid Mistakes"

What we need to do now is take this simplified statement and eliminate all the redundant letters so that we have a collection of the nonrepeating, unique letters in this statement. That set of letters would look like this:

GUIDEBSNCAVOMTK

The final two steps are where you reduce the form down to the nonrepeating letter shapes and using them to create the final sigil formulation. Here is my example of how this sigil would look:

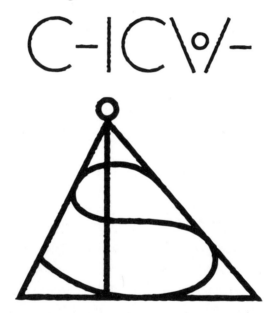

Figure 27: Diagram of Sigil Shapes and Sigil Form for
"Guide Business Success Avoid Mistakes"

Now you have a basic sigil functioning as the intent and link for this working. You will need some additional items in order for it to be fully representative of a talismanic intelligence associated with an astrological septan.

The basic components of a septan invocation working are the element associated with the astrological sign, the quadruplicity of the sign, and the sub-element defining the septan segment. The spiritual hierarchy associated with the septan is the archetypal deity associated with the ruling planet of the zodiacal sign, the Olympian Spirit associated with the ruling planet, the archangel of the sign, the ruling angel of the sign, the ruling angel of the house, the element emperor, and the septan duke. For this particular working, the following hierarchy would be used:

Archetypal Deity: Aphrodite: goddess of love, beauty, elegance, partnerships

Olympian Spirit: Hagith

Archangel of Taurus: Asmodel

Ruling Angel of Taurus: Araziel

Ruling Angel of the Second House: Tual

Emperor Element Ruler: Carnesiel

Duke Septan Ruler: Ornich

The Olympian spirit attributes and seals are found in chapter 4, pages 69–70; the zodiacal angels and septan Duke are in chapter 5, page 85, and in chapter 8, pages 134–137, respectively. Since the second house is the house associated with Taurus, that is the ruling angel of the house we will select. This way, we have three angels associated with the underworld gateway.

In addition to the parchment sigil, you would also use the Hebrew alphabet wheel (located in appendix 1) to derive the name sigils for the three angelic names and use the seal for the Olympian spirit. The emperor and duke have traditional seals associated with them, so you could use those.[69] You can also use the English alphabet wheel to derive sigils for those spirits.

These drawings should be added to the sigil parchment so that the objective is joined with the specific spirit-hierarchy definition of the septan. Since there are a lot of sigils or signatures that would be applied to the parchment, you can omit the Emperor as long as he is summoned in the invocation. The rest of the five renderings should be organized on the parchment along with the sigil objective. Here is what it would look like with the five components:

---

69 Skinner and Rankine, "Sixteen [Grand] Dukes" in *Goetia of Dr. Rudd*, 223–277.

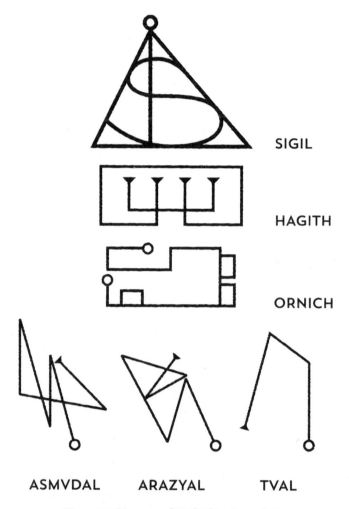

SIGIL

HAGITH

ORNICH

ASMVDAL   ARAZYAL   TVAL

Figure 28: Diagram of Sigil Objective and Five
Components of the Septan Talisman

When crafting the metallic talisman, use the same set of sigils and seals as used on the parchment sigil, perhaps with exception to the sigil of the objective. Since this is a working where Venus is the ruling planet, the metal used to create the talisman would be copper.

Now that we have the objective defined, the object sigil designed, the angelic name sigils designed, and the six components assembled for the parchment sigil and the metallic talisman, we will need to determine an auspicious date and time to perform this working.

Selecting a date for a septan working will be the same as finding the date for a decan working. The only difference is that the septan period will last seven days instead of ten. The optimal date for this particular working would be when the Sun is in Taurus. Since this working is based on the element air, the range of the septan would be from 15 degrees to 22 degrees 30 minutes. The dates are from May 6 through May 13 for 2021. The ruling planet for this septan is Venus, so the working should be performed on a Friday during the hour of Venus. However, since I strongly believe that Venus should be complimented with Saturn so that the quality will be more material based, cautious, and shrewd, Saturday would be optimal. The only Saturday during this seven-day period is May 8, but the entire period for the septan is unfortunately when the moon is waning. It would seem that this date is not a good time to perform the working.

Although we have a perfect date, the moon phase doesn't work—in fact, the full moon occurs before the Sun even enters the septan segment. What can we do? This situation is not uncommon, and we can take three approaches to get a better date. We can just pick the nearest Saturday and do the working during the hour of Venus, we can select a date that is just before the date when the Sun enters the septan and the moon is not yet full, or we can wait a year or two when the septan aligns with the moon's position, which is not a very strategic decision.

What I decided to do was choose a date close to the septan period that was still before the full Moon. That date would be April 24, a Saturday. May 15 or May 22, also Saturdays, could work too. For selecting a date for a decan or septan, getting close to the seasonal period of the zodiacal segment is acceptable. It would not be acceptable for a lunar mansion, where the focus would then be on the planetary hour elected for the working instead of on the date of the septan.

We can check the date on the online planetary hour calculator for Richmond, Virginia, and find the following times. The time of sunrise for April 24, 2021, is 6:23 a.m. EDT and the time of sunset is 7:52 p.m. EDT. Daylight Saving Time is in effect, so that would determine the time of the event. Since we want to perform this rite during the planetary hour of Venus, we will look at our list of planetary hours to determine that the hour of Venus occurs on the fifth and twelfth hours of the day, and on the seventh hour of night. Since the first planetary hour of Venus of day starts at 10:53 a.m. EDT, the second hour of Venus at 6:46 p.m. EDT, and the first planetary hour of Venus of night at 1:09 a.m. EDT the next morning, I would recommend the working be performed starting at 6:46 p.m. You could perform this working starting at 1:09 a.m. if you were quite the night owl, but most people would prefer an earlier time. The working will be performed just before the sunset, which is perfectly acceptable. The day is Saturday, so it shouldn't be difficult to set aside the time to do the working at that time.

Examining the auspices for April 24 shows a fair amount of activity and some cautionary considerations. The Moon is void course until 3:50 a.m. when the first aspect of the Moon occurs as it enters Libra. The Moon in Libra acts as an emotional stabilizer, helping keep one's emotions in check, which is an important factor when the Moon squares Mars at around 1:19 p.m. The Moon square Mars in Cancer can cause irritability, rashness, and hastiness, but that negative aspect will be balanced with the Moon in Libra and calm it down. Additionally, Venus is in Taurus on this day, which is quite auspicious, since Venus and Taurus are the planetary and zodiacal determiners for this working. There is an aspect where Venus squares Saturn later in the evening, which would have a cooling effect on the passions of Venus, but would also be indicative of a need to reassess one's life situation. This, of course, is the very nature of the objective of this working. Overall, the auspices look good for choosing this date.

Now that we have the objective defined, the sigil parchment and metallic talisman constructed, and an elected date and time with good auspices, we need to determine the spiritual hierarchy and write up an invocation for the working for the Air element septan of Taurus. To craft the sigil, we have already covered the spiritual hierarchy, so let us just repeat it here and move forward with crafting the invocation. Here is the spiritual hierarchy we have determined:

Archetypal Deity: Aphrodite: goddess of love, beauty, elegance, partnerships

Olympian Spirit: Hagith

Archangel of Taurus: Asmodel

Ruling Angel of Taurus: Araziel

Ruling Angel of the Second House: Tual

Emperor Element Ruler: Carnesiel

Duke Septan Ruler: Ornich

The three angels of the zodiacal sign and house are invoked when the western gateway is being erected in the decan invocation ritual. You should insert these names into a copy of the ritual when you write up the custom version that you will use in this working. Using this hierarchy, I would then produce the following invocation:

> I summon you to manifest and appear before me, O Spirit Ornich in the name of Aphrodite whom I worship as my goddess. You are the spirit of the Imperial Dukes whose qualities are shrewdness, intuitive insight into material affairs, and business guidance, and who answers to the spiritual authorities of Aphrodite, goddess of the planet of Venus; Hagith, Olympian spirit of Venus; Asmodel, archangel of Taurus; Araziel, angelic ruler of Taurus; Tual, angelic ruler of the Second House; the Emperor of Air, Carnesiel; and the Air Septan of Taurus. I summon, call, and invoke you, O Spirit Ornich, on this date and planetary hour, to come before me and manifest your virtues, intelligence, and powers. I beseech you, O Spirit, to help me judge business decisions and transactions with shrewdness, insights, and intuition so that I may be successful in all of my material undertakings.

With all four of these tasks completed, the only thing left to do is to write up the ritual using the pattern presented above and then develop it specifically for the septan talismanic working. The invocation will be written on piece of paper or parchment and conveniently placed near the center altar. I would recommend studying and practicing the ritual with the few inserted names until it is committed to memory, and then a week before the scheduled date, begin the preparations as outlined in chapter 11.

The three-point pylon used to build the pylon pyramid energy field for the septan of 15 degrees to 22 degrees 30 minutes of Taurus would position the invoking pentagram to earth at the base, the lesser hexagram of the quality of fixed (Air) at the top, and the invoking pentagram of Air in the center of the pylon. These three qualifying nodes drawn on the pylon would aptly define the components of this septan. Here is an example of how that would look:

Figure 29: Diagram of the Three-Point Pylon Used to Invoke the Septan Air of Taurus

This particular septan is not one that would bring forth immediate results; it is also quite subtle, since it imbues a state of sensitivity and shrewdness about business judgment. What this means is that you probably won't realize it is working until you suddenly realize that your business acumen just saved you from making an expensive mistake. Also, this talismanic field takes a while until it has fully manifested and starts to bring out the results that you want and expect.

Perhaps the biggest hurdle is learning to trust your newfound intuition and sensitivity, and to make certain you use caution and care when approaching possible large financial gain. Patience and openness to your sensitive side and avoiding impulsive and quick decisions will allow this ability a greater chance to unfold.

Chapter Sixteen

APPLYING TALISMANS IN EVERYDAY MAGIC

"Sometimes the meaning beyond the talisman is greater than the talisman itself.
A star has a hint of galaxies."

—Talismanist Giebra

Once you have completed charging and activating a talisman, and you have placed it in a pouch or cloth cover on your altar for seventy-two hours of incubation, the talisman is ready for use. The question that needs to be answered is what do you do with it from that point onward? How do you *use* a talisman? How do you get a talisman to work for a friend, family member, or client? We have spent much of this book discussing the background and the techniques involved in charging and generating a talisman, so now we need to discuss some important directions in using a talisman to properly affect you, a friend, or a client.

When taking the talisman out of its protective covering or pouch after the incubation period, it will be wrapped in the parchment sigil used to generate it. The sigil has served its purpose and can be destroyed, typically by burning it. It is no longer needed now that the talisman itself is fully activated and ready for use. Activation is symbolically determined through the use of sacraments, typically a consecrated oil. If the talisman is not metallic, oil might not be a good idea (e.g., if the talisman is made of ceramic or wood). If it is made of a material that can be damaged by oil, then just a small sprinkling of consecrated salt water that is wiped off will work quite well. The talisman is now officially activated for use.

Since a fully activated talisman has within its core an element charge that perpetually invigorates it, it doesn't ever need to be recharged or somehow fed or tended to with offerings. The combination of planetary intelligence as an imbued spirit and the zodiacal sign as element charge remain active in some manner, whether in a fully utilized or dormant talisman. Once a talisman is activated then it continues to function theoretically forever. A talisman can be muted, allowed to go dormant, or even discarded or lost, but it continues to function to some degree unless it is destroyed.

One important consideration is that once you have generated, charged, incubated, and then activated a talisman, there is a bond or link that exists between you, the maker, and the talisman. That bond automatically ensures that you can communicate and direct the talisman. It is a similar bond that exists between you and your magical tools, except that the talisman has a quantum of spiritual intelligence imbued in it. That means that you can talk to the talisman, direct it to new and different targets within the definition of its magical qualities, or pass it to another person and establish its allegiance accordingly. Communication with the talisman is an important topic, since it represents the foundation for any magical effect that the talisman might manifest.

Left alone and without any maker connection or guidance, a talisman will function at the behest of its maker if it is kept in either a prominent place in relation to or on the person who made it. The key to keeping a talisman operational is that it must be kept in the mind of the person who is making use of it. Displaying the talisman somewhere prominently in your house, on your altar (if it is permanent), in your pocket, or on your person (as jewelry) will sufficiently keep it operational. If you store the talisman into a cloth pouch and put it away in a drawer or cabinet, its effect is muted but (amazingly) not completely stopped. Communicating with the talisman will help you focus the talismanic energy and spiritual intelligence on specific objectives both within the purview of the sigil used to help generate it and beyond.

There are two ways to communicate with the talisman, both of which should be done in the sacred space of a magic circle. The first way is to hold the talisman cupped in your hands while sitting in meditation and use your honed sensitive intuition to directly connect and communicate with the talisman. This will work if you just need to direct the talisman to assist you with the objective established in the magical working used to create it. You will probably feel a slight tingle when you are focusing on the talisman; if you are able, you may even hear its voice answering you, just as if you were conjuring a spirit and attempting to communicate with it. If you don't experience any of these subtle clues from the talisman that the communication link is open and your thoughts are being received, don't worry about it. You are the maker of this talisman; it will do what you direct it to do as long as it is within the purview of the talismanic field generated in the ritual. You can use this approach at any time, and in fact, I would recommend that you meditate with your talisman at least once a month.

The second method used to communicate with the talisman is to link it with a temporary parchment sigil. This is how you can more radically change the function and purpose of the talisman, and it is also how you can transfer a talisman over to another person, replacing your bond as maker with the talisman's recipient. You would use your ability to craft a sigil for a new purpose, write it on parchment, and then consecrate that sigil so that it is active. Then, you would take the parchment, wrap it around the talisman, and put it into a pouch for twenty-four hours to reset it to a new task or new owner.

Start by sitting in the sacred space of a consecrated magic circle with the talisman in the palm of your left hand, the parchment in your right. Join them together while cupping both hands by placing the parchment over the talisman so that it is covered. Commune with the talisman and tell it that you have a new objective for it perform. Holding the parchment over the talisman for a period of time, wrap up the talisman with the parchment and put it into a pouch for a short incubation period.

When transferring the talisman to a friend, family member, or client, produce a sigil instructing the talisman to focus all of its efforts for this person instead of you. It would be based on the following phrase, using the person's first name to indicate the new owner. Here is an example of transferring a talisman to a client named Fritz.

The simple command is: "Work magic for Fritz."

Which would be WORKMAGICF FRITZ, using the letter reduction method.

There would be two sigils produced from this method written on to the parchment. One would be the directive and the other would be the name of the beneficiary. Think of this parchment sigil as a kind of title of ownership, that when consecrated, becomes official.

When transferring a talisman to another person, have them open the pouch, take out the parchment-wrapped talisman, remove the wrapper, and then take the talisman into their hands while they sit in meditation for a while. Afterward, they should destroy the parchment sigil by burning it. The talisman is now in their possession and will work its magic for them.

To help with the bonding, it is important that the new owner keep the talisman on their person for three days, perhaps even putting it under their pillow at night. Then, when they want the talisman to act on a specific objective, they should sit in meditation with the talisman cupped in their hands and mentally ask the talisman to do their bidding. Without direction, the talisman will aid its new owner every single day as long as they own it and keep it prominently displayed or on their person.

If the new owner requires a different objective than the one set at the talisman's creation, tell them to bring it back to you so that you can craft a consecrated parchment sigil for them and perform the same operation done for setting a new objective for the talisman's operation. The only difference is that you would not have to put the person in sacred space; they can do this in a secular manner. They would take the talisman wrapped in the parchment sigil in its pouch home and open and unwrap it after twenty-four hours of incubation. The parchment sigil would thereafter be burned.

If the talisman is put away for a long period of time (several months or a year), it becomes dormant. However, reactivating a talisman is quite simple, depending on the amount of time since its last use. By "use" I am referring to when it was last prominent in the mind of the owner. To reactivate a dormant talisman, all that is required is to take it into a consecrated magic circle, re-anoint it, and then focus on it while holding it cupped in your hands for a period of time while making contact with the spirit imbued within in. If the talisman was only put away for a few months, re-anointing it is not necessary.

Recovering a purchased and verified talisman that would be considered a museum piece or something fashioned in antiquity that was not made by you can be more difficult. Such items can be privately and legally bought and owned even for a fair price. You can use the approach of awakening a long dormant talisman by re-anointing and then communing with it. You will need to attempt to determine if it was ever charged in the first place; if it was, you must determine its original function. If it was charged, you will be successful in reactivating it and able to communicate with the spirit residing within it. Keep in mind that the talisman may have never been charged and imbued with a spirit—it may have had more of a psychological and decorative use than a magical one. Such an object will not respond to reactivation.

Keep in mind that reactivation it is only the first step. You will also need to establish a dialog with the spirit in order to determine its original function and purpose and align that with a known talismanic field, whether lunar mansion or decan.

If you can identify the function of the antique talisman with a specific talismanic field (or at least something as close you can get), you will need to reestablish that talisman with a new spiritual hierarchy and purpose and put that into a parchment sigil. Then, link the sigil with the talisman as if you were redirecting one you had made, wrap the parchment around the talisman, and put it into a pouch to incubate for seventy-two hours. Once that is done and the talisman is liberated, it can be activated, after which you can use it with the knowledge that it has survived the ages to become your instrument of magical accomplishment.

Purchasing an already made talisman is something many practitioners do, particularly if the talisman is made as an exquisite piece of jewelry. If it is sold by a reputable magical practitioner, you should go through the process of re-aligning it to you and setting its purpose. If it is a generalized type of talisman, such as one of the traditional Solomonic talismans, it will not actually have a talismanic field associated with it. You can use it and it will work, of course, but it will not be as effective as one you have charged and imbued with a spirit made by your own magical artifice. While homemade talismans may suffer in terms of aesthetics and can even be a bit crude (if the operator is not skilled at the craft of jewelry making), they have the benefit of being a known quantity and have a specific function directed to them.

What you can do with a purchased already made and charged talisman is threefold: You can completely recharge and imbue it with a selected talismanic field, you can set or establish the talisman with a selected spiritual hierarchy for a lunar mansion or a decan and link it with the spiritual hierarchy (as you would with an antique talisman), *or* you can just use it as it is, understanding and appreciating its limitations. The first method ensures that your charge will overlay and add to what has already been set into the talisman. The second method will bend the existing talismanic charge to a specific talismanic field and purpose that will be adequate but not as satisfactory as the first method. You could also purchase uncharged talismans and charge them yourself if your crafting ability is woefully inadequate.

One other consideration for purchasing talismans is that they can become part of the magical jewelry you use in your normal magical and even liturgical workings. Certainly, something elegant, made of precious or semi-precious metals and incorporating semi-precious gems would become a truly powerful tool and would imbue the user with a charmed quality associated with the talismanic field projected into it. Designing and ordering such a piece of jewelry, with the associated sigils and seals for a specific lunar mansion, decan, or even septan would be the high watermark of any talismanic endeavor. Made-to-order talismanic jewelry is probably the best option for working with elegant and aesthetic talismanic tools. Wearing them on your body is also the ideal kind of connection for making this kind of magic the most effective it can be.

Because they are material based, talismans are not immortal and everlasting. They can cease to function if they are destroyed. I have always crafted talismans that have a positive and constructive use, so I have never had to destroy a talisman. However, it might be necessary to destroy a talisman if the auspices for its generation were somehow malefic, or if you were to discover or encounter a negative talisman set by another party to do harm against you or someone close to you.

A purposefully malefic talisman is very rare; you are very unlikely to encounter one. Probably the only place where such an object could be found is in areas where experts in talisman making commonly reside, (e.g., some ethnic minority communities or foreign countries). It is more likely that you may accidentally generate a talisman when the Moon was waning or some other auspice turned out to make your crafted talisman into a malefic one. This probably wouldn't occur if you have followed the rules I have established for choosing a proper date for a working, and it wouldn't ever be a factor unless the working was to produce a strategic change in your life or your clients. Only a strategically important talisman needs to be done through astrological auspices.

Still, if a talisman must be destroyed for some reason, this is what you would do: Fire and blunt trauma are used to break the talismanic spell and release the spirit imbued in it. Heat the talisman to a melting or softening temperature with a torch if it is metal or ceramic, burning it if it is wood, and then using craft scissors and a hammer, break it into pieces and bury them. Just before taking this action, hold the talisman in your hand and tell the spirit within it that you are going to liberate it, it should return to its source, and you are doing this for a good cause. Without any delay, destroy the talisman and bury the pieces in a neutral place (not your backyard).

Hopefully, you will never have to destroy a talisman; if it was made by your own hand, there is something inexplicably lost when such an action is taken. The same is true when destroying someone else's malefic talisman, except because the intent was negative, that negativity comes back to the maker in some manner. In the many years that I have worked talismanic magic, I have never had to destroy a talisman, and I hope that you never have to perform that ignominious task either. Even when it is done to protect you or your client from harm, the act has a very negative overall quality.

As you can see, the application of talismanic magic has certain obligations if it is to be fully developed and used to the benefit of you or your clients. Oddly enough, these actions are so automatic to me that I wouldn't even consider them important unless I was giving this knowledge to someone who didn't know all the little uses and methods for working with talismans once they were generated. Yet they need to be stated and even emphasized so that you will know what to expect and how to incorporate talismans into your day-to-day magical operations.

Chapter Seventeen

INVOKING SATURN: RITUAL WORKING FOR JUSTICE

In the course of living our lives and experiencing the various vicissitudes of good and bad fortune, and having to deal with all kinds of people and social situations, we will unfailingly meet with individuals who will do harm to us, whether physical or mental. We can try to be virtuous, constructive, tolerant, and forgiving, but sometimes we encounter a person or a situation that begs for some kind of retribution. As Witches and Pagans who are not bound by an obligation similar to the Christian golden rule (i.e., the Wiccan rede), we do have the option of deliberately cursing someone, and celestial magic presents to us all kinds of waning moon talismanic fields to use for just that purpose. I admit that I have worked this kind of magic in my life, although it has been a rare occurrence and was highly justified in my own mind. I have, however, never used celestial magic to curse someone.

There is a kind of morality to working malefic magic—you'd better be fully and cleanly justified before you consider doing a dark deed to someone or some group of people. Projecting a curse has the potential to diminish the operator's intrinsic inner light, and sometimes the rationale for doing that kind of magic is thin or even nonexistent. In my opinion, you need an iron-clad case for working malefic magic, especially if you wish to use celestial magic for that purpose.

Celestial magic used to curse is very unforgiving, and it will often deal a greater amount of damage over a longer period of time than any other curse I am aware of. If a talismanic field casts a perpetual charge into a talisman receptor to materially aid someone and that field lasts practically forever, think about what that kind of working would do when applied to a curse. You would be setting up a malefic field that would be practically perpetual and unstoppable.

If you want to curse someone and everyone around them for their entire lifetime and even affect their later progeny when they are gone, then by all means, go ahead and use a talismanic field invoked during a baleful and waning moon. All you need to do is to bury it on their property or somehow pass it to them anonymously. Once again: I don't recommend using celestial magic to curse an individual or a group since it is so long lasting. I also believe that it would take profound justification, both moral and legal, to do such an operation. Celestial magic used as a curse creates a point of true darkness in the fabric of consciousness that lasts for a long time. The only remedy would be to physically destroy the talisman, but the release of its malefic intelligence would momentarily cause even greater harm.

There is a safer and certainly more temporary magical action one can take using celestial magic to right a wrong. If you aren't sure about who is to blame for a transgression or you are at least open-minded enough to consider your role in this kind of situation, you could invoke the planetary intelligence of Saturn as a means to gain justice. Keep in mind that performing this invocation will bring down justice on all guilty parties—and that includes you. If you have been wronged by someone, a group, company, or institution, you can invoke Saturn to force justice to be made manifest in that situation. I have found that this approach is the best for seeking just retribution because Saturn perfectly weighs all the pros and cons of a given situation and awards justice to all parties. Of course, you would not perform this ritual if you were also guilty of bad behavior or if you instigated the event in the first place. You would do this ritual to right a wrong and for a situation in which you were the party who was innocently harmed.

The invocation of Saturn has more to it than performing an invocation of the planetary intelligence and asking for justice. Although you could certainly take that approach, this rite is more involved and has a zodiacal energy as the foundation or base. I chose the sign Scorpio, since it seemed to have the greatest intensity but also could deliver a level verdict either for retribution or for the offending party to seek forgiveness. Also, the planetary deity of Saturn is called upon in this rite, using votive offerings of black candles and presenting to him what I call a black supper of dark bread; pomegranate seeds; and a dark, vinegary wine. As with a typical talismanic elemental working, you should perform a week of liturgical workings with the planetary deity of Saturn, presenting to him your grievances and what you would like to see happen to fix the situation. Whatever you ask for may not manifest exactly as you would want it, but it is a very effective ritual, and I recommend it much more than using celestial magical curses. Approach this working just as you would a judge in a formal setting, presenting your case and asking for justice.

The ritual pattern is basically the same as presented in the talismanic elemental invocation rite, except the planet is set to Saturn, the spirit invoked is the Olympian spirit Aratron, and the zodiacal sign is set to Scorpio for the pylon pyramid. The talismanic vortex charge is not used, of course, and instead of the inverted pentagrams, a great rose ankh is set in the zenith with lesser hexagrams arrayed in the watchtowers, and another rose ankh is drawn to the parchment sigil. Here is what the simple two-part pylon would look like for this working:

Figure 30: Two-Part Pylon Used in the Saturn Invocation Rite

As for the special parchment sigil, you will want to use the Olympian spirit seal and sigils based on your case and what you want to occur. What I typically do is present the case and then what I want to happen to resolve the issue, meaning two sigils are developed: one based on a succinct statement of the case, and the other for the outcome. If there are specific named individuals, you might want to use the English alphabetic wheel (appendix 1) to create sigils of their names. You can use both names or just their surname to identify them to the Olympian spirit, Aratron. All these sigils and the seal are placed on a single piece of consecrated parchment. Keep the charged sigil until the issue is resolved one way or another, after which it can be burned.

Now that we have the basic ideas covered for this working, we can move on to examining the ritual pattern, the center of the working.

Invocation of the Planetary Intelligence of Saturn in Scorpio for Justice Ritual

This ritual is performed within a fully erected and charged magic circle. The ritual pattern to perform this working is as follows:

1. Take up the wand from the altar and proceed to the eastern watchtower. Facing east, draw an invoking pentagram of water to the base and above it, a lesser hexagram of the zodiacal quality of fixed (air). Join the two points together with a narrow invoking spiral, creating a pylon with the zodiacal sign of Scorpio.

2. Proceed to the southern watchtower. Facing the south, do the same operation.

3. Proceed to the western watchtower. Facing the west, do the same operation.

4. Proceed to the northern watchtower. Facing the north, do the same operation.

5. Proceed to the center of the circle. Facing the center, do the same operation.

6. Return the wand to the altar and pick up the sword. Proceed to the eastern watchtower, and with the sword draw the pylon residing there to the pylon in the center of the circle at the zenith point.

7. Proceed to the southern watchtower, and do the same operation.

8. Proceed to the western watchtower, and do the same operation.

9. Proceed to the northern watchtower, and do the same operation.

10. Proceed to the eastern watchtower and draw a line on the floor from the east to south, then the south to the west, then the west to the north, and then a line to the east.

11. Return the sword to the altar. Take up the staff and proceed to the eastern watchtower. Begin a circumambulation starting from the east and proceeding deosil around the circle with a spiral arc toward the center of the circle, passing the eastern watchtower three times and entering the center of the circle. Place the staff before the center altar

and imagine the energy field fully activated within the circle. Return the staff to the altar and pick up the wand.

12. Using the wand, proceed to the northwestern angle, and therein draw a rose ankh before it, projecting into it a deep violet color.

13. Proceed to the southwestern angle, and do the same operation.

14. Proceed to the southeastern angle, and do the same operation.

15. Proceed to the northeastern angle, and do the same operation.

16. Proceed to the center of the circle to the nadir, and do the same operation.

17. Return the wand to the altar. Take the sword and proceed to the northwestern angle. Using the sword, draw a line of force from the ankh in the angle to the ankh in the center of the circle at the nadir.

18. Proceed to the southwestern angle, and do the same operation.

19. Proceed to the southeastern angle, and do the same operation.

20. Proceed to the northeastern angle, and do the same operation.

21. Return the sword to the altar and pick up the wand. Proceed to the northwestern angle. Starting from there, proceed to walk in around the circle widdershins and slowly arc into the center of the circle, passing the northwestern angle three times, holding the wand out to push the forces to the center of the circle. Once reaching the center, push the combined powers into the nadir. The invoking vortex is now set.

22. Return the wand to the altar. Proceed to the eastern watchtower and face west.

23. Draw invoking spirals to the southeast, northeast, and then the western watchtower—these positions are the guide, guardian, and ordeal respectively. Address each when drawing the invoking spiral.[70]

---

70 Addressing the guide, guardian, and ordeal should include acknowledging the points for and against, in addition to the process of restitution for your case. The guide is the defense attorney, the guardian is the prosecution, and the ordeal is the judge presiding over your case.

24. Draw lines of force with the right hand from the southeast angle, to the western watchtower, to the northeast angle, and then back again to the southeast angle. The gateway is established.

25. Proceed to walk slowly from east to west. When arriving at the west, perform the pantomime of opening the veil or a curtain with a dramatic flourish. Step close into the western watchtower and turn to face east, performing the descending wave of energy from above the head to the feet.

26. Proceed to walk slowly from west to east, imagining you are descending into a chamber. Stop at the center, where the central altar is located.

27. Draw an inner circle around the central altar starting in the north and proceeding widdershins around the circle until ending again at the north. Retrieve the wand and sigil from the altar and proceed to the central altar, standing on the western side. Place the sigil in the center of the septagram icon.

28. Using the wand, draw the invoking pattern for Saturn on the septagram icon. Start at the point opposite the target planetary point and draw a line toward it. Continue to draw following the lines of the septagram until you reach the point just before the target. Draw the last line projecting the energy of the wand to the action. Point the wand at the sigil and draw an invoking spiral on the septagram icon centering on the sigil and exhaling the breath.

29. Standing at the central altar, facing east with the wand in hand, draw a great rose ankh in the zenith point. Project a deep violet color into the ankh.

30. Take one step away from the central altar facing southeast. With the wand, draw a lesser hexagram of union (earth) to the southeastern angle. Draw a line of force with the wand from the hexagram to the sigil in the center of the septagram icon.

31. Turn to face the southwest, with the wand do the same operation.

32. Turn to face the northwest, with the wand do the same operation.

33. Turn to face the northeast, with the wand do the same operation.

34. Draw a rose ankh upon the sigil in the center of the septagram icon and project a deep violet color into it. Then draw a line of force from the ankh in the zenith down to the ankh on the sigil.

35. Intone the prepared invocation of the Olympian spirit of Aratron and then call his name repeatedly using a dramatic voice. Let your voice diminish in volume until it is just a whisper.

36. State your case, name the guilty parties (the accused) and what you are seeking as justice or restitution. Present this case before Aratron, asking for his intervention and assistance.

37. Sit in meditation before the center altar and internally call to Aratron until a response is sensed. Use your imagination to help enhance your experience of this Olympian spirit.

38. When the meditative communion with the spirit is completed, stand before the septagram icon and take up the wand to draw a banishing spiral over it. Give Aratron a warm farewell and thanks for visiting.

39. Place the wand on the septagram icon and then turn around and proceed to the west. Turn again to face east.

40. Draw invoking spirals to the northwest, southwest, and then the eastern watchtower. These positions are the guide, guardian, and ordeal respectively. Address each when drawing the invoking spiral.[71]

41. With the right hand, draw lines of force from the northwest angle, to the eastern watchtower, to the southwest angle, and then back again to the northwest angle. The gateway is established.

42. Proceed to walk slowly from the west to the east. When arriving at the east, perform the pantomime of opening the veil or a curtain with a dramatic flourish. Step close into the eastern watchtower and turn to face west, performing the descending wave of energy from above the head to the feet.

43. Proceed to walk slowly from east to west, imagining you are ascending out of a chamber. Stop at the center, where the central altar is located.

---

71 These themes will be represented by a resolution of the lesson learned, the challenge overcome, and the ordeal accomplished.

44. Take up the wand and proceed to the eastern watchtower. With the wand, draw therein a sealing spiral. Do the same to the southeast, south, southwest, west, northwest, north, and northeast. Return the wand to the altar.

45. The vortex is sealed and the ritual is complete.

I have performed variations of this ritual a number of times and have found that working it helped to deal with the issue; typically, something would happen to resolve the injustice. It wasn't always what I wanted, and it often left me with only partial satisfaction. Although I seldom got everything I asked for, I would get at least something out of the situation, and it would help me experience closure regarding the matter.

In the end, closure is all I could really ask for; working this rite is a lot like going to court without the expenses and the public revelations. In my opinion, performing an invocation of Saturn for justice is far better than just cursing someone, especially if there are two sides to the issue that, in the name of fairness, need to be weighed by the magic spell.

Conclusion

THREE WORLDS OF WITCHCRAFT MASTERY

"The domain of Witchcraft is the realm of the unseen and the point at which it impinges upon man's psyche…"

—PAUL HUSON, MASTERING WITCHCRAFT, 19

Having arrived here, you can congratulate yourself for having read through and grasped a comprehensive explanation of celestial magic. You now have the tools to develop a ritual-based method to forge and generate talismanic artifacts that will magically ensure a charmed and fulfilled existence for you, your family or friends, or even paying clients. I have distilled my knowledge and experience into a framework of Witchcraft magic to make the art of celestial magic accessible. It is the key and the crown jewel that will enrich you and lead to other even greater works and achievements.

Although this book is foundational, it is actually only the beginning of the work of celestial magic. Acquiring competency in celestial magic will draw you into studying the associated arts and scienes of astrology, astronomy, psychology, history, and sociology. The more knowledge you have about these topics, the better your art of celestial magic will become. That knowledge will therefore become a major factor in the many successes and rewards occurring during your life. With this knowledge, you can build for yourself a charmed life, not only for you but for others with whom you share this priceless wisdom.

Now that you have read this book, I am hopeful that you will start exploring the world of celestial magic. Begin your work by invoking a few planetary intelligences and a couple zodiacal intelligences and bask in the consultation and insights these operations will afford you. Then start planning to build for yourself a treasure house of charged and activated talismans. You can begin with some general approaches (e.g., what was written as example workings), and from there you can begin to acquire talismans that will empower you and help you overcome obstacles and achieve all that you desire, both materially and spiritual. Additionally, talismans radiating from your temple and home will affect more than just you—they will also positively affect your spouse, children, or anyone who lives with you.

Celestial magic can be used to help and assist others whether they are family members, friends, or paying clients. This kind of magic lends itself well to developing a paying clientele because you are giving them something tangible in exchange for money. You could, if you wanted, build up a whole business around generating and selling talismans to select clients. I have not taken this path to material success simply because I value my privacy and really don't want to deal with other people's problems whether as a valid means to helping others or not. I prefer to teach and instruct others in this valuable art rather than function as a Witch for hire. To be clear, there is nothing wrong with charging folks for your labor and art; it is really a matter of learning to deal fairly and equitably with the public.

When used in conjunction with my other two books in this series, *Talismanic Magic for Witches* confers upon the Witch a status of knowing the full spectrum of magic as potentially practiced in a ritual magic form of Witchcraft. I believe it is important to read and study all three of my books not because it will enrich me in some manner (it won't), but because it will make you a more capable magical practitioner.

In *Elemental Powers for Witches*, I covered the various threads of magic that existed in antiquity and what happened to them from that time to our present. While witches in antiquity owned the techniques and methods for spirit conjuring in addition to finding and using a spirit helper or familiar, the threads of advanced energy magic and celestial magic were owned by philosophers and ancient astrologers, respectively. Although the philosophers and astrologers practiced forms of theurgy, they were never a part of the repertoire of the witches of antiquity.

Two millennia later and the secret inner teachings of the philosophers had completely disappeared, and astrologers removed the practice of magic and prophecy from their regimen. The beginning of the modern age was a time when the practice of magic in all its guises was rapidly disappearing, having become the provenance of the eccentric or the madman. This made the occult revival more difficult but also exciting when it appeared in the middle and later nineteenth century, since much of the lore from antiquity had been irretrievably lost.

The discovery of Eastern religious and mystical practices had a powerful impact on the West due to the latter's practices and knowledge having been lost. Many of the practices such as yoga, meditation, breath control, and energy work were assimilated into the West and found themselves in the revised practices of Western magic. Modern Witchcraft and Paganism benefited from this appropriation, as did nearly every other practical Western occult system.

Even so, the practice of modern Witchcraft lacked in practices, rites, and lore, particularly in the discipline that was once the hallmark of the Witchcraft of antiquity—spirit conjuration through the agency of a familiar spirit. That entire system of magic was completely missing from the practices I inherited as a young and aspiring Witchling. I had to invent the methodology, mechanism, and tools to be able to perform this magic in the modern age.

We can only guess how the Witches of antiquity believed and practiced magic based on the fragments that we now possess. Trying to reinvent it exactly as it was once practiced would be practically impossible. In the end, we are left with bits and pieces (some of which are quite modern) in addition to the power of our imaginations to build a system that would allow us to once again conjure spirits.

It is in this social and practical context I reinvented the practice of conjuring spirits within a Witchcraft system of magic. I wrote up this methodology anew in *Spirit Conjuring for Witches* with the basic belief that I had completed my work in this subject area.

However, my work was not yet completed, since I decided that the lore that I had used for decades to perform advanced energy workings would be important for Witches to master as well. The result was the production of my second book, *Elemental Powers for Witches*. I spent a couple of years working on that project, and in December of 2021 I published it, thereby adding the second tier to the practice of the modern craft.

At this point, I breathed a sigh of relief that my work was done...but then I knew it was all too soon. In the late 1970s I had developed a system of magic that incorporated the basic set of rituals used to perform celestial magic. I refined those rituals and techniques and shared this work with my fellow magicians in Kansas City in the 1980s. I continued to refine and simplify these ritual operations until the early 2000s, when I finally achieved the level of simplicity and elegance that I could share with the Witchcraft community at large. I realized that my community needed this knowledge to complete the final part of the reclamation and extension of Witchcraft magic found in celestial magic. I spent the last couple of years working on this book and have now finally published what you have completed reading.

As stated in *Elemental Powers,* there were only five basic practices within traditional and modern Witchcraft:

1. Meditation and trance: the ability to adopt altered states of consciousness
2. Energy work (simple): cone of power, cord work, scourging, great rite
3. Liturgical operations: drawing down the Moon and Sun, communion, votive offerings
4. Basic mystery ceremonies, consisting of:
    A. twelve esbats,
    B. eight sabbats, and
    C. two initiation mysteries and the great rite as the third mystery.
5. Folk magic: fithfath, binding, healing, cursing, drugs, potions, herbs, minerals and gemstones, animal parts, etc.

Whatever else could be found in the practice of modern Witchcraft had to be either invented or brought into the craft from other sources. Because the standard Book of Shadows contained so little of the once rich but now lost tradition of Witchcraft, appropriation from other sources was necessary to fill out the practice.

Historical folk magic and hoodoo were one variable source of lore, as were the various ceremonies and folk celebrations that have come down to modern Europeans from the Middle Ages. One source that truly sticks out from the others was the magical practices and lore of the Golden Dawn. It was certainly something that Old Gerald was keenly interested in, but it was the Witches of the 1970s and 1980s who found ways of appropriating some GD lore and practices into their work.

Looking at the large gaps in this list is what motivated me to action; over the last five years, I have added three books and three complete systems of magic to the list of practices, at least for those who would like to practice a more advanced kind of ritual magic. I even proposed that these three disciplines—advanced energy magic, evocation, and celestial magic—would bring the number of magical branches in modern Witchcraft to eight in a recreation of the eightfold path. If there are now eight different magical and liturgical practices in the craft, how would these new spokes added to the wheel interact with what Witches are already doing?

Energy magic, evocation, and celestial magic would represent the full spectrum of ritual magical operations that an individual Witch could be expected to practice. These three disciplines would represent a very potent array of magical work that could be leveraged to handle any need or any situation that might arise. It would make the holder of all eight of these disciplines together a magus or mistress/master of the magical arts. She would be a formidable magical practitioner, capable of leading a charmed and wholly empowered life, almost to a mythic degree. She would be a complete Witch in the classical definition of that term.

Evocation and advanced energy work can combine together easily, with one aiding and intensifying the work of the other. Energy makes conjurations more accessible to the senses, and conjuration makes the generation of energy more intensified. They assist each other as if they were made to go together, and indeed, mastery of both aids in the work of evocation and energy generation.

However, it should be clear at this point that celestial magic stands apart and alone from the other magical arts part of the repertoire of the complete Witch. Energy magic is already used extensively in celestial magic, and evocation is co-opted as the invocation part of the working, where the standard five-part evocation is not needed. Celestial magic contains the attributes of evocation and energy work, but neither can use anything from the workings of talismanic magic. I consider celestial magic the apex of all magical forms simply because learning to work it is such a complex and challenging technique to master.

It will probably take you a few years to be able to learn what you need to know about celestial magic and astrology, assemble the tools, and then practice the ritual forms. Planetary invocations will be easy to learn and will probably be the first workings of this sort you will perform. But those early years will be filled with the wonder and enjoyment of learning something new and trying out new forms of magic. It will be a formative time for you, finding new directions and experimenting with this lore. I both envy the joyful work you are about to engage in and feel empathy for being able to share this lore with you to make that possible.

Practicing celestial magic also has the potential of helping you begin the study and ultimately mastery of modern theurgy. The other two disciplines will not be able to aid you in the pursuit of that kind of magical work, but celestial magic can and will lead to works of theurgy.

Theurgy is where the magician functions as a direct conduit of the deities, causing miraculous and amazing materializations. In celestial magic, the practitioner uses mid-level surrogates or intermediaries for charging and imbuing talismanic artifacts with divine-like powers and intelligence. It is a small but significant step for the practitioner to directly channel the powers and intelligences of the deities into the material world.

Becoming a direct channel of the deities and directing those powers and intelligences to make changes in the material world great and small is where the Witch or Pagan begins to transition from human being to demigod. How far can someone take this kind of magical work? Is it possible to be like a god or goddess in human flesh? If someone can push this kind of magic to that point, then certainly it is possible.

Still, the limitations of our mortal existence probably preclude us from becoming like a living god or goddess in our world, but we could potentially strive to be a lot closer to that goal than what we could do otherwise if we did not first master celestial magic. Imagine too, if a group of Witches or Pagans gathered together as masters of the celestial magic. Think of what they might accomplish as a coven of equals or a grove of fellowship and mastery.

I get giddy just thinking about all of these potentials and possibilities. Yet I also know from my own experience that great magical groups like what I am imagining are very rare and, when they do form, they often don't stay together very long, simply because people come together for a short time and then drift apart. And they drift apart because the nature of the Witch's magical path is for the most part solitary and averse to groups and the intrusion of multiple minds and strong wills.

The challenge for us, as Witches and Pagans, is finding a way to keep our humanity intact without falling prey to the battle of petty egos. We should realize that there is little difference between our beliefs when compared to the world's religions. We are so much alike and truly the same, with only minor differences and opinions separating us. We need to enrich our knowledge and experience of being a human in this world at this time, requiring us to put away our pride and ego to meet with the ideals of fully realized perfect love and perfect trust.

While thinking about these amazing revelations and magical ideas, I am reminded of that cold winter evening on Candlemas Eve in the year 1976 when I was initiated to the first degree of the Alexandrian tradition of Witchcraft. I will never forget the words of my High Priestess, recited to me before I was sworn to be a Witch, taken from the Alexandrian/Gardnerian Book of Shadows:

> Single is the race is men and Gods, from a single source we both draw breath, but a difference of power in everything keeps us apart. For we are as nothing, but the Gods stay forever. Yet we can, in greatness of minds, be like the Gods. Though we know not to what goal by day or in the night, but in the heavens' vast expanse there lies a majesty which is the Domains of the Gods. Great are those who pass through the gates of day and night to that sweet place, which is between the world of men and the Domains of the Lords of the Outer Spaces.[72]

---

72 This tract was plagiarized rather poorly from Pindar's "Nemean Ode 5" with Wiccan notations added to it. The author, however, is unknown; it does not appear to be something

It would seem that as I shivered, naked, bound, and blindfolded hearing those words spoken to me seemingly for the first time, I was told the greatest secret about celestial magic, even though at the time, none of us would understand it as such. It talks about the passage through the double gates (of night and day) while being like the gods with powers and the nobility of mind, and passing from this material world into Elysium, home of the heroes and demigods. Such a transport would likely require the death of the body, but that occurrence is the fate of everyone living a mortal human life, and as such, it is ultimately dispensable, a sacrifice of the outer shell to the apotheosis of human ascendancy.

There is much to ponder in the lore of celestial magic, since it has a very ancient provenance but is practiced with very modern tools. What I have brought together in this work is the apex of the practices of magic, and it is also the beginning of even greater fame and fortune. The secret mystery of celestial magic is that the veritable sky is the limit, which is to say, there are no real limits and that everything is possible, given the right timing and the optimal empowering of the gods' consciousness.

May the goddesses and gods of all pantheons bless you with great fortune!

FRATER BARRABBAS

Doreen Valiente wrote. It doesn't appear in the books written by Stewart and Janet Farrar, but it does appear in Lady Sheba's *Book of Shadows*. My guess is that it was written by Gardner himself.

Appendix 1

ALPHABET WHEELS FOR HEBREW AND ENGLISH

When I perform an invocation of a celestial spirit, I employ a sigil crafted from the name of the target spirit. That sigil can be derived from a number of sources, but I generally use the alphabet wheels based on Hebrew or English/Latin. The Hebrew alphabet wheel has the Hebrew letters drawn on the three concentric circles, representing the triple division of those same letters (three mother letters, seven double letters, and twelve simple letters), can be used to create sigils based on a Hebrew word or name.[73]

---

73 For a more in-depth presentation for the use of alphabet wheels, see Frater Barrabbas, *Spirit Conjuring for Witches*, 116–119.

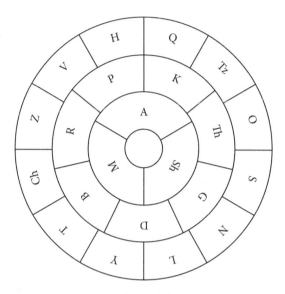

Figure 31: Hebrew Alphabet Wheel

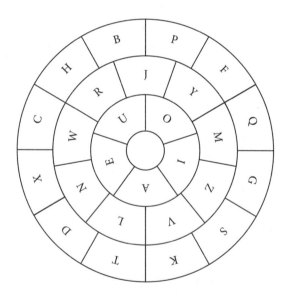

Figure 32: English Alphabet Wheel

ELEMENTAL QUALITIES

Since the elementals are used in the determination of the Septan attribution, I felt that it would be helpful if I put the meanings for the sixteen elementals here without the associated spirit names for the Grand Dukes, as they are presented in chapter 7 of *Elemental Powers for Witches*.

Base Element: Fire
Wisdom, Knowledge—Southern Quadrant

Air of Fire: Pursuit of knowledge, desire to know, thirst for knowledge, act of seeking, sensing and detecting subtle phenomenon

Earth of Fire: Application of knowledge, past experiences, pragmatic outlook or perspective, structural understanding, organization

Fire of Fire: Inspiration, insight, ideals, ethics, moral guidance, breakthrough, reformation of past opinions and beliefs

Water of Fire: Intuition, inner subjective perception of truth, Gnosis, spiritual knowledge, introspection, affirmation of faith

Base Element: Water
Internal Perceptions, Feelings—Western Quadrant

Air of Water: Restlessness, inner stirring, seeking through feeling, emotional regeneration, revitalization of interests and pursuits

Earth of Water: Lust, sexual desire, manifestation of wishes and desires, fantasy, crystallization of one's intuitive needs, possible obsession upon fulfillment of desires

Fire of Water: The desire to give love selflessly, compassion and understanding, the quest for spiritual union, emotional purification

Water of Water: Sensitivity, emotional empathy, psychic and supernatural phenomena, emotional healing and restoration, deep insight of other individuals

Base Element: Air
Volition, Activity—Eastern Quadrant

Air of Air: Action, extreme decisiveness, pursuit of activity, communication, clarity of perception, dispeller of illusion and falsehood

Earth of Air: Discipline, structured or planned action, purposeful activity, goal pursuit, expression of one's personal self or identity, self-discovery, self-control

Fire of Air: Self-direction, self-motivation, realization of one's purpose in life or in any given situation, understanding one's inner motivations

Water of Air: Fantasy, pursuit of illusion for artistic expression, tapping the well-spring of the imagination, the strong desire to express one's inner perceptions

Base Element: Earth
Growth, Acquisition, the Life Force—Northern Quadrant

Air of Earth: Work, building, growth of ambitions, realization of goals through a step by step methodical process, perceiving the method of achieving of one's goals

Earth of Earth: Physical regeneration, healing, self-grounding, medium of physical manifestation of psychic phenomenon, the desire to procreate or heal (medical restoration)

Fire of Earth: Responsibility, understanding the meaning of life in simplistic and basic terms, stewardship of the land, farming, giving of beneficial (monetary) assistance

Water of Earth: Fertility, physical growth, fruitfulness, intuitive understanding of individual physical needs, feeding, nurturing, giving of life (birth or rebirth)

BIBLIOGRAPHY

Alexander, Skye. *Planets in Signs*. Atglen, PA: Whitford Press, 1988.

Attrel, Dan and Porreca, David. *Picatrix: A Medieval Treatise on Astral Magic*. University Park, PA: The Pennsylvania State University Press, 2019.

Campbell, Joseph. *The Hero with a Thousand Faces*. New York: MJF Books, 1949 reprint.

Campion, Nicholas. *A History of Western Astrology Volume 1: The Ancient World*. New York: Bloomsbury Academic, 2013.

———. *A History of Western Astrology Volume 2: The Medieval and Modern Worlds*. New York: Bloomsbury Academic, 2013.

Cornelius, Geoffrey. *The Moment of Astrology*. Bournemouth, UK: The Wessex Astrologer Ltd., 2003.

Crane, Joseph. *Astrological Roots: The Hellenistic Legacy*. Bournemouth, UK: The Wessex Astrologer Ltd., 2007.

Crowley, Aleister. *The Book of Thoth*. New York: Samuel Weiser, 1972.

———. *777 and Other Qabalistic Writings of Aleister Crowley*. York Beach, ME: Samuel Weiser, 1994.

Denning, Melita, and Osborne Phillips. *Planetary Magic: The Heart of Western Magic*. St. Paul, MN: Llewellyn Publications, 1989.

Frater Barrabbas. *Elemental Power for Witches*. Woodbury, MN: Llewellyn Publications, 2021.

———. *Spirit Conjuring for Witches*. Woodbury, MN: Llewellyn Publications, 2017.

———. *Mastering the Art of Ritual Magic: Omnibus Edition*. Stafford, UK: Megalithica Books–Immanion Press, 2013.

Hand, Robert. *Horoscope Symbols*. Rockport, MA: Para Research, 1981.

———. *Planets in Transit: Life Cycles for Living*. Rockport, MA: Para Research, 1976.

March, Marion D. and Joan McEvers. *The Only Way to Learn Astrology: Volume 1, Second Edition: Basic Principles*. San Diego, CA: ACS Publications Inc, 1984.

Roberts, Richard, and Joseph Campbell. *Tarot Revelations*. San Anselmo, CA: Vernal Equinox Press, 1982.

Rogers-Gallagher, Kim. "Introduction to Astrology" in *Llewellyn's 2021 Daily Planetary Guide*. Woodbury, MN: Llewellyn Publications, 2021.

Rudhyar, Dane. *The Lunation Cycle: A Key to Understanding of Personality*. New York: Aurora Press, 1986.

Sassi, Maria Michela. *The Beginnings of Philosophy in Greece*. Translated by Michele Asuni. Princeton, NJ: Princeton University Press, 2018 (eBook).

Schaefer, Bradley E. "The Real Stonehenge" online lecture, part 2 of *Ancient Astronomy* series. Chantilly, VA: The Great Courses, 2017.

———. "Alignments at Maes Howe and Newgrange" online lecture, part 3 of *Ancient Astronomy*. Chantilly, VA: The Great Courses, 2017.

Scheffler, Israel. *Symbolic Worlds: Art, Science, Language, Ritual*. Cambridge, MA: Harvard University Press, 2008.

Schueler, Gerald J. *Enochian Magic: A Practical Guide*. St. Paul, MN: Llewellyn Publications, 1987.

Skinner, Stephen, and David Rankine. *The Goetia of Dr. Rudd (Sourceworks of Ceremonial Magic)*. Singapore: Golden Hoard Press, 2010.

———. *The Veritable Key of Solomon (Sourceworks of Ceremonial Magic)*. Singapore: Golden Hoard Press, 2008.

Skinner, Stephen. *The Complete Magician's Tables*. St. Paul, MN: Llewellyn, 2006.

Warnock, Christopher. *Mansions of the Moon: A Lunar Zodiac for Astrology and Magic*. Columbia, SC: Renaissance Astrology, 2006.

Whitcomb, Bill. *The Magician's Companion: A Practical & Encyclopedic Guide to Magical & Religious Symbolism*. St. Paul, MN: Llewellyn, 1993.

⊙

INDEX

A

Active, 2, 3, 10, 15, 18, 21, 22, 24–26, 29, 42, 44, 47, 59, 72, 92, 112, 132, 140, 150, 168, 172, 206, 207, 213, 215, 220, 264, 265

Agrippa, 24, 37, 67, 92, 121

Akkadians, 22

Al Biruni, 91

Angelic ruler, 85, 86, 98–105, 115, 121, 164, 219, 222, 223, 225, 227, 230, 236, 240, 248, 255, 259

Angels, 17, 24, 44, 52, 62, 86, 114–116, 118, 119, 182, 227, 232, 233, 237, 240, 245, 250, 255, 259

Aphrodite, 56, 61, 87, 222, 223, 255, 258, 259

Aquarius, 82, 83, 85–87, 102, 107, 116–118, 120, 128, 129, 135–137, 201, 239

Aratron, 62, 69, 119, 273, 274, 278

Arbatel, 24, 37, 67, 68

Archangels, 24, 59, 61, 62, 67, 85–87, 114–119, 182, 186, 195, 210, 222, 223, 226, 227, 230, 231, 236, 237, 240, 248, 249, 255, 258, 259

Archetypes, 7, 9, 17, 18, 20, 22, 23, 29, 39, 43, 53, 54, 58, 59, 64, 68, 71–73, 77, 141, 155, 186

Aries, 23, 56, 76, 77, 79, 85–87, 89, 98–100, 106, 112, 116–118, 120, 121, 132, 134–137, 143, 162, 173, 227

Aristotle, 33, 34

Ascendant, 114–118, 120–125, 128, 173, 225, 244

Aspects, 12, 20, 24, 25, 28, 29, 45, 49, 71, 84, 113, 125, 162, 165, 168, 172, 173, 176, 200, 201, 221, 222, 227, 239

B

Babylon, 16

Bethor, 62, 69, 70, 119, 198, 201, 202

C

Cancer, 54, 78, 79, 85–87, 89, 100, 101, 106, 110, 116–118, 120, 123, 124, 132, 134–137, 162, 163, 258

Capricorn, 23, 57, 82, 85–87, 89, 96, 104, 105, 107, 116–118, 120, 127, 128, 132, 135–137, 161, 252

Celestial Magic, 1–12, 15–18, 20, 21, 24, 26–28, 30–32, 34–37, 39, 40, 43–46, 49, 51–53, 59, 64, 67, 72, 73, 90, 133, 139, 140, 145–147, 151, 152, 154, 155, 159–161, 166, 168, 171, 174, 182, 183, 203, 205, 244, 252, 271, 272, 281–288

Chaos Model, 22

Chronos, 22, 23, 30, 48, 49, 63, 64, 178

Chthonie, 48

Cicero, 33

Conjure, 8, 283

Constellations, 1, 2, 16, 20, 32, 52, 87, 88, 109, 110, 181

Correspondences, 11, 21, 43, 44, 51–53, 58–60, 62, 63, 73, 75, 83–86, 88–90, 94, 97, 98, 113, 114, 116, 118, 120, 132, 133, 142, 155, 186, 195

D

Daily Planetary Guide, 13, 54, 72, 77, 200, 201, 221, 239

Decans (definition), 88–89

Delineation, 12

Demigod, 115, 118, 121, 153, 181, 236, 245, 286

Domain, 1, 6, 17, 29, 39–41, 43, 64, 113–115, 118, 121, 150–152, 164, 169, 183, 187, 207, 234, 252, 281

Dukes (list of)

Dodecagram, 143, 145, 187, 189, 194

E

Egypt, 59, 61, 87–89, 109–111, 115, 117, 118, 121, 227, 236

Elective chart, 26, 40, 52, 72, 83, 173

Energy Model *****

Enochian, 16, 93, 222

Ephemeris, 13, 53, 72, 92, 171, 172, 220, 239

Evocation, 5–9, 11, 12, 16, 17, 285, 286

Exemplifying metaphors, 41–43, 54

F

Ficino, 16, 25, 34, 36, 44

G

Gateway, 22, 57, 63, 64, 86, 145, 150, 151, 178, 179, 183–185, 187, 188, 190, 192, 194, 206, 207, 209, 211, 220, 226, 227, 230, 232, 233, 237, 240, 245, 248, 250, 255, 259, 277, 278

Gemini, 55, 76, 78, 85–87, 97, 102, 103, 106, 116–118, 120, 122, 123, 134–137

Geocentric, 5, 34, 53, 54, 112

Godhead Assumption, 156, 179

Golden Dawn, 2–5, 16, 37, 44, 67, 113, 144, 285

Great Kings, 93

Greece, 31, 32, 48

Guardian (definition)

Guide, 13, 28, 54, 55, 64, 72, 77, 91, 150, 160, 178, 179, 184, 185, 188, 189, 192, 194, 200, 201, 209, 211, 220, 221, 227, 230, 232, 234, 235, 239, 248, 250, 253, 254, 276, 278

H

Hagith, 62, 70, 119, 219, 222, 223, 255, 258, 259

Heliocentric, 5, 34, 53

Hermes, 55, 61, 87, 237, 240

Hexagram, 2–5, 93, 144–146, 187, 192, 206, 207, 210, 213, 214, 225, 226, 228, 231, 241, 244, 246, 249, 259, 275, 277

Horary Astrology, 32, 34, 40

Horoscope, 20, 40, 44, 45, 54, 77, 159, 168, 173

Houses, 20, 46, 84, 114, 162

Icon, 4, 10, 65–67, 140, 141, 143, 145, 154, 156, 183–185, 187, 189, 194, 207, 209–211, 214, 230–232, 248–250, 277, 278

I

Information Model, 17, 27, 28

Invoke, 3–5, 10, 26, 58, 59, 61, 64, 68, 86, 140, 141, 143, 144, 164, 182, 183, 187, 197, 202, 206, 207, 217, 223, 225, 228, 234, 240, 243–246, 248, 259, 260, 272

J

John Dee, 16, 37

Jupiter, 3, 4, 23, 46, 56, 57, 60–62, 69, 72, 81, 83, 85, 87, 93–96, 99, 101, 103, 105–107, 112, 117, 119, 120, 122, 124, 126, 127, 129, 135–137, 143, 162–164, 174, 176, 177, 196–202, 239

L

Leo, 23, 35, 54, 79, 85–87, 98, 100, 106, 107, 112, 116–118, 120, 124, 134–137, 162

Lesser Hexagram, 2, 4, 144–146, 187, 192, 206, 207, 210, 213, 214, 225, 226, 228, 231, 241, 244, 246, 249, 259, 275, 277

Libra, 55, 80, 85–87, 89, 102–104, 107, 116–118, 120, 125, 126, 132, 134–137, 221, 222, 258

Lunar Mansions (defintion), 89

Lunar Phases (*see* Moon)

Lunation Cycle, 92, 165–167, 171

M

Magic Circle, 25, 40, 141, 145, 150–153, 156, 172, 180, 182, 183, 187, 191, 196, 203, 207, 216, 228, 246, 265, 266, 275

Mars, 23, 56, 60–62, 70, 72, 77, 81, 85, 87, 89, 93–97, 99, 101, 102, 104, 106, 107, 112, 117, 119–121, 123, 124, 126, 128, 130, 134–137, 142, 174, 176, 177, 199–201, 258

Meditation, 42, 43, 66, 179, 180, 185, 189, 194, 210, 211, 214, 231, 232, 249, 250, 265, 266, 278, 283, 284

Melotheisa, 112

Mercury, 23, 55, 60–62, 70–72, 78, 79, 85, 87, 93–96, 99, 101, 103, 105, 107, 112, 117, 119, 120, 122, 123, 125, 127, 129, 134–137, 142, 143, 174, 176, 177, 199, 200, 238–240

Moon, 9, 23, 28, 47, 53–55, 60–63, 70, 72, 78, 85, 89, 91–100, 102, 104, 107, 112, 117, 119, 120, 122, 124, 125, 127, 129, 134–137, 139, 142, 143, 156, 160, 165–169, 171–174, 176, 199, 201, 205, 207, 213, 220–222, 239, 257, 258, 268, 271, 272, 284

    first quarter, 165–167, 201

    full moon, 9, 92, 156, 165–167, 171, 220, 221, 239, 257

    last quarter, 165–167

    new moon, 92, 156, 165–167, 171

    waning moon, 92, 168, 171, 221, 257, 268, 271, 272

    waxing moon, 92, 171, 173, 220, 221

Mundane Astrology, 19, 32

N

Natal chart, 12, 29, 34, 44–46, 55, 71, 159–163, 169, 200

Neptune, 72, 83, 85, 87

Nile, 110

O

Olympian Spirits, 24, 59, 61, 67, 68, 70, 71, 118, 119, 181, 182, 195, 202

Ophiel, 62, 70, 119, 237, 240

Ordeal, 63, 64, 150, 178, 179, 184, 185, 188, 189, 192, 194, 209, 211, 220, 227, 230, 232, 248, 250, 276, 278

Ouranos, 48

P

Paracelsus, 24, 37, 67, 68

Passive, 2, 3, 15, 18, 21, 22, 24–26, 29, 55, 72, 150

Pentemychos, 48

Persia, 47, 49

Pherecydes, 30, 47–49

Picatrix, 16, 36, 88, 92, 98, 121

Pisces, 23, 73, 83, 85–87, 100, 101, 107, 116–118, 120, 129, 130, 135–137, 199, 201, 239

Planetary days, 10, 26, 27, 174, 239

Planetary deity, 58, 59, 65–68, 71, 72, 86, 155, 156, 178, 179, 181, 196, 201, 202, 216, 222, 236, 273

Planetary hours, 10, 20, 21, 25–27, 45, 46, 65, 66, 71, 132, 160, 169, 171–177, 179, 180, 198–202, 215, 221, 223, 227, 239, 240, 246, 257–259

Planetary intelligence, 4, 24–27, 58, 59, 61, 62, 64, 67, 140, 151, 152, 164, 182, 183, 185–187, 189, 194–197, 201, 206, 207, 264, 272, 275

Plato, 34

Pluto, 72, 81, 85

Psychology model, 15–18, 27, 28, 39–44

Ptolemy, 19, 23, 31, 33, 34, 36, 88, 111

Pylon (definition)

Pyramid, 145, 146, 187, 191, 193, 206, 227, 241, 259, 273

Q

Quadruplicities, 75, 76, 144

R

Receptor, 147, 148, 150, 153, 155, 164, 178, 179, 205, 206, 214, 227, 246, 272

Retrograde, 20, 52, 71, 72

Rose Ankh, 145, 147, 148, 151, 183, 188, 191, 206, 208, 227, 229, 247, 273, 276–278

S

Sagittarius, 57, 81, 82, 85–87, 98, 99, 107, 112, 116–118, 120, 127, 135–137, 162

Saturn, 23, 45, 46, 57, 60–62, 69, 72, 82, 85, 87, 93–97, 100, 101, 103, 105–107, 112, 117, 119, 120, 122, 124, 126, 127, 129, 135–137, 142, 143, 163, 174, 176, 177, 197, 199, 200, 221, 239, 257, 258, 271–275, 277, 279

Scholastic Image Magic, 1

Scorpio, 23, 45, 46, 73, 81, 85–87, 100, 102, 107, 116–118, 120, 126, 135–137, 162, 163, 201, 219–223, 272, 273, 275

Seals, 25, 27, 44, 68, 69, 198, 218, 237, 238, 255, 256, 268

Seniors, 93, 222

Septagram, 4, 5, 10, 29, 72, 140–143, 145, 152, 156, 183–185, 207, 209–211, 214, 227, 230–232, 248–250, 277, 278

Septans, 16, 27–29, 90, 131–134, 165, 243–245

Shrine, 9, 23, 65–67, 156, 178, 196, 216

Sigil, 25, 134, 155, 178, 179, 183–185, 187, 189, 193, 194, 196–198, 201, 202, 207, 209–211, 213–220, 222, 227, 230–232, 235–239, 246, 248–250, 254–256, 258, 263–267, 273, 274, 277, 278, 289

Signs, 20, 22, 23, 25, 27–29, 42–44, 46, 52, 54, 55, 73, 75–77, 83–86, 88, 89, 91, 96, 106, 111, 114, 116, 131, 143, 144, 162, 168, 171, 173, 182, 187, 195, 216, 218–220, 244

Sirius, 110, 111

Sothis, 110

Spiral, 141, 145, 146, 153, 184–186, 188–190, 192–195, 207–211, 228–230, 232, 246–251, 275–279

Spirit, 8, 11, 15, 17, 24, 27, 28, 30, 41, 42, 44, 49, 61–63, 68, 69, 72, 88, 93, 98, 121, 122, 132, 145, 147–151, 153, 155, 156, 161, 178, 182, 183, 186, 187, 196–198, 201, 202, 210, 213, 214, 217–219, 222, 223, 231, 234, 236, 237, 240, 245, 249, 252, 254, 255, 258, 259, 264–267, 269, 273, 274, 278, 282, 283, 289, 291

Spirit Model, 15, 17, 28

Spiritual Hierarchy, 52, 113–115, 152, 155, 196, 201, 202, 216, 222, 226, 236, 239, 240, 243, 254, 258, 267, 268

Star Polygon, 3, 10, 140, 141, 143

Stellar Vortex, 210, 213, 215, 227, 231, 234, 246, 249, 252

Sub-Elemental, 165

Sun, 5, 9, 23, 45–47, 53–55, 60–63, 70, 72, 77, 79, 85, 88, 89, 93–95, 98, 100, 102, 104, 106, 107, 111, 112, 117, 119–121, 123, 125, 126, 128, 132, 134–137, 139, 142, 143, 150, 161, 165, 166, 168, 169, 171–174, 176, 177, 179, 205, 239, 246, 257, 284

T

Talismanic Elementals, 17, 28, 29, 91, 93, 94, 96–98, 106, 132–134, 164, 165, 203, 205–207, 211–213, 215, 217–219, 223, 225, 227, 228, 234, 245, 246, 252, 273

Taurus, 23, 55, 73, 76–78, 85–87, 96, 104, 106, 116–118, 120, 122, 134–137, 173, 245, 252, 255, 257–260

Temporal Model, 15, 28, 30, 39, 40, 44, 45, 47, 49, 168

Tetrabiblos, 19, 33

Theurgia-Goetia, 131, 133, 243, 244, 252

Threshold God, 63

Triplicities, 75

U

Underworld, 37, 63, 150, 151, 183, 187, 206, 220, 237, 255

Uranus, 72, 82, 85

V

Venus, 23, 45, 46, 55–57, 60–62, 70, 72, 73, 77, 80, 85, 87, 93–97, 100, 102, 104–107, 112, 117, 119–121, 123, 125, 126, 128, 134–137, 142, 143, 162, 163, 174, 176, 177, 199, 200, 215, 217, 219–223, 245, 256–259

Virgo, 55, 79, 80, 85–87, 96, 104, 105, 107, 116–118, 120, 125, 134–137, 226, 234, 236, 237, 239–241

Vortex (definition)

Z

Zas, 48, 64

Zeus, 31, 48, 61, 87, 202

Zurvan, 47, 49

⊙

To Write to the Author

If you wish to contact the author or would like more information about this book, please write to the author in care of Llewellyn Worldwide Ltd. and we will forward your request. Both the author and publisher appreciate hearing from you and learning of your enjoyment of this book and how it has helped you. Llewellyn Worldwide Ltd. cannot guarantee that every letter written to the author can be answered, but all will be forwarded. Please write to:

Frater Barrabas
℅ Llewellyn Worldwide
2143 Wooddale Drive
Woodbury, MN 55125-2989
Please enclose a self-addressed stamped envelope for reply,
or $1.00 to cover costs. If outside the U.S.A., enclose
an international postal reply coupon.

Many of Llewellyn's authors have websites with additional information and resources. For more information, please visit our website at http://www.llewellyn.com.